D0058455

Praise ...
THE ESSENTIAL DIFFERENCE

"Baron-Cohen offers curious lay readers a provocative discussion of male-female differences."

—Publishers Weekly

"*The Essential Difference* succeeds in illuminating how fundamental differences between male and female thinking can be blamed on that single, scrawny Y."

—Seed

"Easy and enjoyable to read ... a novel and fascinating idea that seems likely to generate a rich empirical body of literature as its properties are tested.... This book inspires the reader to reconsider traditional assumptions about the skills of each sex."

—Nature

"Well-written science books for a lay audience, such as this one, are a special pleasure. And any book that can change how you see the world and promote greater—dare I say—empathy, is a decidedly good thing."

—The National Post

"*The Essential Difference* is another fascinating entry in what I call self-knowledge science writing. Baron-Cohen's purpose is clearly to give us new tools which we can use to understand ourselves better. What we do with those tools is up to us."

—Edmonton Journal

"Baron-Cohen presents a striking new theory with insightful connections to brain science, evolution, and everyday life. And unlike many books on this vexed subject, it is neither politically correct nor politically oblivious. *The Essential Difference* is essential reading."

—Steven Pinker, author of How the Mind Works and The Blank Slate: The Modern Denial of Human Nature

"The science laid out in *The Essential Difference* is in itself enlightening and Baron-Cohen's practical justification for examining this once virtually taboo subject is admirable."

"I thank Simon Baron-Cohen more than I can say for having written this book. It has explained a good part of my own life to me; it's made men achingly human to me."

"This is an often provocative, compellingly written look at how male and female differences may influence social behavior—both in the mainstream and at the margins—told with a rare combination of wit and insight."

THE
ESSENTIAL
DIFFERENCE

Male and Female Brains
and the Truth About Autism

SIMON BARON-COHEN

BASIC
BOOKS

A Member of the Perseus Books Group
New York

First hardcover edition published in 2003 by Basic Books
A Member of the Perseus Books Group

First paperback edition published in 2004 by Basic Books

Books published by Basic Books are available at special discounts for bulk
purchases in the United States by corporations, institutions, and other
organizations. For more information, please contact the Special Markets
Department at the Perseus Books Group, 11 Cambridge Center,
Cambridge MA 02142, or call (617) 252-5298, (800) 255-1514 or e-mail
special.markets@perseusbooks.com.

Cataloging-in-Publication Data
is available from the Library of Congress
ISBN-10: 0-7382-0844-2 (hc)
ISBN-13: 978-0-7382-0844-2 (hc)
ISBN-10: 0-465-00556-X (pbk.)
ISBN-13: 978-0-465-00556-7

Set in Fairfield Light by the Perseus Books Group

In memory of
Robert Greenblatt
(1906–1987)
(Augusta Georgia Medical School)
who combined endocrinology with humanity

and

Donald Cohen
(1940–2001)
(Yale Child Study Center)
who studied autism and cared for children in need

CONTENTS

LIST OF FIGURES

ACKNOWLEDGMENTS

Bridget Lindley was the first to believe in my ideas about the essential differences between the male and female mind, and about the extreme male brain as an explanation of autism. She supported me when I dipped my toe into these politically dangerous waters, even during the early 1990s when to raise the very idea of psychological sex differences was risky. Like many people, she recognized such sex differences in everyday life, and persuaded me that most readers would now be open-minded enough to look at the evidence dispassionately.

Many people helped me develop my thoughts for this book. They include my talented research students in recent years: Chris Ashwin, Anna Ba'tkti, Livia Colle, Jennifer Connellan, Jaime Craig, Ofer Golan, Rick Griffin, Jessica Hammer, John Herrington, Therese Jolliffe, Rebecca Knickmeyer, Johnny Lawson, and Svetlana Lutchmaya. They also include my valuable research team: Carrie Allison, Matthew Belmonte, Jacqueline Hill, Rosa Hoekstra, Karen McGinty, Catherine Moreno, Jennifer Richler, Fiona Scott, Carol Stott, and Sally Wheelwright. At the risk of embarrassing her, I owe special thanks to Sally. She first came to work with me in 1996, and was as grabbed by the questions in this book as I was. We have enjoyed a long and tremendously productive collaboration, and much of the research behind this book would not have been possible without her.

Some colleagues and friends have been very supportive. They include Patrick Bolton, Kirsten Callesen, Lynn Clemance, Peter Fonagy, Ian Goodyer, Ami Klin, Chantal Martin, Amitta Shah, Luca Surian, Helen Tager-Flusberg, and Esther Tripp. My clinical colleagues Janine Robinson, Emma Weisblatt, and Marc Woodbury-Smith have also helped me enormously in my attempt to understand the nature of Asperger Syndrome.

Last, but not least, are my collaborators: Ralph Adolphs, James Blair, Carol Brayne, Ed Bullmore, Andy Calder, Tony Charman, Livia Colle, Carol Gregory, Gerald Hackett, Melissa Hines, John Hodges, Ioan James, Mark Johnson, John Manning, Michelle O'Riordan, Robert Plomin, Peter Raggatt, Melissa Rutherford, Geoff Sanders, David Skuse, Valerie Stone, Steve Williams, Max Whitby, Andy Young, and Martin Yuille.

Many of the above people gathered new data and tested hypotheses. You will read about some of our discoveries in the pages to come.

I would also like to thank Consulting Psychologists Press, Inc, for permission to reproduce the Adult Embedded Figures Test. The "Reading the Mind in the Eyes" Test (Appendix 1) is based on photographs from commercial sources. The test itself is only used for research and is not distributed for commerical profit. Copyright of each individual photograph cannot be traced from these photo fragments.

I first wrote about the extreme male brain theory of autism in 1997.[1] I didn't dare present the ideas in public until Cure Autism Now organized a scientific meeting at Rutgers University in March 2000. They encouraged their invited speakers, of whom I was one, to present their most provocative ideas. To my surprise, the conference participants did not simply smile politely at my theory, but engaged with it and encouraged me to pursue it. In March 2001 I presented it to the Institutes of Psychiatry and Cognitive Neuroscience in London. The positive reactions I received there, particularly from Uta Frith, encouraged me further to believe that these ideas were ready for a wider audience. Similar reactions at Autism India in Chennai (January 2001) and at the Autism Conference in Madrid (May 2001) gave me the sense that the psychological sex differences in question are universal.[2] Feedback from other such presentations, such as the Child Psychiatry teaching program in Pristina, Kosovo (May 2002), and the Child Psychiatry Conference in Rome (June 2002), resulted in a brief paper to the cognitive science community on this topic.[3] This book expands these early communications for a broader readership.

The following funding agencies have supported my work during the writing of this book: the Medical Research Council (UK), Cure Autism Now, the Shirley Foundation, the Corob Foundation, the Three Guineas Trust, the Gatsby Trust, the Isaac Newton Trust, the NHS Research and Development Fund, the National Alliance for Autism Research, and the James S. McDonnell Foundation.

The following institutions have also fostered my work through their support: Trinity College Cambridge, and within Cambridge University, the Departments of Experimental Psychology and Psychiatry, the Clinical School Department of Biochemistry, the Autism Research Centre, the fMRI Brain Mapping Unit, the Wolfson Brain Imaging Centre, the Section of Developmental Psychiatry, and the Rosie Maternity Hospital; outside the University: the Cambridge Lifespan Asperger Syndrome Service (CLASS), Lifespan NHS Trust (now the Cambridgeshire and Peterborough NHS Partnership Mental Health Trust), the National Autistic Society (UK) and their Cambridge branch, Umbrella.

Certain people have done me the huge favor of commenting on this book in its manuscript stage. They are Helena Cronin, Rick Griffin, Rosa Hoekstra, Johnny Lawson, Esther Tripp, Sally Wheelwright, Geoff Sanders, and Rebecca Knickmeyer. To these kind critics I am more than indebted. Richard Borcherds generously consented to the inclusion of the material in Chapter 11. Alison Clare, Paula Naimi, and Jenny Hannah all provided wonderful secretarial support.

My agents, John Brockman and Katinka Matson, have been wonderfully supportive of this book. My editor at Penguin (UK), Stefan McGrath, and my editor at Basic Books (USA), Amanda Cook, gave me excellent advice on how to finish the final drafts. Helen Guthrie and Mariateresa Boffo at Penguin brought everything together, and my copy editor, Caroline Pretty, did me the great service of patiently turning my words into English. To them I remain indebted.

Finally, my parents, and brothers and sisters, Dan, Ash, Liz, and Suzie, provided much of the humor which any author needs to sustain the writing process. And my children, Sam, Kate, and Robin, each contributed in personal ways to this book, sometimes without even realizing it. To you all, thank you.

1

The Male and Female Brain

The subject of essential sex differences in the mind is clearly very delicate. I could tiptoe around it, but my guess is that you would like the theory of the book stated plainly. So here it is:

> The female brain is predominantly hard-wired for empathy. The male brain is predominantly hard-wired for understanding and building systems.

I hope to persuade you in the rest of this book that this theory has growing support.

Even on page one, however, I can imagine that some readers are alarmed. Will this theory provide grist for those reactionaries who might wish to defend existing inequalities in opportunities for men and women in society? The nervousness of those readers might not dissipate until they are persuaded that this theory can be used progressively. Equally, I can imagine that some readers may be willing to go halfway down the track with me, willing to explore the once-taboo idea that there are sex differences in the mind. Yet, as we discover the ultimate causes of such sex differences, these readers may find things that they would prefer not to see. Some might hope that these sex differences are solely due to experience; but what if they also reflect inborn biological factors? Moreover, if there are indeed fundamental sex differences in the mind, are these differences modifiable? Or should any differences be celebrated, rather than feared?

I will explore issues such as these in the following chapters. But first, let me expand on the two central claims of the theory.

The Female Brain: Empathizing

Empathizing is the drive to identify another person's emotions and thoughts, and to respond to them with an appropriate emotion. Empathizing does not entail just the cold calculation of what someone else thinks and feels (or what is sometimes called mind reading). Psychopaths can do that much. Empathizing occurs when we feel an appropriate emotional reaction, an emotion *triggered by* the other person's emotion, and it is done in order to understand another person, to predict their behavior, and to connect or resonate with them emotionally.

Imagine if you could recognize that Jane is in pain but this left you cold, or detached, or happy, or preoccupied. That would not be empathizing. Now imagine you not only see Jane's pain, but you also automatically feel concern, wince, and feel a desire to run across and help alleviate her pain. This is empathizing. And empathizing extends to recognizing, and responding to, any emotion or state of mind, not just the more obvious ones such as pain. Empathy arises out of a natural desire to *care* about others. Where this desire springs from is a matter of some debate, and one I postpone until Chapters 7 and 8.

In this book I will consider the evidence that, on average, females spontaneously empathize to a greater degree than do males. Note that I am not talking about all females: just about the average female, compared to the average male. Empathy is a skill (or a set of skills). As with any other skill, such as athleticism, or mathematical or musical ability, we all vary in it. In the same way that we can think about why someone is talented, average or even disabled in these other areas, so we can think about individual differences in empathy. We can even think of empathy as a trait, such as height, since that is also something in which we all differ. And in the same way that you can measure someone's height, so you can measure differences in empathizing between individuals. In Chapter 4 I will look at a number of methods used for measuring these differences.

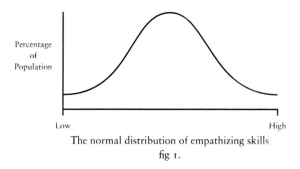

Percentage
of
Population

Low   High

The normal distribution of empathizing skills
fig 1.

Figure 1 shows you this idea visually. Most people fall in the center of the range. But the tails of this bell curve show that some people may have significantly less empathy than others (those at the left-hand tail of the distribution), while those at the right-hand tail may be blessed in this regard. We will discover whether females really are blessed with the brain **type E** (for empathizing) as we go deeper along the trail.

The Male Brain: Systemizing

Systemizing is the drive to analyze, explore, and construct a system. The systemizer intuitively figures out how things work, or extracts the underlying rules that govern the behavior of a system. This is done in order to understand and predict the system, or to invent a new one.

Systems can be as varied as a pond, a vehicle, a plant, a library catalog, a musical composition, a cricket bowl, or even an army unit. They all operate on inputs and deliver outputs, using "if-then" correlational rules. A simple example is a light dimmer. Imagine the light is the input. If you rotate the dimmer clockwise a little (operation), then the bulb on the ceiling gets brighter (output 1). If you rotate it further, the bulb gets even brighter (output 2). "If-then" correlational rules allow you to predict the behavior of most inanimate systems. By monitoring the input, operation, and output you can discover what makes the system work more or less efficiently, and the range of things it can do. Just as empathizing is powerful enough to

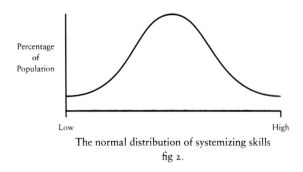

The normal distribution of systemizing skills
fig 2.

cope with the hundreds of emotions that exist, so systemizing is a process that can cope with an enormous number of systems.

I will argue that, on average, males spontaneously systemize to a greater degree than do females. Again, note that I did not say "all males." I am only talking about statistical averages, and we can learn from the exceptions to this rule, too. But for now, let's call the male brain **type S** (for systemizing).

Just as we introduced the notion that in the population we all differ in how much empathy we have, so there are individual differences in our ability to systemize. Most of us fall in the center of the graph in Figure 2, but a few lucky individuals fall in the extreme right-hand end. Others find systems (like car engines, computers, science, math, or engineering) really puzzling, and they are at the other end—the left-hand tail—of the distribution. We will see later on if it really is the case that males (on average) are higher up the scale on measures of systemizing.

Systemizing Versus Empathizing

Is it possible to systemize a person? Systemizing works very well if you are trying to understand a system within a person, such as their ovaries. You can discover, for example, that among twenty-year-old pregnant women, one in ten will have a miscarriage, while among thirty-five-year-old pregnant women, the rate has risen to one in five. At the age of forty, one in three will have a miscarriage, and just two years later, at forty-two, nine out of ten women will miscarry. In this example, I have systemized a woman's fertility, in other words, I have treated it as a system that is lawful. The input is the woman's ovaries, the operation is the increase in a woman's age, and the output is a woman's risk of miscarriage.

Systemizing can also work to a useful degree if you are trying to understand a human group as a system, such as the pattern of traffic accidents on a particular freeway or patterns of voting behavior; hence the term traffic "system" or electoral "system." These systems, like any other, can be lawful, finite, and deterministic.

However, systemizing gets you almost nowhere in most day-to-day social interaction. Some philosophers suggest our everyday understanding of people (our "folk psychology") is rule-based, containing such if-then rules or generalizations as "if someone has a hard day, then they will be grumpy." Yet our behavior and emotions are not governed by rules to any useful degree. How do you explain that some people feel great after a hard day? Furthermore, the kinds of rules you can extract are of almost no use when it comes to making sense of, or predicting, the *moment-by-moment* changes in a person's behavior. Consider the rule "if people get what they want, they will be happy." Say that you followed the rule and gave Julia what she said she wanted for her birthday; why is she *still* not happy? Systemizing just cannot get a foothold into things like a person's fluctuating feelings.

While the natural way to understand and predict the nature of events and objects is to systemize, the natural way to understand a person is to empathize. Let's try empathizing Julia in our last example. Although it was her birthday and she got the present she wanted, it was also the week she was expecting news about her hospital test. Perhaps it wasn't good news. Maybe you should have asked her how she was, and tuned into her feelings, her mental world. Simple laws of how people will behave are next to useless even in this apparently simple interaction.

As you can see, systemizing and empathizing are wholly different kinds of processes. You use one process—empathizing—for making sense of an individual's behavior, and you use the other—systemizing—for predicting almost everything else. To systemize you need detachment in order to monitor information and track which factors cause information to vary. To empathize you need some degree of attachment in order to recognize that you are interacting with a person, not an object, but a person with feelings, and whose feelings affect your own.

Ultimately, systemizing and empathizing depend on independent sets of regions in the human brain. They are not mystical processes but are grounded in our neurophysiology.

The Main Brain Types

In 1987 Vancouver psychologist Doreen Kimura asked the question, "Are men's and women's brains really different?" She continued, "It would be amazing if men's and women's brains were not different, given the gross morphological and often striking behavioral differences between women and men."[1] Kimura is a good example of traditional researchers in this area who have emphasized two different dimensions in defining the male and female brain: language (female superiority) and spatial ability (male superiority). I do not deny the importance of language and spatial ability in defining sex differences, but I do believe that two neglected dimensions are empathizing and systemizing. Moreover, language superiority in women may exist because of their stronger empathizing ability, and good spatial ability in men may be just one instance of their stronger systemizing. But more of that later.

We all have both systemizing and empathizing skills. The question is: How much of each have you got? When it comes to measurement, you need good rulers or tests for each of these domains of skill. Later in the book, you will come across two of our tests: the Systemizing Quotient (SQ) and the Empathy Quotient (EQ). The difference between someone who scores higher than someone else on one of these measures is important, and we will look at such differences. But for now, one can envision three types of brain immediately. Think of these as three broad bands of individuals:

- Individuals in whom empathizing is stronger (more developed) than systemizing. For shorthand, E > S (where > means "greater than"). This is what I will call the female brain, or a brain of type E.
- Individuals in whom systemizing is stronger than empathizing. For shorthand, S > E. This is what I will call the male brain, or a brain of type S.
- Individuals in whom systemizing and empathizing are both equally strong. For shorthand, S = E. This is what I will call the balanced brain, or a brain of type B.

Which are you? Type E, type S, or type B? You can guess for now, but this is not about how you would like to see yourself. It's about how you actually score on different measures of these skills. We might all fantasize or delude ourselves that we are fit and strong, and can run fast enough to catch a bus. But when you are actually put to the test, how do you make out?

Let us now imagine two less common types of brain:

1. Individuals with the extreme male brain, that is, those who are extreme type S. For shorthand, S >> E. (The double-arrow symbol means there is a very large difference between skills in the two areas.) In their case, systemizing is normal or even hyper-developed, while empathizing is hypo-developed. In other words, these individuals may be talented systemizers but at the same time they may be "mindblind."[2] In Chapter 10 I will look at individuals on the autistic spectrum to see if they fit the profile of the extreme male brain.

2. Individuals with the extreme female brain, that is, those who are an extreme of type E. For shorthand, E >> S. These people have normal or even hyper-developed empathizing skills, while their systemizing is hypo-developed. In other words, these individuals may be wonderful empathizers, accurately tuning into the minds of others with amazing rapidity, but at the same time they may be "systemblind." In Chapter 12 I will ask if an extreme of the female brain really exists and, if so, whether this psychological profile leads to any particular difficulties.

Let me stick with the idea of autism as an extreme of the male brain for a moment, while I give you a taster of who you will meet later on our journey. Imagine a person who is so good at systemizing that they notice the same names of cameramen appearing in the credits of different television films. How are they keeping track of so much information in the small print on television? Or imagine a person who is so good at systemizing that they can tell you that if March 22 is a Tuesday, then so will November 22 be. How have they managed to figure out the rules governing calendars to this extraordinary degree of detail? But now imagine that these super-systemizers have major difficulties in empathizing. They may not understand that just because *they* regard someone as their friend, it may not be mutual. Or they may not realize that their wife is upset unless she is actually crying.

Your Sex Does Not
Dictate Your Brain Type

Let's say that I can see you right now. Naturally, just by looking at you, even just at your face, I can tell whether you are male or female. I do not for a moment assume that knowing your sex will tell me anything about which type of brain you, as an individual, have.

The evidence I will review suggests that not all men have the male brain, and not all women have the female brain. In fact, some women have the male brain, and some men have the female brain. The central claim of this book is only that *more* males than females have a brain of type S, and *more* females than males have a brain of type E.

So it should be some reassurance to you if you are male and going for a job interview in the caring professions, or if you are female and going for a job interview in the technical professions, that your interviewer should assume nothing about your skills for these jobs from your sex alone. I, for example, am male, but would be totally unsuited to a job in technical support for any kind of system (computers or otherwise). I was drawn to the helping profession of clinical psychology—a female-dominated world. I rely on a wonderful woman called Traci at Trinity College for advice on how to fix my computer. And I rely on two top women scientists, Svetlana and Rebecca, for advice on how to understand the biochemistry of hormones. (I'll introduce you to Svetlana and Rebecca properly in Chapter 8, as they both have interesting stories to share.)

When I talk about sex differences in the mind, I am dealing only with statistical averages. And if there is one point to get across at the outset, it is this: looking for sex differences is not the same as stereotyping. The search for sex differences enables us to discover how social and biological influences act on the two sexes in different ways, but it does not tell us about individuals. If we find that, on average, men are taller, heavier, stronger, faster, hairier, have larger heads and longer forearms than women, it does not mean that we won't find some women who are exceptions to these norms. (My grandfather's brother, the endocrinologist Robert Greenblatt,

documented some striking examples of such exceptions in his writings.[3])
Stereotyping, in contrast, judges individuals according to a set of assumptions about a group, and is pernicious. We recognize it as such in the context of racism, sexism, ageism, and classism, and for good reasons. Stereotyping reduces individuals to an average, whereas science recognizes that many people fall outside the average range for their group.

Mars and Venus

Some books on sex differences take a rather light-hearted approach. Although it may make amusing reading, it is not helpful scientifically to imagine that "men are from Mars and women are from Venus." For one thing, the joke about our coming from two different planets distracts us from the serious fact that both sexes have evolved on the same planet and yet tend to display differences in the way we think. We need to know why this is, and in Chapter 9 I look at the possibility that the two sexes' minds evolved to be adapted to different niches as a result of different evolutionary pressures. Moreover, the view that men are from Mars and women Venus paints the differences between the two sexes as too extreme. The two sexes are different, but are not so different that we cannot understand each other.[4]

There is a further reason why I think a serious book on this topic is needed. Humor is important, and satire has its place, but light-hearted jibing at the opposite sex can easily spill over into sexism. For example, recently on British television I heard the following joke by a female talk-show host: "Women are from Venus, men are dumb." A few women in the audience laughed. Her female co-presenter then asked, "Do we really need men? What use are they?" To which the first presenter replied, "I've heard men are trainable and can make good house pets." In some ways, this sort of sexist abuse of men by women is astonishing, and would never be tolerated if the subject of the joke was a woman, or was black, Jewish, or gay. Later that day, my teenage son showed me a book he was reading. The book fell open to a page containing the following joke: "Why did God create women? Because dogs can't open the fridge to get the beer." Such sexist humor is deplorable, and when we hear women producing it against men, it comes across as the humor of the victim-turned-victimizer. It is not that I think that the topic of sex differences can't be the focus of humor, but I do think it is important that we do not repeat old forms of oppression in a new guise.

The Politics of
Studying Sex Differences

Responsible scientists in this field are careful not to perpetuate the mistaken attitudes of former generations by assuming that sex differences imply that one sex is inferior overall. At the beginning of the twentieth century Gustav Le Bon made the mistake of concluding that female inferiority "was so obvious that no one can contest it for a minute."[5] One hundred years later, it is easy to contest Le Bon's position. Psychological sex differences are often (though not always) found, yet there are some domains in which women excel compared to men and other domains in which men excel compared to women. *Overall* intelligence is not better in one sex or the other, but the profiles (reflecting relative strengths in specific domains) are *different* between the two sexes. I am investigating the claim that women are better at empathizing and men are better at systemizing, but that this does not mean that one sex is more intelligent overall.

In earlier decades the very idea of psychological sex differences would have triggered a public outcry. The 1960s and 70s saw an ideology that dismissed psychological sex differences as either mythical, or if real, non-essential—that is, not a reflection of any deep differences between the sexes *per se*, but a reflection of different cultural forces acting on the sexes. But the accumulation of evidence from independent laboratories over many decades persuades me that there are essential differences that need to be addressed. The old idea that these might be wholly cultural in origin is nowadays too simplistic.

We must be wary, of course, of assuming that sex differences are only due to biology. To do this would be to commit the opposite error to that seen in the 1960s when it was frequently assumed that all sex differences reflected socialization. Like some people reading this book, I would like to believe that, deep down, men and women's minds do not differ in essence. That would be a very satisfying truth. It would mean that all those centuries of inequality between the sexes that the world has witnessed—inequalities that continue today—could in principle be swept away by fairer and better methods of education and upbringing. I remain a staunch supporter of efforts to eliminate inequality in society. But part of what we consider in Chapters 7 to 9 is whether the differences that have been found between the sexes really can be explained away as a result of socialization, or whether biology plays a significant role too.

Discussing sex differences of course drops you straight into the heart of the political correctness debate. Some people say that even looking for sex differences reveals a sexist mind that is looking for ways to perpetuate the historical inequities women have suffered. There is no doubt at all about the reality of the oppression of women, and the last thing I want is to perpetuate this. Nor for that matter do I want to oppress men, which has been the aim of some authors. Questions about sex differences can still be asked without aiming to oppress either sex.

I have spent more than five years writing this book. This is because the topic was just too politically sensitive to complete in the 1990s. I postponed finishing this book because I was unsure whether a discussion of psychological sex differences could proceed dispassionately. Fortunately there are now growing numbers of people, feminists included, who recognize that asking such questions need not lead to the perpetuation of sexual inequalities. In fact, the opposite can be true. It is by acquiring and using knowledge responsibly that sexism can be eliminated. My women friends, most of whom consider themselves feminists, have persuaded me that the time is ripe for such a discussion. My male friends are also beginning to recognize this.

Sexism, it could be said, occurs when an individual man or woman is judged to be x or y, just by virtue of their sex. If there is any message in this book, it will be to unpack this sexist assumption and to show just how wrong it is. Don't assume that the better parent in a child custody case is the mother, since it could be that the father is a wonderful empathizer who can tune into his child's needs, while the mother cannot. The family law courts typically assume that the better parent will be the mother, but they are wrong to prejudge the case. That is stereotyping. And don't assume that a young woman won't survive the university math course she has applied for. She may be a talented systemizer compared to the young male applicant who is waiting outside. Individuals are just that: individuals.

At the dawn of this new millennium, the picture I saw in the 1990s has changed substantially. Whereas old-style feminists used to assert that there was nothing men could do that a woman could not do equally well, today many feminists have become rather proud that there are things that most women can do that most men cannot do as well. Hosting a large party tactfully, making everyone feel included, is just one example of something that many men may shy away from. It is one that many women would know how to carry off with little effort. Finding out about a friend's personal and delicate problem in a way that makes that friend feel supported, cared for, and rapidly understood is something that many women feel at ease with, but which many men might stumble over or prefer to avoid. These abilities require good empathizing skills.

We have always known that people are drawn to certain subjects when they want something to read. At the newsstand on the train platform or airport departure lounge, those with brain type E will go to the magazine rack featuring fashion, romance, beauty, intimacy, emotional problems, counseling, relationship advice, and parenting. Those with brain type S will go to a different magazine rack (we should thank the shop owners for separating them so clearly for us) featuring computers, cars, boats, photography, consumer guides, science, science fiction, do-it-yourself projects, music equipment, hi-fi, action, guns, tools, and the great outdoors.

Moreover, people with different brain types tend to have very different hobbies. Those with the male brain tend to spend hours happily engaged in car or motorcycle maintenance, small-plane piloting, sailing, bird- or train-spotting, mathematics, tweaking their sound systems, or busy with computer games and programming, do-it-yourself projects, or photography. Those with the female brain tend to prefer to spend their time engaged in coffee mornings or having supper with friends, advising them on relationship problems, or caring for people or pets, or working for volunteer phone-lines listening to depressed, hurt, needy, or even suicidal anonymous callers.

The sorts of topics that distinguish the male and female brain's choice of reading material and hobbies also broadly define their choices of what to watch on television and what to listen to on the radio. We recognize these distinctions. So do magazine publishers, shopkeepers, and television producers. But how early are these differences present? Let's go back to childhood and meet a real boy and a real girl.

2

Boy Meets Girl

The two children I am going to tell you about are brother and sister, and their names have been changed to protect their identities. They are described in the words of their mother.

If you are a parent, judge how closely they resemble your own children. Or see if you recognize your own childhood in either of them. They illustrate in an immediate way the two dimensions of systemizing and empathizing that we will meet repeatedly along our journey. I will consider the psychological evidence for such sex differences in Chapters 4 and 6.

Alex: Cars, Soccer, Music, and Computers

"As a toddler, Alex could concentrate for ages when he was exploring something. He would turn the thing over, open any parts that could be opened and press any buttons that were on the object's surface. He just loved to see what would happen when he poked and prodded different parts of a thing.

"He also loved miniature tractors, fire engines, and cars. If there was a question about what kind of book to buy Alex, people always knew that a book about tractors was a safe present. At the age of three he loved to collect small toy vehicles. He would drag his dad over to the relevant counter in the local toy shop, or rummage through old boxes in the local garage sale. Then he would sift out little cars that he didn't have at home. His favorite video was *Thomas the Tank Engine*—he knew the names of all of the trains backwards.

"Of course, he liked people too. He chatted to them, smiled at them and played nicely with other children. But his real fascination was with little vehicles and how things worked.

"I don't know why he had the vehicle thing. Both of us, his parents, are bored silly by people talking about cars. And our nanny was one of those gentle souls who thought cars were the source of the world's problems. She was more of a hippie—anti-technology, and into Buddhism. So she couldn't have been the one who turned Alex into a vehicle junkie, age two. Nor could it have been playgroup, as he hadn't started there when this 'vehicle virus' invaded his brain.

"He was just two years old when he told us what he liked to look at when he went into a toy shop. His father would lead him over to the other sections of the shop, but it was as if there were only one corner of the universe worth checking out: toy vehicles. And I don't think his grandparents or uncles or our friends introduced him to the joys of vehicles. God knows where he got it from. It went on like that for a couple of years.

"Thankfully, by the age of five his interests had moved on. He still collected things but a little boy he played with introduced him to soccer stickers. You got six in a pack down at the local newsstand on Holloway Road. Little Alex used to drag his dad down there every Saturday. In a frenzy, Alex would rip open the packet, yelping with delight if he got the sticker he needed. He would be so disappointed if he got one he already had. Nevertheless, he would carefully sort the doubles into a different pile, to be swapped with his friends at school. The novel ones were neatly stuck into his soccer album. I remember he would impress visitors by being able to name any player in seconds just from having seen the face on a sticker. There must have been hundreds of names and faces to remember—the whole of the premier league!

"I can recall the exact day his soccer sticker collection started. His friend Matthew, also five years old, showed Alex his sticker album. Matthew told him which shop you could buy the stickers in, and after about half an hour of leafing through the partially filled pages, you could see that Alex was getting hooked. Alex had been exposed to many things, but for whatever reason *this* was the new activity that took root. It was as if Alex's brain were just waiting for something like this to come along.

"For the next three soccer seasons, Alex spent all his pocket money on packs of stickers. He would go to school with a great wad of doubles he could swap with his mates. The unique ones he lovingly placed in their permanent positions in the album. We've still got his albums in the attic somewhere.

"Soccer stickers were a springboard into the wider soccer world, and it wasn't long before Alex *had* to buy the latest issue of *Shoot* from the local newsstand on the street corner. He would pore over the tiny print in this magazine, or in the sports pages of the newspapers, absorbing trivial information. I remember being taken aback when he would talk about it. For example, if you named a team, he could tell you not only its players but also details about them. He knew which teams they had transferred from, for what price, and what their goal averages were this season and last season. Somehow, he had also absorbed the soccer league tables system. I remember being shocked when, at the age of seven, he started talking about aggregates. Seven years old and he comes up with a word like 'aggregates'! When his father asked him what an aggregate was, little Alex pointed to the specific column in the league table data in the newspaper, and explained that *that* was what it was. He then condescended to explain to his father what it meant. His father was flabbergasted that Alex not only had cracked this system so thoroughly but also that he was interested enough to crack it in the first place. And where did he get this interest? His dad and I used to chuck out the sports pages of the newspaper, we had so little interest in all that. Neither of us had ever bothered to explore what those columns of tiny numbers were all about. Thousands of numbers printed in a font so small you had to squint to read them!

"When he was eight years old his soccer interest entered a new level. He had tuned into the fact that each premier league team had at least two different jerseys, one for home and one for away matches. He would drag his dad or grandmother into sports shops and plead for his favorite shirt. And they were expensive! He would also spend hours at his desk, drawing up lists of his dream team players for England. He endlessly revised it as if he were the England manager, thinking of whom he would pick and for which position, even down to who he would put on the bench.

"By the age of ten his interest in soccer had disappeared. His dad and I were rather relieved. But it was almost as if Alex's interest was fueling itself, moving on to a new topic when the current one was exhausted. Soccer was soon replaced by pop music. On Friday nights there was only one thing on Alex's mind. Getting back home in time for *Top of the Pops* on television. Nothing was permitted to get in the way of this. He would pre-set the video recorder so that he didn't miss finding out who was number one, number two, number three, etc. Just like his soccer league table obsession, when he had to see which position each team was in, and how each had moved up or down in this system, so with the pop music charts.

"On Saturday mornings Alex would visit HMV (the local music store) to buy one or two singles on tape. Then he would go home, up to his bedroom and listen to his latest acquisition. After playing it a couple of times, he would master the lyrics, and hum and sing it to himself for the rest of the week. The new tapes then got stored in his tape collection. But not just anywhere in the tape collection. They had to go in their right position, which meant their position in *his* charts. Each week he would draw up his own pop charts according to what was his first, second, and third favorite, etc. I remember we used to quiz him about this. He would tell you that a particular song was, say, number four in the official charts, that it had moved up from number sixteen last week, but that in his own charts, this song was number one.

"During the week he would make a compilation tape, using a tape-to-tape recorder, so that he could give me or a friend a tape of his current favorite songs. The order on the tape was critical. He would write each song's title and author carefully on the outside cover. When Sunday evening came round he would listen to the round-up of the Top 40 on the radio. On Tuesday afternoons he'd be down to the newsstand to pick up his copy of *Smash Hits* magazine. The rest of his leisure time was spent poring over the small print of these teen-zines, accumulating massive amounts of trivial information about pop stars.

"We never had much interest in the pop charts, so, like his soccer interests, he wasn't encouraged to pursue it by us. If anything, like most parents, we tried to direct him to things we thought were good for him: piano practice, tennis lessons, reading novels, and playing with his friends. Don't get me wrong. He did all these things, but they paled in comparison with his true passions. These seemed to come from deep within him.

"His teens saw him getting more and more into computers. How he found all this technical stuff on the computer, I don't know. No one taught him how to do it. He just sat there and worked it all out. And he loved to play with graphics packages. He'd produce all these beautiful-looking documents for his homework.

"For leisure, he played in a band. He's still really into his music. It's nice that they all get together to play. It's funny to watch them because they're all so serious about it. The music is clearly the main reason for getting together, not the chatting. There's not much of that.

"As an adult, Alex is very independent-minded. At home and at work, he likes things to be done the way *he* likes. He does what he wants, and doesn't necessarily follow the group. He is not shy about expressing his views, and can be a bit blunt. He's not reticent to tell another person he thinks they're wrong. Otherwise, he just gets on and pursues his own interests, a bit single-mindedly.

"He will talk about his interests with his friends in the pub. Conversation tends to be about their shared activities. He has a few good friends he sees to play snooker or squash with. But in many ways he's also quite happy being solitary. He just doesn't seem to need to chat for hours on the phone and socialize as frequently as my daughter or me, for example. He's a bit like his dad in that respect."

Hannah (Alex's Sister): Dolls, Cuddlies, Animals, and People

"Hannah was so completely different from Alex. As an eighteen-month-old, whereas Alex was engrossed with *things*, Hannah's big passion was *people*. No miniature tractors for her. No way. We still had Alex's toys in the toy box, but she showed no interest in them. She was just so sociable. She would smile at new people, and take them one of her toys or show them a drawing she had made. She loved to play teasing games: offering things to people, and then withdrawing them at the last minute. Generally, she was always clowning around.

"I remember, at about two years old, she would lay out all her teddy bears. She'd give them all pretend tea, make them drink, and make them talk and walk. We would listen to her having all these pretend conversations with them. It made us laugh so much. She'd use all the emotional intonation that you would toward a person—only it was for her stuffed animals. She would say, 'Ahh. Don't worry,' and comfort them. Or she'd say, 'Hello, Pippa, how're you?' to her cuddly toy dog, and 'Really?' as if chatting to it. She gave names to all her teddies. They corresponded to the people in our neighbor's family. I remember she had a bear called Emma, named after a little girl in the same street. This bear had a sister bear called Clara, a brother bear called Matthew, a mother bear called Sue, and a father bear called Rob. They were all named after the people in Emma's real family. I was amazed at how she paid attention to everyone in this little girl's family.

"She wasn't into things like vehicles or toy cranes, like Alex was. She was into how to make people laugh and smile. I remember, when she was eighteen months old, her favorite game was putting her fingers into her food. She'd paint it delicately on her face, then look up and grin at the adults smiling at her. Or she would put her little hands over her eyes, and then suddenly reveal her eyes. Everyone would join in this game and say, 'Hiyee.' Or she would pout, pretending to be sad. She looked so sweet, and people would say, 'Hannah, what's wrong?' Then, in the next second, she would switch on her sparkling smile.

"Everybody thought she was so cute the way she played with our reactions. She just *loved* an audience. Some of these games were quite subtle. For example, she might slightly turn her eyes away, as if she wasn't listening any more. Then she'd switch her gaze back to you seconds later, slightly raising her eyebrows as if to say, 'Hey, I'm still interested in you, and I want to play with you.' She was such a flirt. Alex wasn't into those games at all.

"I remember she spoke earlier than her brother, and by the age of two her language had really taken off. She didn't like to go round naming things, like Alex had done. Instead, she was into saying little phrases that people loved to reply to. She would say things like 'Hi' and 'How're you?' It always got a response. Or she'd say, 'D'ya know what?' This cute little phrase was irresistible, so that you felt you had to reply, 'What?' And then she would cheekily reply, 'Nothing!' It was just her little game, and she would drive us crazy sometimes. But mostly it got the adults grinning, no matter what sort of mood they had been in. Sometimes she would do it after she had been told off for something, or after there'd been an argument, and it always worked brilliantly. You felt she was winking at you, it diffused tension, and it created a bond between you and her. Most of all she loved humor, and she had the knack of getting everybody to relax and laugh. What a gift.

"At the age of four she was into dolls and small toy animals. She would spend hours dressing and undressing Barbie dolls, brushing their hair. It wasn't the doll's *house*. It was the dolls and animals *themselves* she really liked. It started with little toy horses, toy cats, and toy puppies. She would ask to buy them in toy shops, just as Alex had asked us for toy vehicles. I suppose toy animals were her first collection. If it was soft and cuddly with big eyes, she had to have it. She would coo over these little creatures, saying, 'Oh, but it's *so* cute,' in a voice that was higher than her normal voice, but which sounded like a mother speaking to a real baby.

"She would buy *Pony* magazine at the local newsstand, and cut out the pages with pictures of kittens or foals to stick on her bedroom wall. Her walls ended up looking so different than Alex's. His were plastered with soccer team photos and posters of his warrior heroes. You could read their personalities by what was stuck up on those walls. She also enjoyed going horse riding, and would love to go to the pet shop—just to look.

"Eventually she wanted a real pet. She'd relentlessly ask the same questions each night: 'Daddy, why can't I have my own cat?' or 'Daddy, can I have a puppy?' or 'Daddy, I *really* want a rabbit.' When she was six her dream came true. We gave in and got her a cat. She stroked it, and worried about it. 'Is it cold outside?' she'd ask. 'Have you fed it today? Don't you *care* about her? She might be feeling lonely.'

"She still loved those soft little toy animals. She loved to handle them. I have to admit, they were very strokable. One day, when she was about seven, she and I went into town together. She had brought three of her little toy animals with her in the car. When we parked, she announced she would bring just one of them with her. I told her she could bring another one if she wanted, since she could easily carry two. She replied that if she left two behind, then they wouldn't feel lonely because they would have each other; the other one would be fine because it would be with us. She'd rapidly realized that the best plan would be to leave the other two together, to make sure no one felt left out. I remember thinking how amazing it was that she had this kindness for what her brother thought was just a piece of cloth.

"As an older child, Hannah still loved horses but was also into pop music. She loved to dance with her girlfriends. They'd spend hours doing new hairstyles on each other. Unlike her brother, she wasn't a mine of information about the position of different bands in the charts. For her, it was dancing or singing in front of the mirror with her girlfriends that was important. They would spend time putting on make-up together, telling each other how lovely the other looked. They connected in a special way. That continued into her teens. And she'd always have a huge collection of beautiful felt-tip pens in every color, which she'd use to decorate the covers of her books at school.

"She's an adult now. She's a really sympathetic, supportive person. She would never hurt a fly. She has quite a few close, confiding relationships. She loves to help other people. She's always phoning her friends to find out how they are. Sometimes she's on the phone for hours, whereas Alex can go for weeks without being in touch with some of the people he considers are his close friends.

"Hannah loves to get together with her girlfriends just to chat. She's really good at asking people sensitive questions so that she can explore how they're feeling and find out about their experiences. She does talk about herself, but never in a way that dominates. She's very careful to avoid causing any offense, and tries not to inadvertently hurt someone by neglecting them. She's always concerned to make sure people are relaxed around her, and tries not to stick out too much. When she shows concern, you feel she's really understood what you've been through. And she's so easily moved by hearing a story about someone else's distress or joy. She gets really emotional. As if it had happened to her. Just like me, I suppose."

So now you have met Alex and Hannah. In many ways, they are a very typical boy and girl. Why does one person like small cuddly animals, while the other likes toy cranes? Why does one like computers, while the other prefers to make a best friend? Why does one person like engineering, and another person enjoy caring for others? Alex and Hannah's interests typify the two different brain types we will explore throughout this book.

A brain of type S could be what drove Alex to enjoy playing with toy vehicles, to compile lists of sports teams and lists of pop songs, to be interested in collecting, and to thoroughly explore fact-based systems. A brain of type E could be what drove Hannah to connect in a caring way with, and to read emotions into anything even remotely resembling a person.

But of course, the above accounts are only one mother's anecdotes. They in no way prove that there are real sex differences in empathizing and systemizing, but simply hint at them. In Chapters 4 and 6 we look at the scientific evidence.

3

What Is Empathizing?

In this chapter we will consider what we mean by "empathizing" in more detail. If you think that you know what it is, perhaps because you consider yourself to be an empathic person, you could skip to the next chapter where we will delve into the scientific evidence. However, the funny thing about empathizing is that by definition you would have a hard time realizing that you were short of it. In order to empathize you need to be aware of how other people see you. You may *believe* that you are the most sensitive being on the planet, but none of us can ever really know how we are coming across to others. We can only do our best, and the reality may be that our own evaluation of ourselves falls short of how others *actually* perceive us.

Most of us have some awareness of our empathizing skills, but we may not know when we have reached our limits. In this sense, empathizing is not like athletic ability, where you get direct feedback during your performance about whether you are any good at it or not. You try for that high jump, and if you miss you hit the bar with some force, and see and feel the bar as it falls from its supports. During a conversation you may aim to understand and share the thoughts and feelings of another person, and you may walk away from it believing that you were truly empathic, that you sailed over the bar with plenty of room to spare; however, the person you were just interacting with might never tell you how limited your empathy was, that you hit the bar with such an impact that they could hear the clang for a long time afterwards, but that they were too hurt, or too diplomatic, to tell you.

Empathizing is about spontaneously and naturally tuning into the other person's thoughts and feelings, whatever these might be. It is not just about reacting to a small number of emotions in others, such as their pain or sadness; it is about reading the emotional atmosphere between people. It is about effortlessly putting yourself into another's shoes, sensitively negotiating an interaction with another person so as not to hurt or offend them in any way, caring about another's feelings.

A good empathizer can immediately sense when an emotional change has occurred in someone, what the causes of this might be, and what might make this particular person feel better or worse. A good empathizer responds intuitively to a change in another person's mood with concern, appreciation, understanding, comforting, or whatever the appropriate emotion might be.

Empathizing leads you to pick up the phone and tell someone you are thinking about them and their current situation, even when your own life demands are equally pressing. Empathizing leads you to constantly search people's tone of voice and to scan people's faces, especially their eyes, to pick up how they might be feeling or what they might be thinking. You use the "language of the eyes," and intonation, as windows to their mind.[1] And empathizing drives you to do this because you start from the position that your view of the world may not be the only one, or the true one, and that their views and feelings matter.

The natural empathizer can perceive fine shifts of mood, all the intermediate shades of an emotion in another person that might otherwise go unnoticed. Take hostility, for example. Some people only notice a few shades of hostility (such as aggression, hate, and threat). In contrast, a good empathizer might recognize fifty shades of hostility (such as contempt, cruelty, condescension, and superciliousness). Empathy can be compared to color vision in this way. Some people notice just a few shades of blue, while others notice a hundred. My colleagues Jacqueline Hill, Sally Wheelwright, Ofer Golan, and I recently completed an emotion taxonomy (an encyclopedia of emotions, if you like), and discovered that there are 412 discrete (mutually exclusive, semantically distinct) human emotions. Some people find it easy to define the subtle differences between such shades of emotion, and for others the differences can be very hard to see.[2]

A natural empathizer not only notices others' feelings but also continually thinks about what the other person might be feeling, thinking, or intending. They empathize with people who are present, and with those who aren't present but whose thoughts and feelings have a bearing on the present in some way. They read the emotional weather in this way not because they want to manipulate the person. Rather, the person with the type E brain continually cares how the other might be feeling.

Empathy is a defining feature of human relationships. For example, empathy stops you doing things that would hurt another person's feelings. Empathy makes you bite your lip, rather than say something that may offend someone or make them feel hurt or rejected. Empathy also stops you inflicting physical pain on a person or animal. You may feel angry toward your dog for barking, but you don't hit him because you know he would suffer. Empathy helps you tune in to someone else's world; you have to set aside your own world—your perception, knowledge, assumptions, or feelings. It allows you to see another side of an argument easily. Empathy drives you to care for, or offer comfort to, another person, even if they are unrelated to you and you stand to gain nothing in return. Imagine you are a bystander, witnessing a crash, and you are the first on the scene. Empathy propels you to sit with the victim of the crash, checking how they are, reassuring them that someone is there for them. Seconds before, you had never met each other; minutes later, you might never see that person again; but you still care.

Empathy also makes real communication possible. Talking at a person is not real communication. It is a monologue. If you talk for significantly more than 50 per cent of the time every few sentences, it is not a conversation. It is venting, or story telling, or lecturing, or indoctrinating, or controlling, or persuading, or dominating, or filling silence. In any conversation there is a risk that one party will hijack the topic in an undemocratic manner. They may not intend to be undemocratic, but in hijacking the conversation the speaker does not stop to consider that if they are doing all the talking this is only fulfilling *their* needs, not the listener's. Empathy ensures this risk is minimized by enabling the speaker to check how long to carry on for, and to be receptive to the listener's wish to switch to a different topic.

Real conversation is sensitive to *this* listener at *this* time. Empathy leads you to ask the listener how *they* feel and to check if they want to enter the dialogue, or what *they* think about the topic. Not to check just once, and then ignore their thoughts and feelings while you focus on your own. Rather, to keep asking, frequently, in the dialogue.

Why check? Because otherwise you might be pouring words all over your listener without them being interested. Worse still, they may actually find your torrent of words unpleasant in some way. "Dumping on someone" is an apt expression when someone has vented in a one-sided way rather than being sensitive to or interested in, or fair to, their listener. It is always a good idea to check if the other person wants to hear your words.

Empathy leads you not just to check, but to be able to follow through on what they say, so that they do not feel that you showed an insincere, shallow interest in them. Empathy allows for a reciprocal dialogue, because you are constantly making space in the conversation for the other person, through turn-taking. Empathy allows you to adjust your conversation to be attuned to theirs.

Moreover, empathy involves a leap of imagination into someone else's head. While you can try to figure out another person's thoughts and feelings by reading their face, their voice and their posture, ultimately their internal world is not transparent, and in order to climb inside someone's head one must imagine what it is like to be them.

However, you are not empathizing if you are doing all of the above in order to appear appropriate, or as an intellectual exercise. You do it because you can't help doing it, because you care about the other person's thoughts and feelings, because it matters. Someone who is less skilled at empathizing may be able to do it only when reminded, or if they discover that they are included more often when they do or say the right thing, and they may even rehearse how to empathize to get the benefits. But they may not do it spontaneously. Other people's feelings matter less to them, and it takes an effort to maintain empathic appearances. It's easy for the natural empathizer. It requires no effort at all. They can keep it going for hours.

Empathy ensures that you see a person as a person, with feelings, rather than as a thing to be used to satisfy your own needs and desires. For example, an empathic father may decide not to smack his child, even if he feels outrage at the child's obstinate refusal to cooperate: his feelings of frustration are set aside in the face of the hurt that could be caused to another. Or consider the example of the empathic boss who appreciates that her employees are not production slaves but have personal lives that need their own private time and space, even within working hours.

So empathy triggers you to care how the other person feels and what they think. Why should we care? Through empathy you can identify if someone needs support, and they can do the same for you. You can learn from others, and they from you. You can avoid causing offense, and they can too. You can establish if there is a meeting of minds, and you can engage in genuine communication. Empathy is the glue of social relationships. It motivates you to find out and care about the other person's experience. It leads you to ask about their own problems, to make them feel supported, rather than simply offloading your own difficulties on to them.

Furthermore, empathy provides a framework for the development of a moral code. Despite what the Old Testament tells us, moral codes are not found mysteriously carved on tablets of stone up windswept mountains in the Sinai Desert. People build moral codes from natural empathy, fellow feeling, and compassion. And although some people believe that legal systems determine how we should act (you may have met some lawyers or traffic wardens like this), such systems are simply an attempt to regulate behavior. The legal system underpins a moral code. It would be marvelous if systemizing, the pure process of logic, could give us a sense of justice and injustice, but, as history has shown us, logic and legal systems can be used to defend autocratic, even genocidal, regimes—Nazism is one of the clearest recent examples of this.

One can be a fine scientist, an excellent logician, but without a full quotient of empathy one's moral principles may not be sufficiently developed to determine whether an action could cause harm. A case in point is Professor Konrad Lorenz, widely regarded to be the founding father of ethology, and the master of careful observation and measurement of the natural behavior of animals in the wild. I read his books at the tender age of nineteen, when I was studying psychology at Oxford. A recent book points out that, despite his high intelligence, the esteemed Lorenz was unable to see that the political ideology of ethnic purification in Germany in the 1940s where he worked, and indeed his own views on eugenics, were hurtful and even dangerous.[3]

This is not a complete list of the reasons why empathy is so important, but hopefully it highlights the fact that empathy is central to what it is to be a person, as distinct from any other kind of animal. There may be other species capable of empathy, and the case has been made often enough for dolphins, the great apes and St. Bernard rescue dogs. A famous example is the gorilla Binti, who picked up a three-year-old boy who had fallen into her cage in the zoo, and who comforted the injured child and carried him to a door where zookeepers could remove him.[4] Although this hints that empathy may have an evolutionary lineage visible in the great apes, such evidence is still controversial and I will restrict myself to the clear-cut case of people.

Components of Empathy

There are two major elements to empathy. The first is the cognitive component: understanding the other's feelings and the ability to take their perspective. Swiss developmental psychologist Jean Piaget (1896–1980) called this aspect of empathy "decentering," or "responding non-egocentrically," which are both helpful ways of capturing this cognitive component. More recently developmental psychologists have referred to this aspect of empathy in terms of using a "theory of mind," or "mindreading." Essentially, the cognitive component entails setting aside your own current perspective, attributing a mental state (sometimes called an "attitude") to the other person, and then inferring the likely content of their mental state, given their experience. The cognitive component also allows you to *predict* the other person's behavior or mental state.[5]

The second element to empathy is the affective component. This is an observer's appropriate emotional response to another person's emotional state. Sympathy is just one such type of empathic response, where you feel both an emotional response to someone else's distress and a desire to alleviate their suffering. (You may not actually act on this desire, but at least you feel that you want to reduce the other's distress.) In Figure 3, sympathy is shown as a subset of the affective component in empathy.

Sympathy is perhaps the most easily distinguishable case of empathy. You feel sympathy when you walk past a homeless person in the winter, and you want to help them out of their misfortune. You may do nothing about it, as you may also feel that your action would be futile given the many other homeless people in the same neighborhood, and the difficulty of helping them all. So you walk past. Your reaction was still sympathetic because you felt the desire to alleviate the other person's suffering. It was still sympathy whether or not you took the appropriate action and gave the poor guy your gloves.

But in other empathic reactions there is a different, still appropriate, emotional response to someone else's feelings. Perhaps you feel anger (at the sys-

Empathy

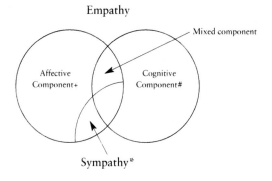

A model of empathy
fig 3.

+ Feeling an appropriate emotion triggered by
  seeing/learning of another's emotion.
Understanding and/or predicting what someone
  else might think, feel or do.
* Feeling an emotion triggered by seeing/learning of
  someone else's distress which moves you to want
  to alleviate their suffering.

tem) in response to the homeless person's sadness, or fear (for his safety), or guilt (over your inability to help him): these feelings are based on empathy. Feeling pleasure, or smugness, or hate toward him would not be empathic reactions, since none of these emotions is appropriate to *his* emotion.

If we accept these two aspects to empathizing (the cognitive and the affective), is it possible to formalize them? Psychologist Alan Leslie now works at Rutgers University; he inspired me when I was a young Ph.D. student and we worked together at London University in the early 1980s. Alan Leslie suggests the cognitive aspect involves what he calls an M-Representation (M for mental state). He characterizes it in this way:[6]

Agent-*Attitude*-Proposition

For example:

John-*thinks*-Sarah is beautiful

Here, the attitude (in the mind of the other person, in this case John's) is highlighted in italic. This tripartite structure captures the cognitive aspect of empathizing but could it be developed to include the affective aspect, namely, that the observer experiences an emotion triggered by the other person's emotion or mental state? To capture this second aspect would require a longer formulation:

Self-**Emotion** (Agent-*Attitude*-Proposition)

Here, the Emotion term is within the observer and is highlighted in bold. It is an appropriate affective reaction to everything that I have enclosed in parentheses, when the Agent is always another person or animal. For example:

Jane-**is concerned** (John-*feels sad*-his mother died)

This notation suggests that empathy is complex, involving chains of information embedded in highly specific ways. But of course what it fails to convey is how immediate and automatic empathy is, that Jane does not have to grind through laborious cognitive reasoning to feel concern at John's sadness. She feels it as clearly as she feels fear if she looks over a cliff edge, or disgust if she sees half a worm in her half-eaten apple.

In the following chapter we look at the evidence from studies of sex differences in a range of very different areas to see if it is predominantly *the female brain* that is hard-wired for this kind of natural, effortless empathizing.

4

The Female Brain as Empathizer: The Evidence

Styles of Play

Even at a very early age, children demonstrate gender differences in their abilities to empathize. Nowhere is this seen more clearly than when they are at play. Indeed, children as young as nineteen months tend to prefer a playmate of the *same* sex, which is believed by some people to reflect the different social styles of the two sexes: children may be selecting a partner whose social style meshes most easily with their own.[1]

Little boys are more physical when they want something than are little girls. Consider this example: when a group of children is given a toy movie player to play with, boys tend to get more than their fair share of looking down its eyepiece. They will just shoulder the girls out of the way: they have less empathy and are more self-centered.[2] If you put girls together with the same toy, the girl who ends up with more than her fair share gets there not by using such obvious physical tactics, but rather by verbal skills. She will bargain and persuade rather than push. This example demonstrates that, on average, young girls show more concern for fairness than boys do, and that even when a young girl's self-interest drives her, she will use mindreading to manipulate the other person into giving her what she wants.

Here's another example, which may strike many parents as familiar. Leave out some of those big plastic cars that children can ride on. You will soon see that young boys tend to play the ramming game: they deliberately

drive the vehicle into another child. The young girls ride around more carefully (when they can get their hands on the vehicles—the boys tend to hog
them), avoiding the other children as much as they can.[3]

American psychologist Eleanor Maccoby calls the boys' behavior "rough-
housing," a term that includes wrestling and mock fighting. I am sure you
will recognize this description of four-year-old boys horsing around:

> They bump, wrestle, and fall on to one another. One child pushes
> another back and forth in playful tussles . . . making machine gun
> sounds, and chasing one another around with space guns and
> spray bottles . . . Boys put clay into one another's hair . . . pretend
> to shoot one another, fall dead and roll on the floor.

Maccoby explains that all this rough stuff is not simply a sign that boys
are more active: girls are just as active when there are other kinds of toys to
play with, such as trampolines and skipping ropes. She also makes it clear
that rough-housing is not aggression; instead it is a good-natured trying out
of each other's toughness. This male style of play could be a lot of fun if you
are a boy who enjoys the same thing. Moreover, if a playful component hurts
or is intrusive, it needs lower empathizing in order to carry it out. Girls tend
to react very differently. If it happens once, she may take it in good spirit.
But if it happens repeatedly, the horsing around can feel insensitive.[4]

Of course, mock fighting is not always just playful. Sometimes it can be
agonistic—not full-blown aggression, but fairly close to it, such as threatening others, or getting into conflict. On average, boys produce much more
agonistic behavior, and shockingly, you can see these differences from as
early as two years old.

As we saw earlier, little boys also tend to have more trouble learning to
share toys. In one study, young boys showed fifty times more competition,
while girls showed twenty times more turn-taking. These are everyday examples of large sex differences in empathizing.[5]

Antisocial Conduct Disorder

A small number of boys end up in the clinics of child psychiatrists where
they are diagnosed with "conduct disorder." What a wonderful Victorian

word: conduct. But this word masks the fact that these children do not merely have a problem with the niceties of the rules of etiquette, such as which fork to use at a posh dinner party. Sometimes such children are described as "hard to manage," which may be a more accurate description. Such children tend to get into a lot of fights. They tend to perceive others as treating them in a hostile or aggressive way, even when to the reasonable observer there was no definite sign of hostility intended. This is an example of inaccurate empathizing: the child misjudges another person's intentions and emotions. Such misattribution of hostile intent is more common in boys.[6]

Concern and Comforting

Baby girls, as young as twelve months old, respond more empathically to the distress of other people, showing greater concern for others through more sad looks, sympathetic vocalizations, and comforting behavior. Interestingly, this echoes what you find at the other end of the age range, where far more women than men report that they frequently share the emotional distress of their friends. Women also show more comforting behavior, even of strangers, than men do.[7]

Theory of Mind

A number of studies suggest that by the age of three young girls are already ahead of boys in their ability to infer what people might be thinking or intending—that is, in using a "theory of mind." This is the cognitive component of empathy that I described in Chapter 3. For example, if you ask children to judge how a character in a story might be feeling on the inside, compared to the emotion that the character is showing on the outside, you will find that girls score more highly than boys. Or when asked how someone should look in different situations, for example if someone gives you a present that you don't like, girls are better at judging when it would be better to suppress showing an emotion, so as not to hurt the other person's feelings. Or when asked to judge when someone might have said something that was inappropriate—when someone committed a *faux pas*—girls from the age of seven score more highly than boys, which again indicates that females are better at empathizing.[8]

Judging Emotion

Women are more sensitive to facial expressions. They are better at decoding non-verbal communication, picking up subtle nuances in tone of voice or facial expression, and using them to judge a person's character.

The most well-known test of sensitivity to non-verbal cues of emotion is called the Profile of Nonverbal Sensitivity (PONS). On this test, women are more accurate in identifying the emotion of an actor. This sex difference holds up in countries as varied as New Guinea, Israel, Australia, and North America.[9]

Sally Wheelwright and I developed a test of empathizing in which the person is presented with photographs of facial expressions of emotions—but only the section of the face around the eyes. We call it the "Reading the Mind in the Eyes" Test. (Have a look at this, as it is reprinted in Appendix 1.) The task is to pick which word, from the four words that surround each photo, best describes what the person is thinking or feeling. Clearly, all you have to go on is the information around the eyes. We designed it in this way to make it a challenging test and to bring out the range of individual differences in empathizing. People are very good at the test, even though they believe they are going to find it really tough. It is a "forced choice" test, so even if you are unsure which word is correct, you are encouraged to guess. And as you may have anticipated, women are more accurate on this task.[10]

Relationships

We all value social relationships, but are there differences in what each sex values about other people? Women tend to value the development of altruistic, reciprocal relationships. Such relationships require good empathizing skills. In contrast, men tend to value power, politics, and competition. This pattern is found across widely different cultures and historical periods, and is even found among chimpanzees.[11]

A similar pattern is found among children, too. Girls are more likely to endorse cooperative items on a questionnaire ("I like to learn by working with other students") and to rate the establishment of intimacy as more important than the establishment of dominance. Boys are more likely than girls to endorse competitive items ("I like to do better work than my friends") and to rate social status as more important than intimacy. When three- to five-year-olds are asked how money should be distributed, more girls suggest sharing it out equally. This suggests that, on average, males value affirmation of their social status (their place in the social hierarchy system), while females value the supportive experience (empathy) that derives from being in an equal relationship.[12]

Sally Wheelwright and I put together the Friendship and Relationship Questionnaire (FQ) as a further way of testing this sex difference. We wanted to discover whether, in social relationships, men and women focused on the other person's feelings, or simply on the shared activity. Only the former involves empathizing. We found that, on average, women are more likely to value empathizing in friendships, while men are more likely to value shared interests. Other studies have reported similar results.[13]

Jealousy and Fantasies

If you ask men and women what their partner would have to do to trigger jealousy, you find that the triggers are very different for the two sexes. Men report relatively more subjective distress (and show more physiological distress) to a partner's imagined sexual infidelity. In contrast, women tend to report that imagining their partner becoming *emotionally* involved with someone else is what would trigger them to feel jealous. These differences seem to suggest that women focus more on the emotional aspects of relationships.

If you ask people about their sexual fantasies, these too reveal how the two sexes think differently about relationships. Women tend to think about the personal and emotional qualities of their fantasy partner, which suggests that they are unable to turn off their empathizing abilities even when they are thinking about sex. In contrast, men tend to focus on the physical characteristics of their partner. Empathizing may or may not figure in their fantasies, which suggests that it is something that they can turn off to varying degrees.[14]

Rape

The fact that some men are capable of sexual pleasure during rape, which by definition involves treating a person with *zero* empathy, demonstrates that for some men sex is entirely independent from an intimate, reciprocal emotional relationship. Consider the phenomenon of "drug rape," where a man poisons a woman's drink with an odorless, tasteless, colorless drug that renders her comatose for up to six hours, so that he can have sex with her as an object. Or consider that in Norway, during the Second World War, there were children raised in orphanages who were the product of sex between Nazi soldiers and Norwegian women. These children were deliberately bred for the sole purpose of spreading Aryan genes. There was no emotional relationship between the soldiers and the women they impregnated. The way these male soldiers thought about these women is sobering evidence for the theory that there are sex differences in empathy. Even more relevant is the fact that Norwegian men queued up for hours to bribe the guards of the orphanage with liquor to let them have sex with these children. Can men's sex drive really lead them to simply ignore people's feelings? Apparently so.

Fortunately, most men are not so lacking in empathy that they could hurt someone to this degree. But the existence of male rape suggests a sex difference in empathy at the extremes. Lower empathy is obviously not the only cause of rape, but it is likely to be a significant factor contributing to its occurrence.

Psychopathic Personality Disorder

Let's consider some seriously unpleasant people, those diagnosed in adulthood as psychopaths. These are people that you really do not want to have as your next-door neighbor. They are the ones who do really nasty things, like holding someone hostage and then cutting them up, or conning an old lady into handing over her life savings. Such people tend to be male. It is presumably uncontroversial that such individuals are low in the affective component of empathy. However, some studies suggest that they have no difficulty with the cognitive kind of empathy, which is why they can lie without feeling any guilt.[15]

Aggression

Let's go back to the ordinary person. Aggression, even in normal quantities, can only occur because of reduced empathizing. You just can't set out to hurt someone if you care about how they feel. If you feel angry, or jealous, however, these emotions can lower your empathy. In some circumstances your empathy is lowered for long enough to fail to inhibit aggression. Good empathy acts as a brake on aggression, but without it, aggression can occur. During aggression you are focused on how *you* feel, more than on how *the other person* feels.

Both sexes of course show aggression, and as such both are capable of reduced empathy at times. But you find a sex difference in how aggression is shown. Males tend to show far more direct aggression (pushing, hitting, punching, and so on). Females tend to show more indirect (or relational, covert) aggression. This occurs between people without them touching each other, or behind people's backs, and it includes things like gossip, exclusion, and bitchy remarks. Indirect aggression is, of course, still aggression. However, it could be said that to punch someone in the face or to wound them physically (the more male style of aggression) requires an even lower level of empathy than a verbal snipe (the more female style of aggression).[16]

Even if you disagree with this rather simplistic distinction—after all, some people think that subtle verbal attacks can hurt as much as sticks and stones—it is still the case that indirect aggression (the more female kind) needs better mindreading skills than does direct aggression (the more male kind). This is because its impact is strategic: you hurt person A by saying something negative about them to person B. Indirect aggression also involves deception: the aggressor can deny any malicious intent if challenged.[17]

Murder

Let's talk murder now, the ultimate in lack of empathy. It is a shocking statistic that in pre-industrial societies one in three young men is killed in a fight, between men. They tend to be men who feel that their reputation has been disrespected. In order that such "loss of face" does not lead to a loss of social status, they stand up for themselves. They send out the signal "Don't f*** with me." And how better to signal that you are a man of action, and not just words, than to kill someone. If you kill someone in a competitive fight, your social status goes rocketing up. Whereas in the developed world a murderer is considered to be a vicious person who should be locked up, in pre-industrial societies a murderer (following the provocation outlined above) is someone who gains respect.

Regarding sex differences in murder, Daly and Wilson wrote, "There is no known human society in which the level of lethal violence among women even approaches that among men."[18] They analyzed homicide records dating back over 700 years, from a range of different societies. They found that male-on-male homicide was thirty to forty times more frequent than female-on-female homicide. Studies show that in a range of different societies, two-thirds of male homicides do not occur during a crime but simply when there is a social conflict, in which the man feels he has been "dissed" (disrespected). Such homicides are carried out to save face and retain status.[19]

This sex difference in aggression and murder could be interpreted as a marker showing that empathizing is lower in males. Of course, the increased rates of physical aggression and homicide among males could reflect several other factors (such as differences in risk-taking), but reduced empathy may be one of the contributing factors. Equally, the male preoccupation with social status may be a useful marker of a higher systemizing drive in males. After all, social hierarchies are systems.

Let's have a closer look at what goes on in these social hierarchies.

Establishing Dominance Hierarchies

In a group, boys are quick to establish a "dominance hierarchy." This might reflect their lower empathizing *and* their higher systemizing skills, because typically a hierarchy is established by one person pushing others around, uncaringly, in order to become the leader.

It is not dissimilar to the way our male non-human primate relatives behave. For example, in a troop of monkeys or apes, males rapidly recognize their place in the system. When two males come across something valuable—food, shelter, or a mate—each male immediately knows whether to go for it, or whether to defer to the other male. How does each monkey know if they are above or below another monkey in the social group? Social hierarchies are not established in any mysterious way. They are not established by God on high handing down a ticket with a number on it, from one to a hundred. Hierarchies are established in a far more straightforward way: by competition. Two male primates (human or non-human) who have both seen a desirable object will face each other. Sometimes it will be clear from the outset that one defers to the other. If not, the *indirect* combat starts. They act tough, and make threatening gestures. They may do "the walk" (walking back and forth, eyeing and sizing each other up), until one of them backs down. Rarely does it become direct combat, but it will accelerate to this if the agonistic behaviors do not cause one of the primates to retreat.

This indirect confrontation, however ritualized, does not need to happen between every pair of males in the group. Other members of the group observing a few such interactions rapidly learn that, in any dispute between A and B, A is superior because B backs down. When the combat is between B and C, the observers learn that B is superior because C backs down. Then the primate uses the inexorable logic of transitive inference. (You may be amazed to discover that even a monkey can compute this logic.) It goes like this: if A is superior to B, and B is superior to C, then A is superior to C. As clear as night follows day, such logic ripples right through the group. This "if-then" rule-based logic is an instance of systemizing (which we look at in detail in the next two chapters). When one sees the same thing going on in humans and monkeys, one realizes that such behavior must have an evolutionary past. More on that in Chapter 9. Let's get back to sex differences in human social hierarchies.

Even among young children in nursery schools, there are more boys at the top of these dominance hierarchies. They are pushier, and they back down less often. In addition, the hierarchies are better established among the boys. The boys spend more time monitoring and maintaining the hierarchy. It seems to matter more to them.

You can test this. Ask a class of children who, of child A or B, determines what happens (who gets the toy, who gets to choose the game, who gets to choose where to sit, who picks the team, and so on). You will find there is better agreement among the boys. This suggests that they notice social rank, that it means a lot to them. Even in pre-school, little boys feel it is important not to appear weak, so as not to lose rank. They care about their own feelings and image more than someone else's, even if this means leaving the other person feeling hurt.

So here we see a trade-off between empathizing and systemizing. To be too empathic would be to let others walk all over you, and you would sink in the social system. To assert your rank, or even try to climb in the system, is to gain in status, often at the expense of someone else. Boys seem more willing to pay the price of putting themselves first, for the obvious personal benefits.

Young girls also establish social rank, but more often this is based on other qualities than simply acting tough. All of this is very relevant to empathizing, of course, since to insist on being right and putting someone else down is to care first and foremost about yourself, not about the other person.

Once again, boys seem to be less empathic than girls.[20]

Summer Camp

If I tell you about anthropologist Ritch Savin-Williams's remarkable study of a teenage summer camp, you will see this sex difference under a magnifying lens. When you read the next few passages, memories of your childhood that you might wish were forgotten could come back to you. It certainly reminds me of my days as a summer camp counselor at Lake Wabikon, in North Bay, Ontario.[21]

The teenagers arrived in the camp, and were put into single-sex cabins with strangers of the same age. As you might imagine, in the cabins dominance hierarchies were established. Some of the tactics used to achieve this were similar in the boys' and in the girls' groups. These tactics included ridiculing someone in the cabin, name-calling, and gossiping. This nasty behavior had an important pay-off: those who ended up higher in the dominance hierarchy also ended up with more control over the group.

So the depressing but realistic conclusion is that nastiness (or lower empathy) gets you higher socially, and gets you more control or power. For example, the teenagers who emerged as natural group leaders had more influence over which activities the group pursued, and got first choice on where they wanted to sleep. They even got offered seconds of food before anyone else.

But regarding the tactics used to climb the social hierarchy, that was as far as the similarities between the sexes went. In contrast, the differences between the sexes were quite startling.

Let's first have a peek into the boys' cabins. Put your eye to the keyhole to see the male mind at work. In some of the boys' groups, there were some boys who made their bid for social dominance within *hours* of arriving in the cabin. No point in wasting time, you might think. Here is how they did it: they would pick on someone in the cabin, not only by ridiculing them but also by picking on them physically, and in full view of the others.

Imagine a child who is just unpacking his rucksack and who is already feeling a bit homesick. He is reading a sweet little card his mother slipped in with his wash bag. Out of the blue, some boy jumps on him, gives him a push and calls him an insulting name. From the perspective of the boy who pushes his weight around in this way, a clear message is sent out to the whole cabin that he is boss. From our perspective of spying through the keyhole, it would be reasonable to wonder if this bully is down a few points in empathy.

In the cabin I supervised at summer camp, the poor child who was picked on was called Stuart. He was a sweet child, scapegoated because he was a bit overweight. Poor old Stuart. As soon as my back was turned, the self-appointed leader of the cabin reverted to planning nasty tricks to play on him. You no doubt remember the kinds of pranks from your own summer camp or school days. Poor Stuart was subjected to that awful trick where other children put his hand in a bowl of water while he was asleep at night, since the local folklore was that this guaranteed that he would urinate in his bed. Were they thinking about Stuart's feelings of embarrassment and victimization, or just their own tough humor, when they did that?

On another occasion, they did the unthinkable. They put a hood over Stuart's head, so that he was unable to see at all. Then they lifted him up and told him they were putting him on a chair. They put a rope around his neck that he was able to feel. They told him that the rope was tied to the ceiling, and that if he attempted to step off the chair he would hang himself. Unknown to poor blindfolded Stuart, he had not been put on a chair at all. They had simply lifted him up and put him back down on the floor. And unknown to Stuart, the rope was not attached to the ceiling but was simply loosely draped around his neck. But that did not stop Stuart feeling terrified at the prospect that if he did not do what they said—namely, stand there on the "chair" in his hooded state—he would hang himself. The boys who had done this nasty trick then left him there, and there he stood, paralyzed with fear and misery at this bullying, until I came into the cabin and found him, some hours later. Knowing afterwards that he had all along simply been standing safely on the floor, in no danger of dying at all, did nothing to reduce the trauma of this experience.

Now let's get back to the experiment and spy through the half-drawn curtains of the girls' cabins, to see the female mind at work. The girls tended to wait at least a week before starting to assert dominance. For them, being nice initially, which helped build friendships, was an equally important priority. Even when some girls did start to hint that they were in control, they mostly did this through subtle strategies—the odd put-down (in words), or the withholding of verbal communication or eye contact. It was rare for a girl to use physical force.

For example, a dominant girl would simply ignore a lower-status girl's suggestions or comments. She might even act as if the lower-status girl was not there, by not looking at her. Eye contact or social exclusion are powerful ways of exerting social control. By dishing out a little or no attention, you can make someone feel invisible, or even of no importance. I am sure that you recognize these tactics.

The girls' verbal means for establishing dominance were usually indirect. In one example, one girl suggested to another that she "take her napkin and clean a piece of food off her face." This apparently caring attitude actually draws attention to the other girl's clumsiness. A boy would simply call the other boy a slob, and invite the other boys to join in a group-ridiculing session of the victim. Both tactics may have the same effect, but the girls' method is more sophisticated.

Such tactics happen so fast that you can hardly pin down how it is that one girl can end up looking superior, and the other looking stupid. Girls more often use tactics such as saying "I won't be your friend any more" or they more often spread negative gossip about a girl—so-called "social alienation." They use more subtle verbal persuasion or even misinformation-based strategies. They are using a "theory of mind" even if they are not fully empathizing. Boys, in contrast, more often use a direct means of aggression: yelling, fighting, and calling each other blatantly offensive names.

You might say that the boys' method is more like using a sledgehammer to crack a nut. A boy in the same situation is more likely to go for the immediate goal, knowing that the net effect will work out in his favor (he rises in the group, while the other child sinks), even if he makes an immediate enemy in the process. But when a girl decides to "put someone else down," she thinks of how this could be done almost invisibly, so as not to risk acquiring the reputation of being a bully. If confronted, the girl can always say that the comment was not intended to be offensive, or that the lack of eye contact was unintended. In this way, she can preserve her reputation of being a nice person even when she has been a touch nasty.

As we saw in the study using the Friendship and Relationship Questionnaire (FQ), girls value intimacy. So this female strategy fulfills both aims: achieving social status without jeopardizing intimacy in her other relationships. Who wants to be intimate with someone who has a reputation for being nasty? The nastiness has to be covert, fleeting, and hard to pin down. In the boy's case, it is clear that that punch is intended. The signal value of the physical force is unambiguous, and the message conveyed is that the aggressor does not much care if the victim feels hurt and offended, nor if it is at the cost of intimacy in other relationships. The overriding aim is control, power, and the access to resources that this brings: reduced empathizing again. (In Chapter 9 we discuss why males and females might have such different priorities in their social lives.)

In the summer camp study they found that, once a boy was put down in this rather blunt way, *other* (lower-status) boys in the cabin jumped in to cement this victim's even-lower status. This was a means of establishing their own dominance over him. This reminds us that dominance hierarchies are dynamic, and that boys tend to be more often on the watch for opportunities to climb socially. So much for empathizing with the victim. More like, kick a guy when he is down. This was true from the lowest to the highest member of the social group.

The girls were also sensitive to opportunities to gain rank, but again the tactics were different. Girls tended to explicitly acknowledge the leadership of another girl, "sucking up" to the dominant girl. They would use flattery, charm, appreciation, and respect. For example, a less dominant girl would ask a more dominant one for advice and support. Or the less dominant one would offer to brush and arrange the dominant one's hair. (If these were non-human primates, consolidating their position in the social group, we would call it "grooming.")

Another difference is that the boys' dominance hierarchies tended to last the whole summer, whereas the girls' groups typically split up much sooner. The result of this was that fairly soon the girls would spend more time in groups of two or three, chatting together in a less rivalrous way, or getting intimate with their "best friend." The boys instead remained largely involved in group-competitive activities against other groups, with the leader directing them.

I have spent a long time on this summer camp experiment because there are obviously a lot of parallels we can draw out for many social situations: the classroom, the office, the committee, the playground. All of these social groupings develop their leaders, and leaders often need "fall guys" to stay on top. It is instructive to look at the role of increased mindreading among females and lower empathizing among males in determining a person's ascent up the social ladder, even if it is a bit depressing.

The other conclusion to emerge from this is that boys are far less reticent about making someone feel less equal than them. They will not lose sleep over the feelings of the poor boy at the bottom of the pile. They even enjoy their higher status. They are also more ready to physically hurt someone, or explicitly hurt their feelings, to increase their status.

Breaking Into a Group of Strangers

Two other ways to reveal a person's empathizing skill are to see how they (as a newcomer) join a group of strangers, and to see how they (as a host) react to a new person joining their group. This has been cleverly investigated in children by introducing a new boy or girl to a group who are already playing together.

Let's start with observing the newcomer. If the newcomer is female, she is more likely to stand and watch for a while in order to find out what is going on, and then try to fit in with the ongoing activity, for example by making helpful suggestions or comments. This usually leads to the newcomer being readily accepted into the group. It shows sensitivity, a desire not just to barge in and interrupt when this might not be wanted: female empathizing.

What happens if the newcomer is a boy? He is more likely to hijack the game by trying to change it, directing everyone's attention on to him. This is less successful than the female style. Children who use this more male style are less likely to be welcomed by the group (unsurprisingly). I mean, would you want someone who you did not yet know to just walk in and take over? Boys tend to act as if they care less about whether others think they are nice, and care more about whether others think they are tough. This fits with the male agenda of climbing the social hierarchy. This newcomer style in males reveals their lower empathizing and higher systemizing.

Now let's switch perspective and look at the children who are already part of the group. How do they react as hosts to the stranger who is trying to join in? It turns out that even by the age of six, girls are better at being hosts. They are more attentive to the newcomer. Boys often just ignore the newcomer's attempt to join in. They are more likely to carry on with what they were already doing, perhaps preoccupied by their own interests, or their own self-importance.

Now let's put these two findings together. The natural consequence of both the newcomer's and the host's strategies is that, if you are a girl, it is easier to join an all-girls group. Girls as hosts show higher levels of emotional sensitivity to the newcomer's predicament. And girls as newcomers show higher levels of emotional sensitivity to the host. Boys, in contrast, do not appear to care at all about the newcomer's or the host's feelings. As Eleanor Maccoby observes, no wonder boys and girls spontaneously segregate into same-sex peer groups: their social styles are so different.[22]

Intimacy and Group Size

Recall that on the Friendship and Relationship Questionnaire (FQ), the two sexes have different agendas in relationships. The female agenda seems to be to enjoy an intimate, one-to-one relationship. Young girls, on average, are reported to show more pleasure in one-to-one interaction. They are more likely to want reciprocal friendships, and to express intimacy. For example, girls are more likely to say sweet things to one another (things you hardly ever hear between boys), or caress or arrange each other's hair, or sit close to or touch the other person. Girls are more likely to have their arm around the other person, and to make direct eye contact.

Another difference is the concern that girls show about the current status of their friendships, and about what would happen if their friendship broke up. And breaking up is more often used as the ultimate threat: "If you don't do this, you won't be my friend." Girls, on average, are more concerned about the potential loss of an intimate friendship.

Girls in later childhood spend a lot of time talking about who is whose best friend, and get very emotional if they are excluded from relationships in the playground. Sulking is not uncommon. For girls, just as it is for many women, the important thing is to spend time *communicating* and nurturing their close relationships, without any necessary focus on an activity.

Girls also tend to spend more time cementing the closeness of their relationships by disclosing secrets, and by confessing their fears and weaknesses. Boys, in contrast, reveal their weaknesses less often, and in some cases never. Paradoxically, although increased self-disclosure between girls leads to closer relationships, it also leaves them more open to gossip—there is more fuel for gossip, as it were. Girls seem to be more willing to take this gamble, however, since the pay-off of self-disclosure is intimacy. The upshot of all this is that relationships between girls, and their break ups, are more emotional.[23]

Most boys in late childhood have relationships based on the game that they want to play. So if the game is soccer, they select one group to play with; if the game is skateboarding, they may select another group of friends. This is not so different for many men, who may play poker with one set of friends, and golf with another set.

This difference in styles of play between girls and boys suggests that girls tend to be more preoccupied with the emotional aspects of relationships, either to become close to someone, or to exclude others from getting between them and their "best friend." In contrast, boys are more preoccupied with the activity itself and its competitive aspects.

The flip side of the coin is that boys' friendships, on average, are less intimate. There is less mutual self-disclosure, less eye contact, and less physical closeness. By the age of eight or so, if boys touch each other at all, it tends to be with an affectionate punch, or to give each other a "high five." While the female agenda is more often directed toward intimacy, the male one is more often directed toward coordinated group activity, based on mutual interests. For example, the boys who enjoy sport, or rock music, or computers magnetically find each other and form themselves into groups.

Boys' main priority seems to be to join a group based on a shared activity. Once inside a group, there is a further priority to establish their individual rank in the dominance hierarchy that will emerge.

An impressive way of climbing in rank, as a welcome alternative to being nasty, is simply to be good at an activity: to be expert, knowledgeable, and skilled at a particular *system*. This earns the respect of the others, and it cements your place in the group activity by being a valued, even indispensable, member of the group. It means that when competition becomes an issue—that is, when there are only a fixed number of places in the group or on the team—you will guarantee yourself a place, and remain in the safety of the group. The less-skilled losers, as it were, by definition end up as outsiders, with all that this brings (less access to resources and support). Both of the male strategies used to acquire social status—the impressive route and the aggressive route—share the same underlying feature: being competitive.

These different social agendas between the sexes have implications for group size, and for degrees of intimacy and empathy. Males may spend their time in larger groups, depending on the nature of the activity. Females may network more, but tend to devote more time to intimacy with a small number of people. The male social agenda is more *self-centered* in relation to the group, with all the benefits this can bring, and it protects one's status within this social system. The female agenda is more *centered on another* person's emotional state (establishing a mutually satisfying and intimate friendship).

Such statements are, of course, open to misunderstanding. Males also have good friends, and these are often close and confiding. We are only talking about differences in degree, not absolute differences. And as with all of these psychological studies, we are only talking about group averages, rather than individuals.[24]

Pretend Play

We have already looked through a few windows into sex differences in empathizing, but do these differences in play continue as children grow older? Boys tend to play group games (such as soccer and baseball) much more than girls do. This is partly a sign of the importance of group membership to boys, and partly a reflection of their interest in rule-based activities. (Just think of how rule-based a system baseball is, both in terms of the rules of the technique and the rules governing play.) And an astonishing 99 percent of girls play with dolls at age six, compared with just 17 percent of boys. Playing with dolls is typically the opposite of rule-based activity, the themes being open-ended and usually involving an enactment of caring, emotional relationships.

When children engage in pretence during play, this is an even more specific window into empathizing. For example, in *social* pretence, one must imagine what another person is imagining. This is a big leap. When a child watches mommy soothing a doll, the child has to keep track that this is all just *in mommy's mind* and that *mommy is imagining the doll's mind*. In reality, dolls do not need soothing. This is a double level of empathizing: imbuing the doll with feelings, in mommy's mind. Girls seem to be more prone to this than are boys.

The *content* of children's pretend play is also relevant here. Girls' pretence tends to involve more cooperative role-taking. They say things like, "I'll be the mommy, you be the child," and they show more reciprocity ("Now it's your turn"). It is as if, within the pretence, they are making space for another person, sensitively adjusting their behavior to accommodate the other person.

In this way they are showing sensitivity to how the other person will feel if they are being included or excluded, being controlled or free, being dominated or treated as an equal. Girls also tend to ensure that the other person understands where the imaginative pursuit is leading. All very empathic.

In contrast, boys show more *solitary* pretence. Even if it is social, their pretence often involves a lone superhero (for example, Batman, Robin Hood, Superman, or Harry Potter) engaging in combat. Mortal combat. Such play typically involves guns, swords, or magical weapons with seriously destructive powers. As any parent knows, if toy guns or swords are not available then boys will use anything as a substitute for them. But the aim of the pretence is to eliminate the other person, the deadly enemy, not to worry about his feelings.

There is the victor, and there is the vanquished. This is certainly evidence of an ability to pretend, but the focus is on the imagined self's strength and power, rather than on being empathic. This male preoccupation with power and strength again suggests that males are less concerned with a sharing of minds and more interested in social rank. Who will win and who will lose. You see the same thing when children tell make-believe stories. In their narratives, boys focus more on lone characters in conflict. In contrast, girls' stories focus more on social and family relationships.[25]

Communication

Listening to people chat is another rich source of evidence for empathy skills. The following section is quite long because there is a lot of evidence for sex differences in communication, across a large number of settings and age ranges.

Girls' speech has been described as more cooperative, more reciprocal, and more collaborative. In concrete terms, this is also reflected in girls being able to keep a conversational exchange with a partner going for longer. It is not to do with how long the conversation is overall, since the conversation of young girls might be quite fragmented. Rather, it is to do with how long an exchange continues, in which the speaker takes turns and maintains a joint theme. Girls, on average, use more of certain kinds of language devices. For example, they use "extending statements" (such as "Oh, you mean x") and "relevant turns" (such as "Oh, that's interesting . . . "), which serve to build on something the other person has just said.

Girls often extend dialogue by expressing agreement with the other person's suggestions. When they disagree, they are more likely to soften the blow by expressing their opinion in the form of a question, rather than an assertion. This comes across as less dominating, less confrontational, and less humiliating for the other person. For example: "You may be right, but could it also be that . . . ?" or "Oh, I'm sure you're right, but I saw it a bit differently." In these examples, the speaker makes space for the other's point of view, and makes it easier for the other person to save face because they feel that their point has been accepted, respecting a difference in opinion.[26]

The male style is more likely to go along these lines: "I'm sorry, but you're wrong," showing no respect for the other person's different opinion.

Or they may be even more blunt: "You're wrong." Indeed, what in a female exchange might be seen as a difference of *opinion* is more likely to be interpreted by males as a matter of *fact*, where there can only be one correct answer—the speaker's. If the other person makes a suggestion, boys are more likely to reject it out of hand by saying, "Rubbish," or "No, it's not," or more rudely, "That's stupid." It is as if the more male style is to assume that there is an objective picture of reality, which happens to be *their* version of the facts; that if their beliefs are true then there can only be one version of the truth. The more female approach seems to be to assume from the outset that there might be subjectivity in the world. Therefore, they make room for multiple interpretations, each of which might have an equal claim to being a valid viewpoint.

Women are much more prepared to say when they feel hurt or offended by the other person in the conversation, and will also talk to each other when they feel offended by somebody else. Men are more likely to simply note an offense and withdraw contact, rather than working at repairing the relationship through conversation.

Girls express their anger less directly, and propose compromises more often. And in their talk, they are more likely to attempt to clarify the feelings and intentions of the other person. They also make softer claims, and use more polite forms of speech, avoiding the blunter forms of power-assertion such as yelling or shouting. In contrast, boys in middle childhood and adolescence produce more challenges in a direct assertion of power. When there are disagreements, boys are less likely to give a reason for their argument, and instead simply to assert it.[27]

Imperatives (direct commands, such as "Do this" or "Give that to me") or prohibitions ("Stop it" or "Don't DO that") are more common in boys' speech. These sorts of "domineering exchanges" are also more likely to end up in conflict. A good empathizer would worry that to order someone to do something is likely to make them feel inferior and devalued, and would avoid such speech styles. Girls are more likely to say, "Would you mind not doing that? It's just that I don't really like it," referring to the other person's feelings while at the same time clarifying their own.

Boys in early childhood are also more likely to do what psychologist Eleanor Maccoby calls "grandstanding"—in other words, giving a running commentary on their own actions, while ignoring what the other person is doing. It has been suggested that boys' talk tends to be "single-voiced discourse." By this it is meant that the speaker presents their own perspective alone. When two boys do this, conflict is likely to escalate.

In contrast, it is suggested that female speech style tends to be "double-voiced discourse." The idea is that while little girls still pursue their own objectives, each also spends more time negotiating with the other person, trying to take the other person's wishes into account. Look at this example: "I know you feel x, but have you thought of y? I realize you might wish that z, but what if . . . ." This female speech style reveals clear empathizing at work in conversation. The "facts" of x, y, and z are all prefaced by mental-state words (feel, think, wish) that immediately set those facts in a multiple-interpretation framework, and make space for both viewpoints. All of these differences in conversational style are seen even more dramatically in middle childhood and in the teenage years.

Boys are also more "egocentric" in their speech, by which I do not mean the "single-voiced discourse" mentioned earlier. I mean that they are more likely to brag, dare each other, taunt, threaten, override the other person's attempt to speak, and ignore the other person's suggestion. They are also less willing to give up the floor to the other speaker.

Males more often use language to assert their social dominance, to display their social status, especially when there are other males around. Here's how Eleanor Maccoby puts it:

> Boys in their groups are more likely than girls in all-girl groups to interrupt one another; use commands, threats, or boasts of authority; refuse to comply with another child's command; give information; heckle a speaker; . . . top someone else's story; or call another child names.[28]

Girls, on the other hand, are said to show "socially enabling" language more frequently. Socially enabling language is speech that is used to ensure that all members of the group talk, and express their views and feelings, encouraging differences in perspective to emerge.[29] Maccoby writes that girls in all-girl groups

> are more likely than boys to express agreement with what another speaker has just said, pause to give another girl a chance to speak, or when starting a speaking turn, acknowledge a point previously

made by another speaker . . . Among girls, conversation is a more socially binding process.

Men spend more time using language to demonstrate their knowledge, skill, and status. They are more likely to show off or try to impress. This leads to more interruptions by men in order to give their opinion, and to their showing less interest in the opinion of the other person. For women, language functions in a different way: it is used to develop and maintain intimate, reciprocal relationships, especially with other females. Women spend more time using language to negotiate understandings, to develop a relationship, and to make people feel listened to. Women's talk often affirms the other person, expressing positive feelings for their friendship, whereas men shy away from telling each other how important they are to each other.[30]

Women in conversation will often include personal reference to each other's appearance (their hair, their jewelry, their clothes) so as to praise the other's looks. It is astonishing how rapidly this will happen, often within seconds of first meeting. Let's say a husband and wife are visiting another couple. One of the women may open a conversation with her female friend by saying something like this:

> Oh, I *love* your dress. You *must* tell me where you got it. You look *so* pretty in it. It really goes well with your bag.

Why do women do this, while men hardly ever do so? One view is that in this way women signal their feelings for the other person, again something that men do much less frequently. For example, the compliment can be taken as implicitly saying "I like you," or "I think you're pretty," or "I think you've got good taste," thus affirming the relationship itself. Another equally positive view is that women implicitly build each other up through mutual compliments, rather than putting each other down. Evidence for this positive view often comes in the reply from the person receiving the compliment, which might go like this:

> Oh, thank you. You *must* come shopping with me to this new shop I've found in Covent Garden, where they have *such* beautiful new

material and designs. You'd *love* the summer dresses. They'd suit
your tan *so* well.

I have often commented to my male friends how stark this particular sex
difference is. That is, that women will not only *talk* about each other's appearances (men do this occasionally, too) but will actually follow through
this chat by going shopping together, and even going into the same changing room to try on new clothes. When was the last time that you heard of
two men going shopping together, getting into the same little booth, undressing in front of each other and asking each other whether this new
shirt suited them? Homophobia may be what leads men to avoid such talk
or avoid issuing such invitations to each other. But between women there
is no suggestion of any sexual interest in such talk or in such shopping
sprees. The shopping is often described as simple fun, and a chance to
spend time together in a close way.

So this exchange of compliments could be taken as signaling a desire to
get closer in the friendship, or to remain close, and it involves a fairly explicit removal of barriers between the two women (verbally undressing
each other, as it were).

A less rosy view of this compliment exchange, however, is that women
are drawing attention to appearances, reminding each other, and any observers, that appearances matter in the competition between women. This
view is corroborated when compliments are laced with a fleeting but razor-
sharp aside, such as:

> Oh, that dress makes you look *so* thin, I *hate* you! Look at how fat
> my butt is in this dress!

The reference to "hate" is typically delivered with jokey or affectionate
intonation, but nevertheless might be revealing a touch of rivalry, jealousy,
and competitiveness. Yet one thing is clear: often within *seconds* of a reuni-
fication with a woman friend, women talk about personal, even intimate,
things (the size of body parts, and their dissatisfaction with their shape,
etc.), and this demonstrates that women waste no time on impersonal dia-
log but immediately move the conversation on to the point where they can
share personal feelings and closeness.

Women's conversation also involves much more talk about feelings and relationships than men's, while men's conversation with each other tends to be more object-focused, such as discussion of sports, cars, routes, and new acquisitions. Let's go back to my example of a husband and wife visiting another couple. While the women have quickly started to compliment each other and are talking about personal appearances, the two men's opening gambit might go something like this:

> How was the traffic on the M11? I usually find going up the A1M through Royston and Baldock can save a lot of time. Especially now they have the roadworks just beyond Stansted.

Male talk about traffic and routes is of course a clear example of talk about systems, but more on that in Chapter 6.

A study of the stories told by two-year-old children found that people were the focus in the vast majority of the stories told by girls but were the focus in only a small minority of the stories told by boys. By four years of age, every story told by girls was people-centered, but still only about half of the boys' stories were. Girls seem to be far more people-centered than boys.

A well-substantiated sex difference in language content is found in self-disclosure and intimacy. Whereas men and women do not differ in their willingness to self-disclose to a female conversation partner, men use far less intimate language when talking to another man. This mirrors the finding that I discussed in relation to girls' and boys' styles of relationships, and may reflect the pressure that men feel to appear in control. It is of interest that even when men are in conversation with a woman, and are talking intimately, they offer less supportive communication when the woman takes her turn to talk intimately. Women, on the other hand, are more likely to respond with words conveying that they have understood what the other person has said, offering sympathy spontaneously.[31]

Men tend to refer less frequently to their relationships, tending to live them through joint activities rather than talking about them. These sorts of conversational differences mirror the differences we saw between the sexes on the Friendship and Relationship Questionnaire (FQ).

Deborah Tannen documents the differences in how men and women talk with each other. In her book *You Just Don't Understand* she wrote about her studies in the context of couples' interactions. In *Talking 9 to 5* she dealt with talk in the workplace. Her key finding is that there is a lot more informal chatting in the office among women, chat that is not work-related. She argues that this forms and reinforces social bonds. These in turn keep communication channels open so that any tensions that arise are then easier to defuse.[32]

Amusingly, Tannen finds that in the workplace men more often talk to each other about *systems*: technology (such as their latest power-tools, or computer, or music system), cars (such as the differences between one model and another: their engine capacity, fuel consumption, speed, or accessories), and sport (such as the best places to windsurf, or soccer rankings, or the big game last night, or their new golf clubs). Women talk to each other more often about social themes: clothes, hairstyles, social gatherings, relationships, domestic concerns and children. (Just like the magazines that men and women tend to buy at the newsstand, reflecting their different interests or what matters to them.) These differences are referred to as "guy talk" and "girl talk." Not surprisingly, people find it easier to get to know someone if they are a member of the same sex, arguably because it is easier to establish an informal topic of mutual interest. It may also be because male and female humor differs, in the office at least: male humor tends to involve more teasing and pretend hostility, while female humor tends to involve more self-mockery.

These differences also affect how management operates at work. Female managers tend to soften the blow tactfully when delivering criticism, while male managers tend to be more willing to deliver direct criticism without sugar-coating the pill. Female management-style also tends to be more consultative and inclusive, ensuring that no one feels left out, while men's management-style tends to be more directive and task-oriented. A final difference in women's style of talk in the workplace is women's use of "we" in describing work as a collaboration, while men will more often talk about "I" or "my," acknowledging less often the role that others have played.

It seems reasonable to conclude this section as follows: differences in speech styles suggest that there are key differences in how self- and other-centered each sex is. The speech styles of each sex suggest that there are sex differences in how much speakers set aside their own desires to consider sensitively someone else's. Empathy again.

Parenting Styles

Parenting style is another good place to test if women are more empathic than men. Here again, sex differences are found. Fathers are less likely than mothers to hold their infant in a face-to-face position. One consequence of this is that there is less exchange of emotional information via the face between fathers and infants. Mothers are more likely to follow through the child's choice of topic in play, while fathers are more likely to impose their own topic.

Moreover, mothers fine-tune their speech more often to match what the child can understand. For example, a mother's mean length of utterance tends to correlate with her child's comprehension level, while fathers tend to use unfamiliar or difficult words more often. Finally, when a father and child are talking, they take turns less often. These examples from parenting again suggest that women are better at empathizing than men.

An experimental demonstration of this is seen in a study by Eleanor Maccoby and her colleagues. They used a communication task in which a parent and his or her six-year-old child were given four ambiguous pictures. The parent described the picture and the child was asked to pick out which of the four pictures was being described. Mother-child pairs were more successful than father-child pairs at identifying the intended picture, presumably because of women's greater communicative clarity.[33]

Eye Contact and Face Perception

Do babies show sex differences in how people-centered and how object-centered they are? There are claims that from birth, female infants look longer at faces, and particularly at people's eyes, while male infants are more likely to look at inanimate objects.[34] Interestingly, when you try to track down an original study to test this claim it is very hard to put your hands on any concrete data. I was fortunate enough to work with a talented Ph.D. student, Svetlana Lutchmaya, who tested this claim with one-year-olds.

Svetlana invited the infants into our lab, and filmed them while they played on the floor, and their mothers sat in a chair nearby. She then painstakingly coded all of the videotapes to ascertain how many times the

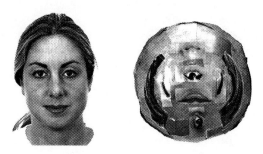

The face and mobile presented to newborns
fig 4.

infants looked up at their mother's face during a twenty-minute period. She found that the girls looked up significantly more often than the boys did. And when she gave them a choice of a film of a face to watch, or a film of cars, the boys looked for longer at the cars and the girls looked for longer at the face.[35]

Two other enterprising students of mine, Jennifer Connellan and Anna Ba'tki, decided to take this question a little further. They videotaped over 100 babies who were just one day old, in the Rosie Maternity Hospital in Cambridge, England. Little did these babies know what lay in store for them. No sooner had they emerged from the womb than they were recruited into this scientific study. The babies were shown Jennifer's tanned Californian face, smiling over their crib. Her face moved in the natural way that faces do. They were also shown a mobile. But this mobile was no ordinary mobile. It was made from a ball the same size as Jennifer's head, with the same coloring (tanned), but with her features rearranged, so that the overall impression was no longer face-like. Around the lab we called it The Alien. To make it look more mechanical, we hung some material from it that moved every time the larger mobile moved. In this way, we could compare the baby's interest in a social object (a face) and a mechanical object (a mobile). Finally, in order for the experimenters to remain unbiased, mothers were asked not to tell the researchers the sex of her baby. This information was only checked after the videotapes had been coded for how long each baby looked at each type of object.

So the question was, would babies look longer at Jennifer's face, or at the mobile? When we analyzed the videotapes, we found that girls looked for longer at the face, and that boys looked for longer at the mobile. And this sex difference in social interest was on the first day of life.[36]

This difference at birth echoes a pattern we have seen right across the human lifespan. For example, on average, women engage in more "consistent" social smiling and "maintained" eye contact than does the average man. The fact that this difference is present at birth strongly suggests that biology plays a role. We return to examine this possibility in Chapter 8.[37]

The Empathy Quotient (EQ)

There are a number of questionnaires that purport to measure empathy. Many of these find that women score higher than men. My research team and I developed a measure in this area, called the Empathy Quotient (or EQ; have a look at it in Appendix 2), which also found that women score higher than men.[38] We developed our test because of a worry that earlier tests were not "pure" tests of empathy, since they included items in their questionnaires that involved self-control or fantasy. If you take a look at the EQ you will see that the questions are intended to measure how easily you can pick up on other people's feelings, and also how strongly you are affected by other people's feelings. Figure 5 shows a schematic of the results we found on the EQ, for men and women.

As you can see, the female scores are positioned toward the right, and are higher up the scale than the male scores, which provides strong evidence that females are better empathizers. Note, though, that this test only collects information from self-reports, so the higher scores may just reflect that women are less modest. We think this is unlikely, since when we ask someone to fill out the questionnaire on behalf of another person that they know very well, we find that reports by others correlate very closely with self-reports. However, as this chapter indicates, to test the idea that females are better at empathizing it is important to look at a range of indicators to see if they provide converging evidence for this conclusion.

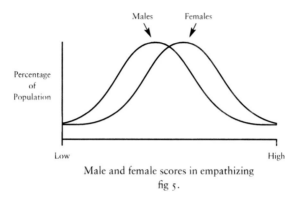

Male and female scores in empathizing
fig 5.

Language Ability:
An Alternative View of the Female Brain?

Females are clearly better than males at empathizing. But perhaps they are better not just at communication but at all aspects of language. When you look at even low-level language tests, females are superior in many of these, too. Before closing this chapter, we look at whether this is necessarily a problem for the empathizing theory.

But first, what is the evidence for sex differences in language? On average, women produce more words in a given period, fewer speech errors (such as using the wrong word), and perform better in the ability to discriminate speech sounds (such as consonants and vowels) than do men. Their average sentences are also longer, and their utterances show standard grammatical structure and correct pronunciation more often. They also find it easier to articulate words, and do this faster than men. Women can also recall words more easily. Most men have more pauses in their speech. And at the clinical level of severity, males are at least two times more likely to develop language disorders, such as stuttering.[39]

In addition, girls start talking earlier than boys, by about one month, and their vocabulary size is greater. It is not clear whether receptive vocabulary size (how many words a child understands) differs between the sexes, but it seems that girls use language more at an earlier age. For example, they initiate talk more often with their parents, with other children, and with teachers. This greater use of language by girls may not be seen when in the company of boys, whose effect is usually to render girls quieter or more inhibited.

Girls are also better spellers and readers. Boys tend to be faster at repeating a single syllable (e.g., ba-ba-ba), while girls tend to produce more syllables when the task is to repeat a sequence of different sounds (e.g., ba-da-ga). Girls are also better on tests of verbal memory, or recall of words. This female superiority is seen in older women, too, including those who are well into their eighties. The female advantage is even seen when the task is to recall a string of numbers spoken aloud (the Digit Span Test). Women are not better at the spatial equivalent of this test—where one is asked to tap a long series of blocks into the same irregular sequence as the experimenter.

Women taking medical school entrance exams do better on an assessment called "Learning Facts," which you could think of as a verbal memory test. And women, given a lot of words read aloud, learn them more easily. Women also tend to cluster the words reported into meaningful categories, while men tend to report them in the order in which they were presented. Women are better at recalling the meaning of a paragraph, and this has been found in widely differing cultures—for example, in South Africa, America, and Japan. On a control test of recalling irregular nonsense shapes, where the shapes cannot be named, no sex difference is seen.[40]

In a landmark study that sparked a lot of interest, Bennett Shaywitz and his colleagues at Yale University found that certain regions of the prefrontal cortex of the brain, including Broca's area, were activated differently in men and women during a language task. The subject was asked to decide if a pair of written nonsense words rhymed or not. About half of the women showed activation of Broca's area in both the right *and* left frontal lobes, while the men only showed left hemisphere activation. The same research group has replicated its own work, finding a similar effect even if the task is simply to listen to speech sounds (though this has not been found in all studies).[41]

This short detour into differences in language competence tells us that the female brain may not only be a natural empathizer but also have a flair for language. Is this a problem for the characterization of the female brain in terms of superior empathizing? My view is that it need not be, for several reasons.

It is noteworthy that the very idea that females have better language skills has been questioned,[42] whereas the idea that females have better empathy remains unchallenged. But let us accept it as true that they also have better language skills. First, it is possible that a female superiority in all these broader language skills may be part and parcel of developing good empathizing skills. Language skills (including good verbal memory) are essential in seamless chatting and establishing intimacy, to make the interaction smooth, fluent, and socially binding. Long pauses in conversation do not help partners to feel connected or in tune with one another.

Second, some measures of language, such as reading comprehension, may actually reflect empathizing ability. For example, girls tend to perform better than boys on reading achievement tests overall, but this is because they are particularly better at understanding *social* storylines, compared to non-social ones.[43]

Third, the greater emotional sensitivity in females is unlikely to be just a by-product of their better language skills, because we all know people who have excellent language skills but poor social sensitivity, or vice versa. I'm sure you can think of some people who are verbally fluent, but who won't stop talking. The fact that you can't get a word in edgewise suggests that their turn-taking and empathy skills are at a lower level compared to their verbal skills.

Equally, you can probably think of someone who is a patient and sensitive listener, who responds very warmly and empathically to other people's problems, but who is a person of few words. So good language ability need have nothing to do with good communication ability, or good empathy.

Indeed, a Darwinian view might be that rather than good empathy stemming from good language skills, it is the other way around. Females may have evolved better language systems because their survival depended on a more empathic, rapid, tactful, and strategic use of language.

But the safest conclusion at this point is that females are *both* better empathizers and better in many aspects of language use, and that the relationship between these two skills is likely to have been complex and two-way, both in ontogeny (development) and phylogeny (evolution): good language could promote good empathy (since the drive to communicate would bring one more social experience), and good empathy could promote good language (since social sensitivity would make the pragmatics of communication easier). But as domains, language and empathy are likely to be independent of each other.

So our main conclusion still stands: when you look at different aspects of social behavior and communication, a large body of evidence points to females being better empathizers. But what about the other main claim of this book? Are males better systemizers?

5

What Is Systemizing?

In the last chapter we considered the evidence for a female superiority in empathizing. In the next chapter we encounter the evidence for a male superiority in systemizing. But first let's take a short pause on our journey to examine what systemizing is.

Systemizing is the drive to understand a system and to build one. By a system I do not just mean a machine (like a tool, or a musical instrument, or the insides of your watch). Nor do I even just mean things that you can build (like a house, a town, or a legal code). I mean by a system anything which is governed by rules specifying input-operation-output relationships. This definition takes in systems beyond machines, such as math, physics, chemistry, astronomy, logic, music, military strategy, the climate, sailing, horticulture, and computer programming. It also includes systems like libraries, economics, companies, taxonomies, board games, or sports. The system might be tiny (like an individual cell), or larger (like a whole animal), or larger still (like a social group or a political system).

Systemizing involves first the analysis of the features in a system that can vary, followed by close, detailed observation of the effects that occur when each feature is varied ("systematically"). Repeating such observations leads one to discover the input-operation-output rules governing the behavior of the system.

Here's a simple example: "If I push the red button, the projector advances to the next slide." Here, the red button is the input, pushing it is the operation, and the next slide popping up is the output.

Sometimes the operation is not performed by an animate agent (you or anyone else) but is an impersonal event. Here's a simple example: "At 10 A.M., the sun casts a shadow on my bedroom wall at this particular point." Here, the sun is the input, and its position is the operation. The shadow from the sun's previous position is one output, and the shadow from the sun's present position is a new output.

Systemizing therefore needs an exact eye for detail, since it makes a world of difference if you confuse one input or operation for another. If the operation is a mouse-click on a computer screen, or if the input is a digit in a mathematical formula, one tiny change at this stage can lead to a completely different output—it can lead the system to behave completely differently. The pay-off of good systemizing is not only being able to understand the system but also being able to predict what it will do next.

The key thing about systemizing is that the system your brain is trying to understand is finite, deterministic, and lawful. Once you have identified the rules and regularities of the system, then you can predict its workings absolutely. This holds true even for more complex systems, where there are many more parameters, or where the rules are much more elaborate. But the rules are in principle specifiable.

You might feel, as a reader, that I am using such a broad notion of "system" that it includes almost everything. This is a reasonable worry. In fact, systemizing (and empathizing) are *processes in the mind*, and as such they can indeed be applied to almost any aspect of the environment. In practice, empathizing is most easily applied to agents (i.e., entities that are capable of self-propulsion, even virtual ones, such as cartoon characters),[1] while systemizing is most easily applied to lawful aspects of the environment. And there are many lawful aspects of the environment to discover, using this process.

We can draft a classification of the six major kinds of system that exist, which the brain can analyze and/or build. (Here I am, systemizing systems.)

Technical Systems

We often think of systems in the world of technology as "man-made." (My guess is that most of these were indeed invented by men, and as this book will go on to explore, this may be no coincidence.) Technical systems may be complex, such as computers, vehicles, tools, and other machines. They also include the complex systems of the kind that academics would study in branches of physics, electronic and mechanical engineering, computer science, and material science. But a technical system can be as basic as a roof, a sail, a plane wing, or a compass. For example:

- A musician might discover that playing an instrument (the input) in an auditorium with a dome roof (the operation) causes one note (output 1) to reverberate and interact with the present note (output 2) to create a new combination of notes (output 3)—an auditory salad.

- Or a music-lover might discover that by connecting the speakers with an electrical cable (the input) one centimeter thicker (the operation), the sound is no longer muffled (output 1) but clear (output 2).

- Or a surfer might discover that by using a surfboard (the input) three inches wider (the operation), the board is no longer unstable (output 1) but stable (output 2).

Natural Systems

These include the complex systems in nature of the kind that academics study in ecology, geography, chemistry, physics, astronomy, medicine, meteorology, biology, or geology. But systemizing nature is not just carried out by academics. We all systemize nature. Just think how we analyze an animal or a plant, an ecosystem, or the climate. And again, these systems can include quite ordinary things like soil, rivers, rocks, an insect, or a leaf. For example:

- A gardener might discover that if he grows a hydrangea (the input) in alkaline soil (the operation), the flower color changes from pink (output 1) to blue (output 2).

- Or a forest-dweller might discover that the presence of a tiger (the input) within 50 meters (the operation) leads a langur monkey's vocalizations to change from relaxed (output 1) to a specific alarm call (output 2).

- Or a walk on the beach might lead you to notice that the tide throws stones (the input) that are smaller (the operation) higher up the beach (output).

Abstract Systems

Complex examples of abstract systems include things such as math, logic, grammar, music, computer programs, taxation, mortgages, pensions, stocks and shares, or maps. Some abstract systems are really quite ordinary, such as the rules for reading text, or the account book of a business, or a train timetable. For example:

- A programmer might notice that an extra bracket (the operation) in a computer program (the input) changes what was otherwise an endless loop (output 1) to quit (output 2).
- Or a child encountering math might notice that when you cube (the operation) the numbers 1, 2, 3, and 4 (the input), you get the numbers 1, 8, 27, and 64 (the output).
- Or an English-language learner might realize that when words that end in a consonant (the input) are affixed with an "e" (the operation), the pronunciation of the previous vowel changes from one of its forms (output 1) to the other (output 2).

Social Systems

These are groups of people or, more precisely, the rules describing these groups. Complex social systems include those studied by academics in politics, business, law, theology, the military, economics, history, and social science. Simpler social systems include a committee, a political group, a group of friends, an institution, or charts such as a soccer league table, a pop-music chart, or a list of players in the sports team. For example:

- A businessman might discover that when selling a particular product (the input), the month of the year (the operation) causes the sales to increase (the output).

- Or a politician might realize that redrawing the constituency boundary on the map (the operation) leads the number of votes for his party (the input) to increase (the output).
- Or a soccer manager might notice that when he plays his team (the input) with three particular players in offensive positions (the operation), the average number of goals scored is increased (the output).

Organizable Systems

Some of these systems are vast, such as encyclopedias, museums, or second-hand-record shops and book shops; some of them are more limited, such as sets of coins or stamps in an album. But they all need to be organized according to some criteria or taxonomy, and there can be many different ways to cut the cake, as it were. This is because members of a category can be grouped in different ways. For example:

- A birdspotter might discover that eagles' tail colors (the input) in Scotland (the operation) are patterned with a brown and white stripe (the output). This might lead the birdspotter to create a new category in his bird photography collection.
- Or a music enthusiast might decide that her CD collection (the input) should be reorganized according to the chronological release dates (the operation), producing a new sequence (the output) on the shelf.
- Or a child might decide that his toy cars and boats (the input) should be separated into two boxes according to type (the operation) so that the toys end up in new places.

Motoric Systems

Again, some of these systems are complex, such as the finger movements required to play a Beethoven sonata on the piano. Others are simpler, such as the ability to throw a dart at the bullseye, or the golf swing. The golf swing lasts just two seconds, but what goes on during those two seconds (the operation) can make the difference between the ball (the input) ending up in the hole (output 1) or in the lake (output 2). For example:

- A skier might work out that if she raises her arms just slightly (the operation), her balance (the input) is no longer unstable (output 1) but far more stable (output 2).
- Or a tennis player might realize that if he changes the top-spin (the operation), the ball (the input) bounces right (the output).
- Or a pianist might discover that a trill with the third and fourth fingers (the input) practiced repeatedly (the operation) becomes more precise (the output).

So we have (at least) six different kinds of systems. You can see that, despite their surface differences, there are some deep, underlying similarities. In each case, the systemizer explores how a particular input produces a particular output following a particular operation. This provides us with more or less useful if-then rules. You use a narrower canoe, it goes faster. You prune your roses in March, they grow stronger next season. You fly above a cloud, you experience less turbulence. You swing the golf club higher, the ball travels along a steeper trajectory. You focus on the jaws of the crocodiles, the reptile classification changes. You divide some numbers by others, they leave no remainder. The outcome is noted and stored as a possible underlying rule or regularity governing the system. The rules are nothing more than input-operation-output relations.

Behaviorist psychologists of the early twentieth century called this kind of learning "association" learning, which is a partial description of systemizing. Typically in association learning (in other words, classical or operant conditioning) we extract the rule because there is sufficient reward or punishment. For example, a child learns that touching a hot radiator leads to pain, or a motorist discovers that a particular parking meter takes his money and credits him with twice the expected amount of time. In these examples the motivation for learning is an external reward (x) or punishment (y).

Systemizing is different from classical or operant conditioning, in that the motivation is not external but intrinsic—to understand the system itself. The buzz is not derived from some tangible reward (such as a food pellet when you press a lever, or a salary when you do a job). Rather, the buzz is in *discovering the causes* of things, not because you want to collect causal information for the sake of it, but because discovering causes gives you control over the world.

And a second big difference between association learning and systemizing is that the former is within the capability of most organisms with a nervous system, from a worm to an American president, whereas the latter may be a uniquely human or higher primate capability. This needs to be investigated in a range of species, but one conclusion is that causal cognition is rarely, if ever, seen outside of humans.[1]

Philosophers worry about whether such correlation-based observations could ever distinguish between "common cause" (where two things appear to be causally related, but in reality they are both caused by a third, common factor) and "causation" proper. My guess is that this is a nicety that in practice the brain ignores, because even mistaking a common cause for causation gives you valuable leverage over events in the world. It allows you to begin designing systems or intervening in nature, to get control in the world.

So the big pay-off of systemizing is control. If you want to harness energy with a water wheel or a windmill, you had better understand how water or wind pressure causes your technical system to move. If you can figure out what controls what, you can build any machine to do anything for you: a spear that flies straight, or a rocket that can get to the moon. The principles—systemizing—are the same, but the list of if-then rules gets longer as the system becomes more complex.

Systemizing is an inductive process. You watch what happens each time you click that mouse, and after a series of reliably predictable results, you form your rule. Systemizing is also an empirical process. You need a keen eye and an orderly mind. An exact mind. Without them, essential variables or parameters, and the pattern of their effects, will be missed, or the rules will not have been carefully checked and tested. If one exception occurs which violates the rule, the systemizer notes it, rechecks the rule, and refines or revises it. If he or she has identified the rule governing the system correctly, the system works. The test is repeatability. Of course, this only works with events which repeat or are repeatable, and where the output can change.[2]

In the next chapter we look at the evidence relevant to the claim that there is a male superiority in systemizing.

6

The Male Brain as Systemizer: The Evidence

Mechanical and Constructional Play

There is a lot of evidence to show that there are big differences in the ways the two sexes play. Boys, even as toddlers, are more interested in cars, trucks, planes, guns, and swords, and the noises that they make while they play tend to be appropriate to these sorts of toys (motor sounds, bangs, and sirens). Even at two years of age, boys show a stronger interest in building blocks and mechanical toys, while girls show a stronger interest in dolls, jewelry, dressing up, and adornment.

In a classic test of this one leaves a choice of toys out on the carpet, and waits to see which ones a child picks. By two years of age, little boys are far more likely to select toy vehicles and building bricks to play with, leaving the dolls to one side. Girls of this age tend to choose the dolls.

As children grow older, one can see the same pattern: boys spend more time engaged in mechanical play (for example, with toy cars) and construction play (for example, building with blocks) than do girls. Boys seem to love putting things together, to build toy towers or towns or vehicles. Often, when they have sat and admired their wonderful construction, they will simply take it apart again. Boys also enjoy playing with toys that have clear functions—things with buttons to press, things that will light up, or devices that will cause another object to move: systems.

Although you might think that this is only true of boys living in a Western or technological society, the same broad pattern has also been found in pre-industrial societies. For example, a study of drawings showed that boys in a pre-industrial society more often drew machines of some kind. They did not draw machines that we are more familiar with, such as electrical devices, but machines that are far more universal, such as tools, weapons, and vehicles.

This interest in the mechanical and the constructional is not simply a sign that boys are more object-oriented, since girls play with some objects (like clay and marker pens) more often than boys. Rather, it seems that boys are more interested in mechanical and constructional systems. They are more interested in systemizing.[1] Recall from Chapter 4 that this pattern is seen in twelve-month-old boys, who look longer at a film of cars than do girls, and even in one-day-old baby boys, who look for longer at a mechanical mobile.[2]

Interestingly, you see the same sort of pattern in the adult workplace, too. Some occupations are almost entirely male. Take, for example, the fields of metalworking, weapon-making, or crafting musical instruments. Or the construction industries, such as boat-building. These occupations are almost always carried out by men, and this sex difference is seen universally, not just in the Western world. This sex difference does not reflect the greater physical strength in males since, in many of these occupations (making a violin or a knife are good examples), strength is not the key factor. The focus of these occupations is on constructing systems.[3]

How can we draw a link between the observations of infants, children, and adults that I have described? One link is that *attention* in males and females is being drawn to different aspects of the environment. In one fascinating test, men and women were shown a series of human figures and mechanical objects, using a stereoscope. This equipment allows the human-figure picture and the mechanical-object picture to fall on the same part of the observer's visual field. The two stimuli compete for the observer's attention. Guess the results? Male observers reported seeing more mechanical objects than people, compared to the females. Female observers reported seeing more people than mechanical objects, compared to the males. And, of course, mechanical objects are systems.[4]

Math, Physics, and Engineering

Professions (in the industrialized world) such as math, physics, and engineering require high systemizing abilities. In musical-instrument-making, or building a tool or a boat, if one changes a detail in the input to the system, or the operation it performs, the output can be radically affected. So it is in math, physics, or engineering. Change one number in the formula, or the width of the device, and the whole system may no longer work, or may function suboptimally.

Physics and engineering are, of course, the adult equivalent of children's play with mechanical and constructional toys. Indeed, all the sciences utilize systemizing as their basis, and all are dominated by men. According to a headline in the *Times Higher*, only three of the 170 living Nobel Prize-winners in science are women.[5] In the 1970s the sex ratio of those working in the fields of math, physics, and engineering was about 9:1 (male:female) and this remains the case today. So, too, those fields where math is applied, such as mathematical modeling in economics or statistics.

Some have argued that this is because these disciplines are unfriendly to women. However, the pattern across the different sciences suggests that something more subtle is going on. For example, in one survey conducted by the National Science Foundation in the USA, 23 percent of scientists in biology were women, whereas in physics only 5 percent were women, and in engineering only 3 percent. A similar pattern has been found in other countries. Although there is no evidence that physics and engineering are less friendly to women applicants than biology,[6] it could be that some pernicious, unconscious sexism operates at the point of selection. For example, interviewers may expect male applicants to make better students, given their experience from teaching male-dominated classes in the past. This would be hard to test as interviewers are hardly going to express any conscious sexism of this kind freely. And if the sexism is unconscious, the interviewers by definition will be unaware of it.

I work at Trinity College Cambridge in England, where there is a wonderful concentration of mathematicians, physicists, and engineers. Chatting at lunch with my colleagues in these disciplines leads me to suspect that if anything, many of them hold the opposite bias: that if they catch a glimpse of a talented female applicant, they try extra hard to accept her into the course, to reverse centuries of discrimination.

A less sexist possible explanation for the sex difference in physics and engineering is that there could be an inadvertent selection bias into these two disciplines if a mathematical reasoning test is used as a selection criterion. This would not be unreasonable on the part of physics and engineering departments, given that mathematical ability is a good predictor of success in these fields. However, it may be math that skews the sex ratio in these fields. Corroborating evidence can be found in the ratio of ten males to every female who perform at the top end of the SAT-M, the Scholastic Aptitude Math Test that is administered nationally to college applicants in the USA.[7]

An alternative explanation is that there is no external selection bias. Rather, perhaps men and women are simply choosing areas of science where they feel they have greater natural aptitude, or interest. "Choosing" of course is a loaded term here, because the occupations we end up in may not always be the result of any conscious choice but simply the result of opportunities presented. But I use the word "interest" because obviously our choice of occupation may be guided not simply by our aptitude, but also by our preferences and fascinations.

My creative Ph.D. student Johnny Lawson used a test which he called the Physical Prediction Questionnaire (PPQ) to see if there is a sex difference in understanding how levers (input) attached to different mechanisms (cog wheels joined in different ways) affect the movement of rods (output). Would the rods go up or down? Men were better at predicting these outcomes, and this cannot have been related to any sexist interviewers, since the tasks were presented by questionnaire through the mail, and completed by the person alone.[8]

So while not denying the existence of possible social factors that are creating inequalities between male and female scientists at the higher levels, I think we need to remain open to the possibility that, on average, men are more often drawn to pursue these interests.

Let's have a closer look at math. Boys at school tend to receive lower grades in mathematics than do girls. On the face of it, this looks like counter-evidence for the male brain being a better systemizer. However, although they score lower on *accuracy* in math, boys tend to score higher on tests of mathematical *ability*. Teachers will tell you that, on average, girls are the better students, but that boys score higher in exams. Despite their work being less neat, and more erratic, boys tend to see mathematical solutions more readily. No justice, you might think.

Girls do not score worse than boys in all aspects of math ability, though. Across the school years, girls score better in tests of mathematical *sentences*, and in tests of mathematical *reasoning*, such as calculation. Some people have wondered if this is because these are math tasks on which it is easier to use verbal strategies. As we saw in Chapter 4, females tend to have better verbal skills. When you look at the math tasks where verbal strategies are arguably less useful (for example, geometry, probability, and statistics), girls score lower than boys.

Sex differences in math have been documented in children as young as seven years old. As psychologist Doreen Kimura points out, the *same* teachers teach both the calculation (in which girls excel) and mathematical problem-solving (in which boys excel), so it is hard to see how a teacher's *general* expectations or teaching style could produce a different pattern of scores in the two sexes. The same argument makes parental expectations a poor explanation of this sex difference.[9]

Cross-cultural studies suggest that, in childhood, there are no sex differences in primary mathematical abilities. These are the aspects of math found in children in all cultures, such as basic counting, numerosity (the idea of more or less), ordinality (the idea of what comes after what), and simple arithmetic (addition and subtraction). The sex differences only emerge in secondary domains. These are the aspects of math that are first encountered at school, such as geometry and mathematical word problems.

Since sex differences in math only appear later in childhood, you might be tempted to conclude that this shows the role of culture and education in producing sex differences. However, cross-cultural studies reveal the same pattern of sex differences worldwide. Girls perform better at the calculation and computational components of math tests; boys perform better at mathematical problem-solving. This is seen across cultures as diverse as those in the USA, Thailand, Taiwan, and Japan.[10] So if it is just a matter of culture, why should most cultures be producing the same pattern?

I mentioned earlier that a sex difference is also seen in the math component of the Scholastic Aptitude Test (SAT-M). Males on average score *fifty points higher* than females on this test. When the results are examined by bands, the sex differences become more marked as one approaches the highest bands. For example, if you look at all those people who score above 500, you find a sex ratio of 2:1 (men to women). If you look at those people scoring above 600, you find a sex ratio of 6:1. And by the time you look at those people scoring above 700, the sex ratio is 13:1 (men to women).

A similar picture emerges if you look at the International Mathematical Olympiad, in which the world's best mathematicians compete against each other. Here's how it works: eighty-five countries put forward their best six mathematicians, selected through national competitions. You can look up the winners on the Web if you are interested. You will notice immediately that they are nearly all male. The Olympiad winners are listed by name, not by sex, but one can have a good guess at the sex of someone called Sanjay, David, Sergei, or Adam. This male bias is true of all countries and across the years that the competition has been run. Interestingly, China always manages to include a woman on its team: women are able to do math at this level. However, taking a look at group averages for the two sexes, it is much more likely that top mathematicians will be male. Looking at the broad picture suggests that males outperform females in mathematics (that is stripped of any verbal component) from school right through to the highest level.[11]

Understanding Other Systems

Let's leave math to one side and think about other examples of systemizing. Systemizing involves the prediction of output from a system when you apply some variable operation on the input. Have a look at the Water Level Task, originally devised by Swiss child psychologist Jean Piaget. The result he obtained may shock you. You show someone a bottle, tipped at an angle, and ask that person to predict the water level. Women more often draw the water level aligned with the tilt of the bottle, whereas the true water level, no matter what the tilt of the bottle, will always be horizontal.[12]

The same male advantage is seen in another similar test, the Rod and Frame Test. You sit the person being tested in a darkened room, and show them a 3-D model of a luminous rectangle (the frame) with a luminous rod inside it. The rectangle is rotated to different orientations, and you ask the person to position the rod so that it is vertical. Your sense of the vertical should be an absolute judgment, or perhaps relative to your sense of your

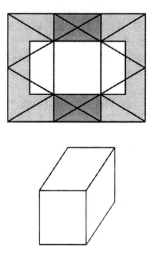

An item from the Adult Embedded Figures Test
fig 6.

body's verticality. Certainly, changing the tilt of the frame should not affect the tilt of the rod, if you understand the meaning of verticality. If your judgment of verticality is influenced by the tilt of the frame, you are said to be "field dependent": your judgment is easily swayed by (irrelevant) input from the surrounding context. If you are not influenced by the tilt of the frame, you are said to be "field independent": your understanding takes account only of the relevant factors intrinsic to that system. Most studies show that females are more field dependent. In plain English, it means that women are relatively more distracted by irrelevant cues, rather than considering the system in isolation. They are more likely than men to say (erroneously) that the rod is upright if it is aligned with its frame.[13]

Consider next the Embedded Figures Test. (An example of the Adult Embedded Figures Test is shown in Figure 6.) In this test someone is asked to look at a simple shape (the target), and to pick it out from a more complex pattern (the background in which it is embedded). On average, males are quicker and more accurate in locating the target from the larger, complex pattern.[14] This can be seen as a systemizing test because the target shape can *only* fit into its slot in one way; in other words, there is a rule that describes this relationship. If you think of the complex background pattern as a car engine, for example, and the target as a component part, it is only possible to fit the part into the engine in one way in order to complete the system.

Attention to Detail

The above tasks require not only an understanding of the system but also attention to relevant detail and an ability to ignore irrelevant detail. This is indeed a general feature of systemizing—not the only factor, but a necessary part of it—and it proves to be the case that attention to relevant detail is superior in men.

Men, on average, are also better at detecting a particular feature (static or moving). For example, if someone is shown a film of a forest and asked whether they can detect any movements created by an animal or person in that forest, one finds that most men and boys are better able to spot movement than are girls and women.[15]

Systems Under Changing
Orientation or Topography

Another frequently used measure is the Mental Rotation Test. You show someone two shapes and ask them whether one of the shapes is a rotation or a mirror image of the other. Men are both quicker and more accurate at this test than are women. This sex difference can even be seen in children as young as five who are set a rotation task using a clock face, or are asked to judge if Teddy has the same arm raised when he is rotated. The male advantage has been found in many different cultures in the UK, the USA, Africa, the East Indies, and Asia. This test involves systemizing because one has to run the input through an operation (a rotation) to predict the output.[16] The test may benefit from good visualization skills, but at a minimum one also has to keep track of rules of the type *if operation a, then b changes to c.*

Reading maps is another everyday test of systemizing—you have to operate on 3-D input in order to predict how it will appear in 2-D. Consider also how we tend to think of the train network, highways, waterways, aviation, and other route-based maps as traffic "systems." In these examples, one motorway (the input) leads into another (the output), or one river (the input) flows into another (the output). So you can predict, using simple if-then rules, where a given route will take you. If I turn left at Junction 12 (the operation), I leave the M11 (input) and end up on the Barton Road (output). The flow of traffic (its speed and density) can also be understood as a system.

In one study, children were asked to describe if they would be turning left or right at a particular intersection on a city map, to reach a particular destination. To make it a touch harder, they were not allowed to rotate the map. (Try this next time you are out in a new area, if you can stop yourself turning the road atlas around.) Boys performed at a higher level than girls.

If you ask people to put together a 3-D mechanical apparatus in an assembly task, on average men score higher than women. And in relation to construction tests, boys are also better at constructing block buildings from 2-D blueprints.

Men can also learn a route in fewer trials, just from looking at a map, correctly recalling more details about direction and distance. If you ask boys to make a map of an area that they have only visited once, their maps are more accurately laid out in terms of the features in the environment, for example, showing which landmark is south-east of another. If you score these maps as either disorganized or organized, more of the boys' maps are classified as organized. More of the girls' maps make serious errors in the location of important landmarks.

The boys tend to emphasize directions, routes, or roads, whereas the girls tend to emphasize specific landmarks (the corner shop, for example). These two strategies—using directional cues versus using landmark cues—have been widely studied. The directional strategy is an instance of understanding space as a geometric system, and the focus on roads or routes is an instance of considering space in terms of another system, in this case a transport system.[17]

You might wonder if this reflects a less accurate visual memory in women, rather than a less accurate understanding of the system. In fact, women do better on one aspect of visuospatial memory, namely the ability to remember the relative locations of objects. This is tested in the following way: men and women are shown an array of objects for one minute, and then are given two sheets of paper with objects drawn on them. On the first sheet are all the objects they were shown originally, together with some that they were not. They are asked to name the objects that they were shown originally. On the second sheet are all the original items, but some of them have been sneakily moved to a different position. They are then asked to name the objects that have moved.

Women do better at both of these tasks. And if men and women are asked to turn over two cards to find matching pairs, correct pairs then being removed from the array, women succeed in finding all the matching pairs in fewer trials. Women can also recall more details about landmarks and street names from maps. So there is clearly nothing wrong with their memory for the important components. Rather, their spontaneous recall of the systematic properties of maps (for example, geometric or network aspects) is not as good as men's.[18]

In another study, people were shown a map of an unfamiliar town (a made-up one). They were then tested on their ability to learn a route within this fictional town—how good they were at being taxi-drivers, if you will. Results showed that men learned the route more quickly (they needed less time and fewer attempts) and made fewer errors. Once again, women tended to recall more landmarks, while the men had a better directional understanding of the map. Other studies have found similar results. For example, take a group of children (even as young as eight) to a new area, give them a map, and then later ask them to reconstruct the map of the area through drawing. You will find that the girls include more landmarks, while the boys include more routes (roads, and so on). If you repeat the experiment with a second group of children but this time give them just half the map and interrupt their tour of the area (to make the test a bit tougher), boys are still better at recalling the relative positions of places. The two sexes seem to be approaching the task very differently. The male brain puts the features into a geometric or network system; the female brain marks the features descriptively.

Let's put it a little more concretely. If you are shown a route from A to B to C, and you are a systemizer, you might work out that it would be quicker (and shorter) to go from C straight back to A, without needing to take a route via B at all. To do this, you would have to work out the compass directions, which comprise the system. For example, if C is north-east of A, then A must be south-west of C. If you are not a systemizer and simply stick to your landmark strategy, how would you get back from C to A? You

would have to retrace your path via B, since that was your key landmark on
the way from A to C (you would turn left at B). These are clearly two very
different strategies and the former is significantly more powerful.[19]

Building and Copying a System

Children's play with Legos is another good example to look at, because
Lego bricks can be combined and recombined into an infinite number of
systems. In this case the systems involve an understanding of what will
support what, as well as the design and redesign of buildings or objects.
And as the toy industry knows, boys love it. As young as three, boys are also
faster at copying 3-D models of outsized Lego pieces, and older boys, from
age nine, are better at imagining what a 3-D object will look like if it is laid
out flat. Boys are also better at constructing a 3-D structure from just an
aerial and frontal view in a picture. These examples of male superiority in
systemizing abilities are reported right across the age range.[20]

Systemizing Object Motion:
Playing Darts and Catching Balls

In Chapter 5, we mentioned another class of system, motor systems. Systemizing in this case includes things such as perfecting your swing with a
golf club, or your technique with a squash racquet, or your finger speed on
a musical instrument, or flying a kite, or juggling. If you understand the
physics of the system, the ball will end up exactly where you want it (in
that little area in the corner of the squash court where the other guy has no
chance of returning it), or each note in a rapid sequence on the piano will
end up of equal pressure and volume, or that wrist action will flip the kite
into a beautiful figure of eight. Is there any evidence that males are better
at this kind of systemizing?

If you are asked to throw objects at a target, such as playing darts, men
are more accurate in such throwing accuracy. My favorite example is frisbee-
throwing. Men are also better at intercepting balls flung from a launcher.
Equally, if people are asked to judge which of two moving objects is traveling faster, on average men are more accurate. They are also better at

estimating when an object moving toward them will hit them. In one study, the object could only be seen, not heard, and the task was to say when the object would arrive. In a related study, judging object velocity from sound alone also revealed a male advantage. This must be systemizing par excellence. Presumably the systemizer is analyzing the auditory input in terms of how it correlates with speed.[21]

Could all this just be a male advantage in motor skills? This explanation does not hold, since if one designs a motor task that involves minimal or no systemizing, such as simple "fine-motor" accuracy, women actually score better than men. An example of this kind of task involves asking men and women to put pegs into holes as rapidly as possible (the Purdue Peg Board Task).[22]

Classification and Organizable Systems

What about organizable systems? In one unusual study, people were asked to classify over a hundred examples of local specimens into related species. The people who took part in this experiment were the Aguaruna, a tribal people living in the forest in northern Peru. The following results were found: men's classification systems had more sub-categories (in other words, they introduced greater differentiation) and more consistency. More striking, the criteria that the Aguaruna men used to decide which animals belonged together more closely resembled the taxonomic criteria used by Western (mostly male) biologists. Another culture that has been studied is that of the Itza-Maya, in Guatemala. Here, as in the Peruvian example, men used a more complex set of criteria to classify local animals. Women were more likely to use "static" morphological features (such as the color or shape of the animal's body); men were more likely to use a cluster of related features (such as the animal's habitat, diet and even their relationship to humans).[23]

You will remember from Chapter 2 that Alex enjoyed collecting things from a very early age. Studies of children's rituals support the idea that boys are more into collecting and focusing on the fine differences between the components of their collection. Nick Hornby presents an interesting account of the male mind in his book *Fever Pitch*, in which the author documents his obsession with the details of the soccer club he supports. His obsession does not simply involve knowing the names of players in his team (Arsenal) but all of the club's characteristics, such as knowing the players' goal averages and the scores of matches, going back years.

In sports enthusiasts, you see at work the combination of an organizable system (classifying players or teams), a rule-based system (the rules of the game), a motoric system (the techniques behind skill), and a statistical system (statistic information). Four forms of systemizing converging on one topic (sport). If men enjoy systemizing, no wonder they cannot get enough of league sports. My recent experience watching a baseball game in Toronto (the Blue Jays versus the Red Sox) persuades me that the trivial information people collect about their team's players is not restricted to an English obsession with soccer. In baseball you keep track of the pitcher's ERA (earned runs average), the players' RBI (runs batted in), and many other fascinating and constantly shifting statistics.

In Nick Hornby's novel, *High Fidelity*, the male protagonist is obsessed with his record collection, and works in a second-hand-record shop catering for (almost all male) customers searching for that one missing item in their collections of music. The character's main leisure pursuit is listening to his favorite records and making his own compilation recordings, putting together his own lists of songs according to type (ten best blues songs, ten best jazz songs, ten best Irish folk songs, and so on).

Such an interest in classification and organization involves systemizing because one is confronted with a mass of input (for example, dogs, players, songs) and one has to generate one's own categories (to predict how each dog, player, or song will behave). The categories are therefore not just a way of organizing information into lists: they are more than that. The categories (for example, marsupials) are the operations performed on the input (for example, koala) which then predict the output (for example, has a pouch). The more finely differentiated your categories, the better your system of prediction will be.

Knowing that the erne is not just an eagle but a sea eagle will allow you to predict its habitat, its prey, and its behavior more accurately. Knowing that this snake is poisonous and that snake is not will allow you to react with fear to the right animal. Knowing that this pitcher has a higher earned runs average allows you to predict which team is likely to win the game. Knowing that this musician is a 1970s Czech rock musician allows you to predict which section of the music store you will find his album in.

The world's leading birdwatcher, according to the *Guinness Book of Records*, was a woman, Phoebe Snetsinger, the American ornithologist. This might appear to contradict the claim that males are more prone to collect things and compile lists of facts. As it turns out, Phoebe was the exception to the rule. Most birdwatchers, trainspotters, and plane-spotters are male. Cath Jeffs is an ornithologist and project officer with the Royal Society for the Protection of Birds, and was interviewed by the *Guardian* newspaper:

> Birding is still very male—it's all about collecting information and obsessively putting it into lists. Women just can't get that passionate about lists, can they? . . . It can be very stressful with all these men around. If a bird is supposed to appear and they miss it, things can get tense. Pretty often fights break out, usually because someone has made a noise and scared away a really rare species before everyone's had a chance to record it.[24]

But the existence of some female birdwatchers in no way undermines the theory, because the claim is only that, on average, males will be more strongly drawn to systemize (birds, or any other aspect of the environment) compared to females. Part of what we will also need to explain, however, are such exceptions, as well as these differences between the majority of each sex. Why is this particular woman a talented physicist or an obsessive plane-spotter? Why is this particular man a wonderful counselor or a caring nurse? I will look at possible reasons for these exceptions later in the book.

The Systemizing Quotient (SQ)

In this chapter we have seen a pattern emerging: on average, males seem be drawn more strongly to many different aspects of systemizing—machines, mathematics, maps, birdwatching, and sports statistics, to name just a few. To draw these ostensibly varied types of systemizing together, my research team and I designed the Systemizing Quotient (or SQ). The SQ gives an individual a total score based on how strongly drawn they are to systemize each of these aspects of the world. It may come as no surprise to learn that men score significantly higher than females on the SQ (Appendix 3).[25]

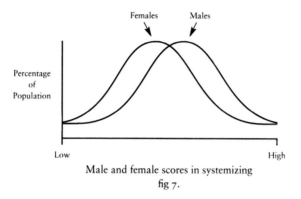

Male and female scores in systemizing

fig 7.

Babies: The Ultimate Test

Before we leave this part of the journey—our voyage into systemizing—it is worth perhaps just thinking about how early we see sex differences in this domain. Recall that in the Cambridge study reported in Chapter 4, we found that one-day-old boys looked longer at a mechanical mobile (a system with predictable laws of motion) than at a person's face (an object that is next to impossible to systemize). Even on the first day of life, a subtle trace is evident of what we see magnified later in development. This is signaling that from birth, boys' attention is being drawn more strongly to a non-personal system, while girls' attention is being drawn more strongly to a face.[26] Recall also that at one year old, boys showed a stronger preference to watch a video of cars (predictable mechanical systems) than to watch a film showing a talking head (with the sound switched off). One-year-old girls showed the opposite preference.[27]

These sex differences are therefore present very early in life. There has hardly been any opportunity for socialization and experience to shape these sex differences. We of course know that, with time, culture and socialization do play a role in determining if you develop a male brain (stronger interest in systems) or a female brain (stronger interest in empathy). But these studies of infancy strongly suggest that biology may also partly determine this.

We have deferred the question of causality for long enough. We have reached a certain point on our journey where we now have to leave the safe path of behavioral differences, and turn into the rocky terrain where we confront what is causing these sex differences, head on.

7

Culture

What might be causing the female brain to empathize at a superior level, and the male brain to systemize at a superior level? Most people are likely to assume that such sex differences are due to a mix of cultural and biological factors. There are, of course, more extreme claims which propose that the sex differences can be reduced to just one of these factors. If these extreme theories were true, this would be important since it would mean that the other set of factors was ruled out.

As I pointed out in Chapter 1, it would be politically attractive if the cultural theory were true. If it really were the case that cultural factors (such as sexism in education or the workplace, or differential child-rearing styles, or the media, or the toy industry) made little boys and girls turn out differently, it would at least mean that we could try to eliminate these differences through new social or educational programs. So just how persuasive is the cultural theory?

Cultural Stereotyping and Biases

If you are shown a videotape in which a child appears upset, and you are told the child is male, you are more likely to label the child's emotion as anger. If you are told the child in the video is female, you are more likely to label the child's emotion as fear. This is an example of what has come to be known as the Baby X experiment. One conclusion to draw from this is that we are not very good at judging if a baby is male or female. But that is not the important conclusion, and sex recognition becomes easier as the person we are observing gets older. The more important conclusion is that, despite believing that we are perceiving people in an unbiased fashion, we must be unwittingly carrying a set of sexist biases. These could be biases we have picked up from the way society stereotypes the sexes, or simply associations we have formed in relation to each sex. Whatever their origin, such biases may lead us to react differently to a person, depending on what we believe their sex to be.

The implication of this is that the psychological sex differences discussed previously could be just the result of gender expectations by adults of children throughout their upbringing. I will look at parenting shortly, to test this idea. The other implication is that sex differences could be the result of the subjective biases of the researchers who make the observations in the experiments. It is therefore imperative for those conducting studies in this area to attempt to remain "blind" to the sex of the participants.

In practice, this is very hard. In the Cambridge newborn study, the observers made strenuous efforts to remain blind to the babies' sex. They asked the mothers who consented to participate in the study while they were in the hospital, on the first day of their new baby's life, *not* to tell the researchers the sex of their baby, so as to avoid being influenced by this information when they were filming or testing the baby. Mothers agreed to withhold this information until after the filming and data recording was complete.

In the vast majority of cases, this information did not leak out. In a few cases it was hard to remain completely blind because the mother's hospital bed would be surrounded with cards from well-wishers saying things such as "Congratulations! It's a boy!" or the baby would be dressed in pink or blue pajamas and blankets. Nevertheless, the experimenters ensured that they filmed only the baby's face, to record where the baby's eyes were looking when he or she was shown the two types of objects (a human face and a mechanical mobile). By the time the judges came to analyze each tape, none of the potential cues (such as the color of baby's clothing) were visible, and they could not tell if they were looking at the face of a male or female baby. And yet the sex difference in looking preference was still found; cultural stereotyping cannot explain the result of this experiment.[1]

The Baby X experiments have not always produced consistent results, but let's assume that it really is true that our expectations of the sexes shape how we interact with boys and girls, or what opportunities we offer them. Despite the influence of such biases, there are examples of well-controlled studies suggesting that this is not necessarily the only cause of observed sex differences in behavior.[2]

Parenting

Could differences in parenting toward boys and girls cause the observed sex differences in children? Could these differences be linked to the fact that mothers are frequently the primary caregiver? This is a valid consideration since, in all societies studied, children (on average) spend more time with their mother than with their father. In some cultures (such as those in Kenya or Japan), children spend about three times as much time with their mother, while in others (such as those in India), children spend more than ten times as much time with their mother. Are mothers doing something to make young girls better empathizers and young boys better systemizers? Or are fathers to blame, treating their sons and daughters differently?[3]

Boys certainly receive more punishments, prohibitions, and threats from parents, as forms of control. Parents tend to forbid their sons from doing something, and tell them what will happen if they transgress those orders far more frequently than they tell their daughters. Do the following examples sound familiar?

> "Max, come back here!"
> "Max, stop!"
> "Max, don't DO that!"
> "No! I've told you before!"
> "Max, do what I say or you'll be in trouble!"
> "Max, if you do that ONE more time, I'll take away your remote-controlled jeep for a week!"

Of course, girls are spoken to in an admonitory way, too, but it is interesting that in most cultures this style of speaking is more often directed toward boys. Is it a sign of sex-typing (in other words, the different treatment of boys and girls for purely cultural reasons)? If so, what on earth are parents doing?

One view is that parents hold in their mind some notion that boys are wilder or greater risk-takers and therefore need more restrictions. Are boys living up to such assumptions? Have parents unconsciously encouraged their sons to take more risks, or to push back the boundaries more often, and then find themselves having to police their sons more often when their child goes too far? There is, of course, an opposite view. It may be that boys are poorer empathizers than girls, which leads them to be less socially compliant, less skilled at picking up the social cues of boundaries, and requiring more frequent disciplining.

There is some evidence for both views. For example, in one study, fathers were videotaped in the waiting room with their one-year-old children, a good set-up for a naturalistic experiment. The investigators found that fathers reprimanded their sons twice as often as they reprimanded their daughters. But this was not without reason: the boys tried to touch forbidden things more often. Girls seemed to pick up on subtle cues—for example, their father looking somewhat disapproving. Such "social referencing"—looking at a parent's face to detect whether something is permitted or not—was enough for many girls to get the message of what was, or was not, allowed.

You can imagine these subtle signals in the parent's face: the father's eyebrows narrow a touch; or maybe his eyes shoot a quick stern stare at the child, as he wanders further than he is allowed to, or tries to take something that is not appropriate; or the father's lips purse just slightly into a silent "shhh," to signal that the child is being a bit too noisy. While girls look up more frequently to pick up these signals, and are more accurate at decoding them, boys may miss them more often. This may be because they are not checking back to see them, or because the signals are being seen but are unread or ignored. In this study boys seemed to get the message that they were doing something that was not allowed only when an explicit verbal expression of disapproval was given.

However, this does not prove that boys are inherently less empathic than girls. The subject of this book is essential differences in the minds of men and women, but perhaps the observed differences in empathizing in this chapter do not reflect any differences in "essence." There is evidence that we have encouraged young boys to be less emotional and more independent by giving them messages such as these:

"Who's a tough boy? Well done!"

"That's my big lad! You did it!"
"Ooh, you're strong! Look at those muscles! You can do it!"
"Want to try climbing a bit higher? You're so big and brave!"
"Don't cry. Boys don't cry!"
"Stop being babyish! None of the other boys are being clingy! It's time for me to go now."

Parents do use phrases like these more often toward their sons. Fathers in particular are less sympathetic to their sons showing emotional dependency.

Such findings are, of course, open to multiple interpretations. Parents might be discouraging boys from showing emotion, thus socializing them into different sex roles; or they might be more tolerant of emotional dependency and clinginess in their daughters, compared to their sons; or they might be giving their sons a description of themselves that portrays them as independent explorers more often than they do their daughters. Yet another interpretation is that girls are better at self-control (we will see some evidence for this in the next chapter), so they do not need to be told to control their emotional outbursts or to inhibit their impulses as often. Young boys are therefore judged by the norms set by young girls, and are thus told more often not to cry or not to touch anything they want. So this difference in parental behavior toward the two sexes could actually be driven by an essential difference between males and females.

In summary, one can see parents' differential behavior as either a cause of observed differences in children, or as a consequence of them.[4]

Although there is some evidence for the two sexes being treated differently by their parents in terms of rough-and-tumble play, with boys being given more opportunities and invitations to horse around and to be more physical than girls, systematic studies reveal more similarities than differences in how the two sexes are handled. For example, parents do not differ in how they treat their sons and daughters in terms of the amount of warmth, responsiveness, talking, or restrictions that they provide. Parents also do not differ in how they handle their sons and daughters when it comes to how much encouragement they give. This suggests that sex-typing may not exist as strongly as many people suspect. There is even evidence that, if anything, parents devote more energy toward encouraging their *sons* to be more empathic. For example, mothers devote more time to copying their baby's facial expressions if the baby is a boy than if it is a girl. It is difficult to correlate such evidence with a female superiority in empathy resulting from parenting styles.[5]

Mothers do, however, speak to their toddler daughters with more emotion words, compared with the number of emotion words they use with their sons. There are also differences in the type of emotion words that mothers use when talking to their toddler sons or daughters, and they tend to discuss positive emotions more with their daughters. Look at these examples of mothers talking to daughters:

> "Oh, that was so *kind* of you to have made that for me."
> "Maybe she didn't want to play with you because she thinks you're best friends with Sally now? She might be feeling a bit jealous. Why don't you invite her round on the weekend and make her feel a bit special as your friend?"

Mothers also use more "other-oriented" talk with their daughters when they have done something wrong, compared to how they talk to their sons. For example, they might say to daughters:

> "How do you think *she* might have felt?"
> "Imagine if *you* were the one who had gone off with a new best friend. You might also feel like her."
> "Do you think she'd like this as a present? It'd be nice to make her feel really special after her illness."

Such differences in style of speech could lead girls to develop better empathy than boys. However, Maccoby makes the important point that this may not be the result of mothers' unwitting sexism. Rather, it may reflect what mothers perceive their particular child is capable of understanding.[6]

Children's Gender Stereotypes

We saw in Chapter 4 that young girls are more likely to play with dolls, and young boys are more likely to play with toy vehicles, or with mechanical toys, or with building blocks such as Legos. Could this be because they have somehow picked up gender stereotypes of what are considered to be "boy toys" or "girl toys"? Certainly, these messages are out there. Consider fathers who say, "I'm not having my son playing with dolls. He'll get laughed at at school for being a sissy." Or consider the toy industry that fills children's television with constant advertisements. In these advertisements, Spider-Man toys are depicted as the ideal present for a child (who is always male) and Barbie dolls are depicted as the most desirable present for a child (who invariably is female). And as the toy business knows, nagging-power by children ("Oh, can't I have one of those, Dad? All the other children have got one.") is a powerful economic force in consumer activity. It is hard for parents to keep saying "No" to their child. And now consider how the influences from parents or the media are strengthened because their older sibling or other children in their peer group have been exposed to the same messages. Sibling rivalry, and the strong need to belong to the peer group, to fit in, might be some of the pressures making children believe that they need these sex-typical toys.

This may well be happening by school age, when the peer group gives signals of approval or disapproval of a child's interests. But the idea that such social influences *determine* toy choices is unlikely. Here's why. If you ask two-year-olds which toys are for boys and which for girls, they will not be able to tell you. Children do not yet know the gender stereotypes; they are as likely to suggest a toy car or a doll for a girl or a boy. Yet at this age they already show the sex-typical toy preferences through the toys that they themselves choose to play with. This suggests that their toy preferences *predate* their gender stereotypes. The latter cannot be causing the former, not unless you believe in backward-causation, in which case we are not living on the same planet.

In addition, by four years of age children are able to distinguish between their own preferences and those of others. Consider the little girl in one study who had been left with a male-typical toy (a truck) to play with, and who said, "My mommy would want me to play with this, but I don't want to." This strongly suggests that children are making choices that are not simply the result of what their parents want for them, but reflect other factors.[7]

Imitation and Practice

Could the sex differences in toy choice and behavior be the result of early imitation of same-sex peers, or of adults? There is no doubt that imitation plays a powerful role by school age. For example, even in cultures where there is no school, older children's play tends to involve enacting the roles of the same-sex parent. But as an account of the *origins* of these sex differences in *toddlers*, this is insufficient. This is because children younger than school age do not consistently imitate someone of the same sex more than they imitate someone of the opposite sex. Imitation of peers cannot be the relevant factor determining early toy preferences.

Psychologist Eleanor Maccoby makes the important point that when children choose to play with a peer of the same sex, and thereby play with toys that the same-sex peer is playing with, this is unlikely to be due to imitation of adults. This is because, when you stop to think about it, adults interact with the *opposite* sex all the time. Certainly, there is no evidence that parents encourage their children to *avoid* the opposite sex. Yet this is what children are choosing to do.[8]

Leaving aside imitation as an explanation of how sex differences arise, what about the obvious explanation of practice? Take the male superiority in motor skills (such as hitting targets). The common-sense view is that it is due to the greater amount of practice males get, through games such as darts and other male-typical sports. Practice may partly explain why the sexes diverge in their skills with age, but problematic for this view of the *origin* of these sex differences is the fact that the male superiority in throwing accuracy is present even in children as young as two years old. At this age, we can safely assume there has been little difference in opportunities to practice, and yet the two-year-old boys clearly outstrip the girls. At older ages, these sex differences are found even when the experimenter obtains information about each individual's sports history and implements controls for this.[9]

Gender Roles

Another explanation of sex differences is the perpetuation of "gender roles." The basic idea is that we hold different beliefs about our genders that affect our behavior and interests. For example, women are believed to be more "communal" (more selfless, more concerned for others), while men are believed to be more "agentive" (more self-assertive, self-expansive, with a stronger urge to master). These beliefs about gender are held to arise from men's and women's different social and economic roles: women's greater involvement in domestic and childcare activities gives rise to them being more communal, and men's greater involvement in paid employment gives rise to them being more self-assertive.

Certainly, there is plenty of evidence for the existence of these gender roles. Given a choice, more men choose to work in "dominance-oriented" occupations (i.e., those emphasizing social hierarchies and the control over others), while more women choose to work in "dominance-attenuating" jobs (i.e., working in a team of equals with others, and/or working with disadvantaged people).[10]

It may be that we hold gender-role beliefs (such as men have a stronger urge to master), but where do such beliefs come from? The systemizing theory would say that men, on average, have a stronger drive to understand systems as thoroughly as possible, whether this is a physical technique to master, or a new computer to understand. But *why* this is present is a wide-open question.

How can we test if it is our gender-role beliefs that cause the observed sex differences (in behavior, emotion, interests, and skills) or if they arise for Darwinian reasons? The Darwinian David Geary argues that more males are agentive because males depend for their reproductive success on a drive to establish social dominance. For the gender-roles theory to work, it would have to disprove such Darwinian factors. This has not yet been done. In fact, the gender-roles theory runs into specific problems quite quickly. For example, it fails to explain striking similarities across very different societies. Thus, of 122 societies studied, weapon-making (a clear example of a systemizing skill) is an exclusively male activity in 121 of these. (In the one society where women work in weapon-making, the women help the men rather than being involved exclusively.) This must be more than a coincidence.[11]

To summarize, there is some support for cultural determinism. A clear example can be found in the different ways that parents speak to their sons and their daughters, something that could contribute to the differences we observe in the development of empathy. But some of the sex differences are present so early (at birth) that it is hard to see how culture could be the *sole* cause. In addition, some parents try to do everything to avoid such cultural influences on their child. They buy their sons dolls, and their daughters toy trucks, only to find that the child still chooses to play with sex-typical toys. And even if we think that this simply shows that peer and media influences are stronger than parental ones, this still seems insufficient to explain all the observed sex differences, because of their *early* onset—before the media or the peer group have taken root in the young child's mind.

For these and other reasons, it seems possible that the development of sex differences in behavior are due to factors other than, and additional to, the cultural ones. Biological factors are the only other candidates. Let's have a look at what these could be.

8

Biology

Social or cultural explanations seem to be incomplete accounts of why the female brain is, on average, better at empathizing and why the male brain is, on average, better at systemizing. Can biology account for these sex differences? In this chapter I will examine studies of animals, hormones, the brain, and finally genetics. Let's start with animals.

From Rats to Monkeys

Are there sex differences in other species which mirror what we see in humans? If there are, then since other species are by definition outside of human culture (leaving aside dogs in England), this could implicate a biological cause.

The key danger here is, of course, anthropocentrism—the age-old tendency to assume that other animals have attributes just like ours. This is an important risk to keep in mind, since it is hotly contested whether other animals (apart from humans) are capable of empathizing or systemizing at all.[1] But other animals do have simpler forms of sociability and spatial ability than humans, which may be relevant.

Let's start with the great apes, baboons, and rhesus monkeys. Males in all these species show more "play-fighting" than the females—what would be called "rough-and-tumble play" in human children. One can see this kind of behavior in very young animals, for example in one-year-old male rhesus monkeys. As we saw in Chapter 4, human male toddlers also show more rough-and-tumble play than human female toddlers. Some people interpret this difference in human behavior as a sign of males' reduced social sensitivity to others, males having a stronger drive to assert their strength and their social status, rather than tiptoeing cautiously around others' feelings. The fact that we see this behavior across different primates suggests it may have some shared biological cause(s).

Another apparent similarity across humans, monkeys, and apes is the greater interest that females on average show in babies (of their own species). Females like to look at them, cuddle them, care for them, and worry about them. One might think that this does not reflect biology but same-sex imitation (of mothers by daughters) in all three kinds of animal. A problem for the imitation account, however, is that it is *juvenile* female monkeys and apes who show more interest in babies, and yet juvenile monkeys are not great imitators in general.[2] So the stronger interest by females in babies may be a marker of their increased emotional sensitivity to others, especially vulnerable others.

What about animal studies of systemizing? We acknowledged above that systemizing may be a uniquely human ability, since it is a method of establishing causal information, and causal thinking has not been convincingly demonstrated in species other than humans. Nevertheless, studies of simpler behaviors in the rat, such as spatial ability, may teach us something about the animal equivalent of systemizing. After all, we have already seen that spatial skills in humans can involve systemizing.

Male rats generally find their way through mazes more quickly and with fewer errors. In one test called the radial maze, for example, the animal has to remember which of the radiating paths from the center they must use to find food. Mazes are traditional tests of spatial ability, but of course a maze is also a system. If one travels along arm A of the radial maze, it leads to output X. Travel along arm B, and it leads to a different output (Y). In both the human and rat studies, a male superiority has been established when geometric (systemic) cues are available. Females tend to rely on landmarks (objects) in the room.

One could say that when it comes to understanding space, using the landmark strategy is not very systematic. Simply telling yourself to turn right at the church to find the shop might help if you always approach the church from the same direction. But consider what happens if you ap-

proach the church from the opposite direction. The correct move to make
is to turn *left* at the church to find the shop. The landmark is still important, but systemizing is needed as well. You will need to follow rules such as
"If A (input) is to the *right* of B (output 1), then under a rotation of 180 degrees (operation), A will be to the *left* of B (output 2)." These are systematic
rules governing space. There is some evidence that males are better at this
approach to spatial tasks.

A further human sex difference that is hinted at in another species is the
male superiority in throwing accuracy, evident even by the age of two. In
Chapter 6 I explained that this ability involved systemizing, in terms of
both understanding the rules governing object motion and the rules governing actions. Although it is not known if male chimpanzees are more *accurate* in their throwing (as we see in human males), they throw objects much
more than female chimps do. If this throwing behavior is arising in human
and chimp males for the same reason, it would again suggest an evolved, bi-
ologically based sex difference. Certainly, chimps are not subject to human
cultural influences, such as watching darts championships on television,
and nor are most human two-year-olds.[3]

So animal studies hint at the role of biology in empathizing and systemizing, but the hints are no more than that, at this stage. What about studies
of hormones? Can they teach us anything relevant?

Topping Up Your Hormone Levels

An obvious biological factor that might be causing sex differences in the
mind is the hormone (or endocrine) system. From soon after conception, the
testes in male fetuses secrete testosterone at a high rate. Testosterone is also
secreted from the adrenal glands, which explains why girls also produce it;
however, boys, even before birth, obviously produce more testosterone.

It is worth backtracking to remind you of a very basic point about your
sex. When you think about your sex, you have to distinguish five different
levels:

1. Your *genetic sex*: you are male if you have one X and one Y chromosome (XY), and you are female if you have two X chromosomes (XX).

2. Your *gonadal sex*: you are male if you have a normal set of testes (producing male hormones), and you are female if you have a normal set of ovaries (producing female hormones).

3. Your *genital sex*: you are male if you have a normal penis, and you are female if you have a normal vagina.

4. Your *brain type*: you are male if your systemizing is stronger than your empathizing, and you are female if your empathizing is stronger than your systemizing.

5. Your *sex-typical behavior*: this follows from your brain type. You are male if your interests involve things such as gadgets, CD collections, and sports statistics, and you are female if your interests involve things such as caring for friends, worrying about their feelings, and striving for intimacy.

Your brain type is not entirely distinct from your sex-typical behavior, but it is a summary of information derived from your behavior. Psychologists would say that your brain type is a description at the "cognitive" level, while behavior is what you can be observed to do. Your genetic sex is set at the point of conception, and is straightforward to determine. Most people who want to determine whether a person is male or female stop at this first level. But even if you are genetically female, and even if you are genitally female, you could be more male gonadally, and have a male brain and male sex-typical behavior. Conversely, even if you are genetically and genitally male, you could be more female gonadally, or you could have a female brain and female sex-typical behavior. And pre-natal testosterone, an androgen, oozing from your testes if you are genetically and gonadally male, or dripping out of your adrenal glands if you are genetically and gonadally female, appears to be one important variable in determining your brain type or your sex-typical behavior.

There appear to be three points in development when testosterone secretion really surges. The first is the pre-natal period, between eight and twenty-four weeks into the pregnancy. The next one is around five months after birth. A final peak is at puberty. These periods are referred to as the "activational" periods, because it is at these times that the brain is thought to be most sensitive to such hormonal changes. The sex hormones are said to have a pre-natal activating effect on the brain.[4]

Norman Geschwind, a neurologist, drew on this observation to formulate a brilliantly simple idea. He speculated that fetal testosterone affects the growth rate of the two hemispheres of the brain. The more testosterone you have the faster your right hemisphere develops and, correspondingly, the slower your left hemisphere develops. We will come back to the two hemispheres shortly, since although Geschwind's theory has been criticized in different ways, there is evidence in support of his prediction that males have superior right hemisphere skills and females have superior left hemisphere skills.[5]

But first, has fetal testosterone got anything to do with empathizing?

Scientists injected pregnant rhesus monkeys with testosterone. The daughters of these monkeys, although *genetically* female (they had two X chromosomes), were *genitally* male. As they grew older, these daughters showed more male forms of play, such as more rough-and-tumble play (play-fighting). As we discussed earlier, play-fighting can be a sign of lower empathy. Conversely, scientists have injected virgin female mammals with estrogen and progesterone. They demonstrated more maternal behavior, such as an increased interest in babies. Again, this suggests increased empathizing. Moreover, human fetuses exposed to synthetic androgen-based compounds show increased aggression post-natally. These clues indicate that hormones can affect these social behaviors.[6]

There was a time when women were prescribed a synthetic female hormone (diesthylstilbestrol) in an attempt to prevent repeated spontaneous miscarriages. Boys born to such women are likely to show more female-typical behaviors—enacting social themes in their play as toddlers, for example, or caring for dolls. This is a further indication that hormone levels can affect the ability to empathize.[7]

The study of male-to-female transsexuals can also teach us about the effects of hormones on empathizing. They show a reduction in "direct" forms of aggression (the physical assaults that are more common in males) and an increase in indirect or "relational" aggression (the style of aggression that is more common in females). This is strong evidence that testosterone affects the form that aggression takes. Recall that direct aggression is likely to require even lower empathizing. Of course, this only tells us about post-natal androgens.[8] How could we learn more about pre-natal androgens?

Svetlana Lutchmaya was my talented Ph.D. student. Peter Raggatt is a biochemist at Addenbrooke's Hospital in Cambridge who has a contagious enthusiasm for testing how testosterone affects behavior. Together, Svetlana, Peter, and I decided to test the pre-natal testosterone theory directly. We studied babies whose mothers had undergone amniocentesis during the first trimester of pregnancy. As you probably know, amniocentesis is a routine medical procedure administered to women who are thought to be at raised risk of having a baby with Down's Syndrome (usually because of the mother's age).

Addenbrooke's Hospital in Cambridge is, among other things, a regional center for the analysis of amniotic fluid from hospitals in the east of England. Most importantly for our study, Addenbrooke's Hospital stores the amniotic fluid from each pregnancy in a deep freezer until each baby is born. It is therefore possible to analyze the amniotic fluid for levels of pre-natal testosterone, although it is not usually retained for this purpose. The testosterone that one finds in that fluid is fetal in origin.

We took advantage of this situation by getting in touch with the mothers whose amniotic fluid was in the deep freezer, and asking them to bring their healthy, bouncing toddlers into our lab. We found that the toddlers (at twelve and twenty-four months of age) who we had identified as having lower fetal testosterone, now had higher levels of eye contact and a larger vocabulary; or, putting it the other way around, the higher your levels of pre-natal testosterone, the less eye contact you now make and the smaller your vocabulary. This is exactly as Geschwind had predicted.

When we got these results, I had one of those strange feelings, like a shiver down the spine. A few drops more of this little chemical could affect your sociability or your language ability. I found it extraordinary. My only regret is that I cannot share the excitement of this result with Geschwind himself. Unfortunately he died of a heart-attack some years ago. But back to the result: if eye contact and communication are early signs of empathizing, this is a further indication that fetal testosterone is an important biological factor in individual differences in empathizing.[9]

We decided to embark on a follow-up study of the children whose mothers had undergone amniocentesis. By the time they were four years old, I had a new Ph.D. student, Rebecca Knickmeyer, a naturally gifted scientist. We gave these four-year-old children the Childhood Communication Checklist (CCC). This measures your social skill and how narrow your interests are. (The latter is an index of your systemizing ability, since systemizing typically involves a deep interest in one topic.) We found that those children who had had higher pre-natal testosterone now had lower social skills, and were more restricted in their interests, compared with those who had had lower pre-natal testosterone.[10]

So lower levels of fetal testosterone (seen more commonly in females) lead to better levels of language, communication skills, eye contact, and social skills—all signs of better empathizing. And if restricted interests are an indicator of in-depth systemizing, these results clearly show that good systemizing abilities are linked to higher levels of fetal testosterone. But there are other clues that indicate that fetal testosterone is linked to systemizing.

For example, if you castrate a male rat at birth, his testosterone stops flowing from his testes to his brain. (I do not suggest that you try this at home, but the experiment has been done in the lab.) Such rats end up without the typical male thickness difference between the left and right cortex. Male fetuses (human or rat) have a larger right hemisphere volume. If pre-natal testosterone is responsible for accelerating the growth of the right side of the body, and the right hemisphere in particular, then castration should lead to less-well-developed spatial systemizing, given that the right hemisphere is more strongly implicated in this ability. This is indeed the case.[11] If a female rat is injected at birth with testosterone, she shows faster maze-learning and makes fewer errors compared with a female rat who has not been given such an injection: masculinizing the rat hormonally improves her spatial systemizing. Amazingly, the testosterone-injected female rats perform as well as normal male rats (whose testes have been secreting testosterone all along). The normal male rats and the hormonally treated female rats use a directional strategy to find their way through the mazes. This strongly suggests a good systemizing ability. The normal females and the castrated males depend heavily on landmarks as cues. Not surprisingly, using landmarks leads to a poorer rate of maze-learning since, as we discussed earlier, landmarks can be unreliable. This suggests that systemizing ability is influenced by pre- and peri-natal testosterone.[12]

A final group who demonstrate the effect of hormones on systemizing are older men with lower testosterone levels. If one gives them testosterone treatment for therapeutic reasons, they perform better on the Block Design Task compared with men given a placebo. The Block Design Task requires one to predict how a design will look when it is rotated. The systemizing element within the task is something like this: if I do x, a changes to b (for example, if I turn the design around by 90 degrees, then the edge that was vertical becomes horizontal). Good performance tends to be predicated on a systemizing approach.[13] Furthermore, one group of Canadian researchers, led by Gina Grimshaw, has found that the higher a child's pre-natal testosterone, the better they perform the Mental Rotation Test. Like the Block Design Test, performance on this also benefits from good systemizing.

Incidentally, the relationship between pre-natal testosterone and systemizing is not endlessly linear. If your pre-natal testosterone levels were too high, your performance on the Mental Rotation Task is *worse* than if your pre-natal testosterone levels were lower. So there may be an optimal level of pre-natal testosterone for the development of systemizing—somewhere in the low–normal male range. Even if you look at current levels of testosterone, as it circulates in the blood or saliva in adult volunteers, men with low–normal levels of testosterone also do best on systemizing tests involving mathematics and spatial ability.[14]

Some male babies are born with a condition called IHH (idiopathic hypogonadotropic hypogonadism). People with IHH have very small testes. IHH is caused by a deficiency in the hypothalamic gonadotrophic hormone, which regulates the production and release of sex hormones. People with IHH are worse at spatial aspects of systemizing than normal males. These again are further clues that early levels of testosterone do indeed influence systemizing abilities.[15]

Then there are those with Androgen Insensitivity (AI) Syndrome. These people are genetically male. They are also gonadally male, so they produce normal amounts of androgen. But because of a genetic defect, they are not sensitive to androgens at a cellular level. At birth, they look genitally female, so their parents and doctors assume that they are indeed female. They are therefore given girls' names and reared as girls from birth. It is only later, at puberty, that their AI is detected. This is because, although they have normal breasts, they do not menstruate—they are amenorrhoeic (not surprising, given that they have no internal female organs). People with AI are, as you might predict, worse at systemizing.[16]

Yet other babies are born with a condition called CAH (congenital adrenal hyperplasia). They have unusually high levels of androgens due to an overproduction of a testosterone-like androgen called androstenedione. As a result, a *genetically* female baby with CAH ends up *genitally* male. Surgery is typically carried out in the first year of life, and corrective hormonal therapy is started in order to block the flow of androgens. This is naturally very worrying for parents, but with this treatment these children develop without further medical complications.

From the scientific perspective, children with CAH are an experiment of nature. They make it possible to investigate the effects of unusually high levels of androgens occurring before birth. (Individuals with HHH are less clear-cut, scientifically, as they are not typically diagnosed until puberty. This means that many post-natal factors may operate, which are difficult to monitor.) As one would predict, girls with CAH have enhanced spatial systemizing, compared with their sisters or other close female relatives without CAH, who act as controls.

You can obtain these results using the Mental Rotation Test or visualizing tests, such as paper-folding. You also obtain the same results if you ask them to find the target on the Embedded Figures Test. You may recall that these are all tests on which males typically score higher than females. Girls with CAH score as well as normal boys, and dramatically better than normal girls. Girls with CAH also tend to participate more often in athletic competitions and physical play, where competition is the main goal. This might reflect their focus on rank in the social system, and their focus on themselves as individual competitors—something that requires reduced empathy. Young girls with CAH also prefer to play with toys like cars (mechanical systems) more than is typically seen in girls without CAH. In short, they have stronger systemizing abilities.

Boys with CAH are a different story. Despite the fact that they were exposed to excess androgens, their spatial ability is no better than that seen in normal boys. In some studies it is even impaired. This fits with the earlier finding that spatial or systemizing abilities do not simply get better and better if one is exposed to more pre-natal androgens. Rather, the function is an inverted U-shaped curve. In plain language, if you have very high *or* very low androgen levels, this can impair your systemizing abilities. If you are somewhere in the middle (in the low male range), you do best.[17]

In sex-change operations, women are given extra androgens to masculinize them, while men are given anti-androgen (estrogen) therapy to feminize them. What happens? The female-to-male transsexuals improve on spatial rotation tests. The male-to-female transsexuals may actually get worse on this task (the results are tricky to interpret).[18]

All the evidence above leads us down one path on our journey. Namely, to suspect that testosterone (especially early in development) is affecting the brain and thus affecting behavior. More specifically, the more you have of this special substance, the more your brain is tuned into systems and the less your brain is tuned into emotional relationships.

Testosterone and the
Two Hemispheres of the Brain

Geschwind's idea was that fetal testosterone affects the rate of growth of the two hemispheres of the brain, with the higher level of fetal testosterone in men leading to earlier, faster growth of the right hemisphere.

The right hemisphere is involved in spatial ability, which, as we have seen, is assisted by the ability to systemize. The left hemisphere is involved in language and communication, which, as we have seen, is assisted by the ability to empathize. If the right hemisphere in the male brain develops faster than it does in the female brain, this could explain why men's ability to systemize develops faster too. Equally, if the left hemisphere develops faster in the female brain than it does in the male brain, this could explain why women's language and empathizing skills might develop faster too. Is this what is found in studies?

The two hemispheres' specialization is referred to as the "laterality" of different brain functions. The laterality of language has been extensively studied. Language skills play a major role in our social life, and in empathizing. From as early as six months old, girls show more electrical activity in the left than in the right hemisphere when listening to speech sounds. As people get older, the left hemisphere in most individuals becomes "dominant" for language. The fact that in early infancy little girls are already showing left-hemisphere dominance for speech perception may help explain why girls develop speech faster than boys, and is consistent with Geschwind's theory.[19]

If you are played speech through headphones, you recall words played in your right ear more accurately than those played in your left ear. This is called the "right-ear advantage," and it is thought to be due to the auditory nerve fibers from the cochlear ascending to the contralateral (or opposite) side of the brain. The ears are connected to both hemispheres of your brain, but the connections are greater on the contralateral side. So the right ear sends its strongest auditory signal to the left hemisphere of the brain. This may be one reason why the left hemisphere of the brain is dominant for language perception.[20]

There are sex differences in such laterality effects. For example, men can attend more accurately to words heard in the right ear than they can to words heard in the left. This suggests that men are more lateralized for language than are women. It may seem contradictory that men are more lateralized for language, yet perform at a lower level on many language tests in relation to women, but there may, in fact, be no contradiction: bilateral representation for language (i.e., using *both* hemispheres rather than one) may be why women show better performance.[21] One view is that because females are devoting less of their right hemisphere to spatial or systemizing skills, they have spare cortex available in their right hemisphere for language functions.

A clue that women are making use of both hemispheres for language can be discerned from the fact that when they have left-hemisphere damage (for example, after a stroke), they are less likely to develop aphasia (language difficulties). If they do develop aphasia after brain damage, they tend to recover more quickly. This may be because the right-hemisphere language areas in women (not present in men to the same extent) take over some of the damaged left-hemisphere language areas.

Consistent with this, the language test scores of women who are brain damaged are not affected by whether the damage is on the right or left hemisphere of the brain, whereas in men, left-hemisphere damage typically carries more risk for developing aphasia.[22]

A final clue comes from the Wada Test. In this test the patient is injected with an anesthetic (sodium amytal), which quickly flows into one hemisphere of his or her brain. It is therefore possible to put the left hemisphere of the patient's brain to sleep. One can then examine the patient's ability to understand words when all they have to rely on is their right hemisphere. By repeating this test on the other side of the brain, one can test what each hemisphere of the brain is capable of doing, in turn. When groups of both men and women are tested, one finds something very interesting. Women's language ability becomes markedly less fluent when the anesthetic is injected into either hemisphere. Men's verbal fluency only decreases when they have a left-hemisphere injection. This fits with the other evidence from studies of laterality.[23] My late friend Donald Cohen, a leading child psychiatrist working at Yale University, listened to all this evidence and called it the "spare tire" theory of women and language. "Hey, guys," he quipped in his characteristically jovial style to an amused group of scientists gathered together for a research meeting in (of all places) an austere monastery in Venice, in 2001. "Don't rely on just using one tire. Get smart and do what the girls do: carry a spare."

Norman Geschwind also theorized that fetal androgens enhance the development of the right side of the body more generally (in other words, not just the right hemisphere of the brain). Thus, in men, some (but not all) studies find that the right foot is larger than the left, and the right testis is larger than the left one. In women, the left foot tends to be larger than the right, the left ovary larger than the right one, and women on average report having a larger left breast.[24] Of course, these are statistical averages. They do not apply to every man or woman.

Doreen Kimura had the imaginative idea of separating her subjects into two groups, according to whether they had a larger testis or breast on the left or right side. In this way, she was able to compare the "left-greater" individuals to the "right-greater" individuals (irrespective of whether they were male or female). When she gave them language tests (purportedly performed better by the female brain), the group with the left-larger testis or breast performed better than the group with the right-larger testis or breast. These results help explain why a woman might show a more male brain type, or why a man might show a more female brain type. The explanation is in terms of the person's early fetal androgen levels, and their consequent neural asymmetric development. The "right-greater" individuals are assumed to have had higher levels of fetal androgens.

Even scientists feel uncomfortable about asking their volunteers to strip off to measure the size of their breasts or testes. So Doreen Kimura measured a less intrusive marker of fetal asymmetry, namely the fingerprint. The traditional system for classifying fingerprints involves counting the number of ridges on the fingertips of the left and right hands.[25] Using counts from the thumb and little finger on each hand, Kimura confirmed the finding that most people have more ridges on the right hand. She calls this the "right-greater" (or R>) pattern. But she also confirmed that more females have the minority "left-greater" (or L>) pattern. This fits with the earlier broad finding that women are more likely to have enhanced left-sided growth.[26]

Since our fingerprints are laid down during the first four months of fetal life, and do not change for the rest of our life (barring major injury), they serve as a sort of fossil record of which half of our body developed earlier, while we were in the womb. They are thought to be a marker of levels of fetal testosterone, which drive asymmetric body development. Just as with the measures of testis or breast size, those individuals (irrespective of their sex) who showed the L> pattern did better on the tests that women usually do better on.

Language ability is likely to be related to empathizing (since both are involved in communication). Certain aspects of language are more closely linked to empathizing—especially those aspects relating to "pragmatics," interpreting a speaker's intentions and meaning. Other aspects of language involve systemizing—especially syntax (grammar) and lexicon (vocabulary). It will therefore be important to repeat Kimura's interesting observations with tests that measure empathizing more directly, and with tests that distinguish between the empathizing and systemizing aspects of language. Certainly, there is evidence that when it comes to matching faces in terms of emotional expression, boys show more right-hemisphere brain activity, while girls show more left-hemisphere activity.[27]

Almost everyone knows that the right hemisphere of the brain is more involved in spatial abilities, such as route-learning. This idea is backed up by neuroimaging studies. For example, if you measure blood flow in the brain while volunteers are doing a verbal task, you see more blood flow in the left hemisphere. And when they are doing a spatial task (for example, judging the orientation of lines), you see more blood flow in the right hemisphere. This tells us that there is hemispheric specialization. As we discussed earlier, spatial tasks can be solved using systemizing (directional cues). This predicts that your systemizing score might change if the task involved your left or right hand, given that your left hand is controlled by the right hemisphere of your brain, and vice versa.[28]

In one large study of this, children were asked to feel several meaningless objects, one at a time, while the objects were out of sight. You know the old party game: stick your hand inside the bag and try to formulate a picture of an object from the way it feels. Because these shapes are given no context, it is difficult to name them. After the child had had a good feel around, one of the objects was removed from the bag (while the child's eyes were still closed) and put into a display with five other objects that the child had not felt. The child was then allowed to open their eyes and asked to identify, using sight alone, which object they had felt in the bag. A tough test. It involves systemizing because you have to take tactile-shape information (the input), and transform it (the operation) to predict its visual-shape information (output). The question is, does it make a difference if you use your right or left hand? Here is what you find: boys are better at identifying the object with their left hand, suggesting that their right hemisphere is controlling their ability. Girls are equally good with either hand, suggesting that their right hemisphere is less specialized for this activity and that they are equally able to use the left hemisphere. In the jargon used earlier, girls appear to have "bilateral representation" for this ability. The fact that, overall, boys' and girls' accuracy is very similar suggests that this is nothing to do with how enjoyable the game is, or how motivated each sex is.[29]

As you might guess, whether you are left- or right-handed adds an extra twist. Left-handers show less of a difference between the two hemispheres when they are doing verbal or spatial tasks. This suggests that they are less strongly specialized, perhaps because they have already devoted some of their right hemisphere to controlling their left-handedness, so there is less cortex remaining for strong specialization in systemizing in the right hemisphere. This would result in more of these abilities also being located in the left hemisphere. The consequence of this would be to deprive the left hemisphere of becoming specialized in verbal processing.

However, when you take handedness into account, you find the same sex difference: males are more right-lateralized for systemizing ability. All these results are consistent with Geschwind's theory of how testosterone shapes brain development.[30]

The study of rats allows us to look directly at lateralization in the brain—at brain tissue itself rather than performance of tasks. In male rats the cortex is thicker on the right side, perhaps because it is required to support their superior spatial (systemizing) abilities. Once again, we find that the cause of the sex difference in cortical thickness is fetal testosterone, the masculinizing hormone.[31]

Finally, recall the idea of splitting the human population into those who are right-greater (R>), in other words, those who have a right-larger testis or a right-larger breast, and those who are left-greater (L>). The R> do better than the L> group at systemizing tests, such as the Mental Rotation Test. This is irrespective of the subject's sex. Interestingly, architects and visual artists (who presumably need a good spatial or right-hemisphere ability) are more likely to be left-handed (this being under the control of the right hemisphere) than would be expected from chance. But this is also true of musicians and mathematicians, who need to be good systemizers.[32]

All this is telling us that testosterone affects the laterality of both the body and the brain. The more you have of this special substance early on in development, the faster the right side of your body and brain develops. And if systemizing is a right-hemisphere function, this could explain why males tend to be better at systemizing.

You might be wondering if the male superiority in skills like throwing accuracy or spatial ability arises *not* because of a specific advantage in systemizing, and not because the right hemisphere develops quickly, but because boys mature faster than girls. In fact, girls mature faster than boys. At birth, girls are on average four to six weeks more mature physically than boys, and by puberty, girls are an astonishing two years ahead of boys. So general maturity cannot explain a male superiority in systemizing.[33] Rather, pre-natal testosterone plays an important role in the development of individual differences in empathizing, language, and systemizing ability. The role of other hormones (such as estrogen) may also be important in relation to sex differences in the mind, but this is a topic for another book.[34]

Surfing the Brain

A different way to explore how these sex differences in the brain arise is to focus on which brain regions are known to play a role in empathizing and which play a role in systemizing, and then to look for sex differences in these brain regions.

Here are the regions that Leslie Brothers suggests together form the "social brain."[35] The first is the *amygdala*, an almond-shaped region in the brain (hence its name: Greek, for almond). Like most regions in the primate brain, there are two of them. They lie at the back of the temporal lobes, in the subcortical area of the brain called the limbic system. Although the amygdala is involved in functions other than empathizing—such as attaching emotional significance to stimuli—it nevertheless has a clear role in judging emotions in others. We know this because the amygdala becomes active when someone responds to emotional facial expressions while their brain is being imaged in a scanner, and because damage to this region causes the person or animal to lose their empathizing skills.

Sex differences have been found in the amygdala. For example, when studied using fMRI (functional magnetic resonance imaging), boys looking at photographs of fearful faces show a different pattern of amygdala responsiveness, compared with girls. The amygdala is also rich in testosterone receptor cells. Thus, if you inject testosterone into the amygdala of a female rat soon after birth, her play becomes much more typical of males. The male rat has a larger section of the amygdala (posterodorsal nucleus of the medial amygdala, or MePD). If you castrate the adult male rat, in just four weeks the MePD shrinks back to the size usually seen in a female. Treating a female rat with testosterone, the MePD swells to the size normally seen in males. Damage to the amygdala in the rat and the human causes social abnormalities.[36]

The amygdala does not operate alone. It is strongly connected to the rest of the brain, and to areas of the prefrontal cortex in particular. Two parts of the prefrontal cortex that play a role in empathizing are the *orbito-* and *medial-frontal* areas (often on the left side of the brain). Again, these areas become active when the human brain is being scanned while the person is figuring out what people are thinking or intending, and damage to these brain regions leads to difficulties with just these sorts of tests.[37]

Another brain region that appears to be important in empathizing is the *superior temporal sulcus* (STS), located in the temporal lobes, on both sides of the brain. Here, cells have been discovered that respond specifically to another person or animal looking at you. When you look at someone else's eyes to determine if they are aggressive, friendly, flirtatious, or interested in you for some other reason, what happens in the brain? That is to say, when you try to get inside someone's mind, to work out their intentions and moods, which regions "light up"? Connections from the STS to the amygdala are activated, as shown by neuroimaging studies.[38]

These functional neuroimaging methods typically measure blood flow in different regions of the brain, as a proxy for brain activity. The relevant brain regions do not literally "light up," but can be identified following in-depth computing analysis to be regions with greater blood flow during critical events. Fancy computer graphics are what make these regions appear as if they are "lighting up." The methods are not without their limitations and involve many assumptions, but they are giving us important clues about which brain regions are involved in different functions.

Another important structure of the brain to look at is the *corpus callosum*. This is the set of neural connections that transfers information across the two hemispheres of the brain. Some (but not all) studies have found that women have a larger posterior section of the corpus callosum. The controversy hinges on whether the absolute or relative size of the corpus callosum is measured. That is, whether overall brain size is controlled for.

This sex difference is revealed by dissecting brains at post-mortem. Some studies have found that it is the splenium section of the corpus callosum that is bigger in women, while others have found that the anterior commissure (another point of transfer between the hemispheres) is bigger in women. Homosexual men are also reported to have a larger anterior commissure than heterosexual men, and as large as heterosexual women. The massa intermedia (which connects the two sides of the thalamus) is also relevant here: it is absent more often in men and, when it is present, it is smaller than in women.

Those studies that do find a bigger corpus callosum in women have revealed that its size is the result of a greater number of nerve fibers connecting the two hemispheres of the brain. So on tasks that benefit from rapid inter-hemispheric transfer of information (such as communication and empathizing), individuals with larger connecting areas should do better. This has been found in some (but not all) studies of women. In one study, those with larger splenial areas in the corpus callosum performed better on a verbal fluency task, for example.[39]

Self-control is crucial to empathy. It is hard to consider someone else's emotional state if all you can do is think about yourself. Of course, when you empathize, you do not switch off your feelings, since having an appropriate emotional response to the other person's feelings *is* empathy, but you do need self-control to set aside your current (self-centered) goal in order to attend to someone else.

Studies have been carried out into self-control in male and female infants, using child psychologist Jean Piaget's famous "A not B" task. In this task, you hide an object (in location A) and let the infant retrieve it. Next, you hide it somewhere different (in location B). Boys before their first birthday persist for longer in searching for the object in location A. Some people interpret this as boys having a delay in the maturation of the prefrontal cortex, the region of the brain that has been linked to planning sequences of actions. This could be relevant to boys' less patient verbal style (ordering rather than negotiating) and their social bluntness (using less politeness in their speech). Both negotiation and politeness require strategies across a series of steps to achieve a goal, rather than just a quick conclusion (grab, or hit). Some further examples are relevant to self-control differences between the sexes: girls on average are toilet-trained earlier, and boys are more at risk for disorders of impulsivity, attention, and hyperactivity (ADHD).

One particularly wicked test of self-control involved asking children as young as three years old to leave a candy on their tongue for as long as they could before swallowing or chewing it. There were a couple of other tests of self-control included too, such as asking the child to lower his or her voice, or to wait for a "go" signal. Boys scored lower in their self-control than girls. Quite what is causing the girls' superior self-control is not immediately obvious. It is only an inference that this has anything to do with the maturity of the prefrontal cortex.[40]

Men's brains are larger and heavier than women's brains. When the ratio of brain to body size is taken into account by comparing men and women of the same height, men's brains are still heavier. Post-mortem examination shows that men's brains contain about 4 billion more neurons in the cortex than women's. So men's heavier brains may be due to having more brain cells. Having more brain cells may lead to greater attention to detail, which itself would lead to better systemizing. The cost of such increased attention to detail could be a slower grasp of the overall picture. This remains to be fully tested.[41]

There is an area at the back of the parietal lobe called the *planum parietale*. We all have two of these areas, on the right and left sides of our brain. The right planum parietale is bigger than the left equivalent area, and this right-sided bias is larger in men. In right-handers, the left planum parietale is involved in speech and hand movement, and the right planum parietale in spatial ability. For left-handers, the pattern is exactly the reverse.[42] It is not known if the sex difference in the planum parietale is affected by pre-natal testosterone. It will be important for future research to test if this region of the brain is involved in systemizing.

In the rat brain there is also a sex difference in the *hippocampus*, males having a bigger one. When this structure is damaged, rats find it more diffi-cult to remember their way through mazes. This suggests that the hip-pocampus plays a role in systemizing. Birds who hide their food widely across their terrain (and therefore need a good spatial memory to remem-ber exactly where they left it) have a larger hippocampus than those that do not have to hide their food. Once again, the more pre-natal testosterone an animal has, the larger their hippocampus. As far as I know, there is as yet no demonstrated equivalent sex difference in human hippocampal size.[43]

Finally, the *hypothalamus* has a region called the preoptic area (POA), and a part of this is larger in male rats. For this reason, it is called the "sex-ually dimorphic nucleus of the preoptic area" (SDN-POA). The more pre-natal testosterone the rat has, the larger their SDN-POA. The human equivalent of the SDN-POA region is thought to be the "interstitial nuclei of the anterior of the hypothalamus" (INAH). From post-mortem studies, women have smaller INAH areas (though this may only be in areas INAH2 and INAH3, not the key area INAH1). Whether this has anything to do with systemizing is an interesting question for future research.[44]

Genes

We have considered sex differences in the brain, but the other big source of variation between the sexes is the genes. We know that some genes are sex-linked and this may be a major determinant of the male and female brain types. Furthermore, genetic and hormonal effects need not be mutu-ally exclusive. Genes may affect testosterone secretion, for example.

There are genes on both the sex chromosomes (X and Y) and on some of the other chromosomes that can affect sex-typical brain development and behavior. These have been studied in the rodent, but an important human medical condition, Turner's Syndrome, has also highlighted the role of the X chromosome in producing sex differences in human behavior.[45]

Turner's Syndrome (TS) is a genetic disorder in which a girl inherits one X chromosome instead of the usual two. In most cases of TS, the X chromosome is inherited from the mother, but in some cases, the X comes from the father. On a questionnaire measuring social skills, normally developing girls typically score higher than boys, and so do girls with TS who inherit their X from their father, compared with girls with TS who get their X from their mother. These results suggest that it is genes on the paternal X that *partially* contribute to social skills, and they help us to understand why sex differences should occur in sociability, given that in the normal case, boys only inherit their mother's X.[46]

One of the few studies of empathizing in twins was carried out by psychologist Claire Hughes, with her colleagues in London. Studying twins is a familiar strategy in genetics research when the specific genes have not yet been identified but when heritability of a trait is being tested. Comparison was made between identical twins and non-identical twins in terms of their scores on a "theory of mind" test. This test assesses one aspect of empathizing: the cognitive. The "concordance" or similarity in scores among the identical twins was significantly higher than among the non-identical twins, leading the researchers to conclude that empathizing is in part heritable. A measure of social skills in a separate study of twins also suggests that this ability is heritable.[47]

Little is known about the genetics of systemizing, but there are clues that genes play a role. For example, studies of mathematical ability in twins (one of the clearest examples of systemizing) show that identical twins are more alike in their mathematical ability than are non-identical twins. And children with developmental dyscalculia are "born not to count," as Brian Butterworth at UCL puts it. They are of normal intelligence and are sociable, but cannot systemize for genetic reasons.[48]

With the human genome mapped, and the determination of the functions of genes now a major industry, we can be confident that genes controlling empathizing and systemizing will be identified. Such genes will not rule out the role of culture and environment. Genetically and/or hormonally based neural systems underlying empathizing and systemizing still require the right environmental input (sensitive parenting, for example, in the case of empathizing) in order to develop normally. But identifying such genes or hormones will help us understand why, despite all the relevant environmental factors, some children are worse at empathizing, or better at systemizing, than others.

As the genetics of both systemizing and empathizing become better understood, this will raise an obvious question: Why should these abilities have become encoded in our genes? The traditional answer to this type of question is the one that Charles Darwin formulated, in terms of evolutionary theory: traits usually only come under genetic control when they confer some survival and reproductive advantage to the organism in two battles: surviving to reach adulthood, and being selected to become a parent. In the next chapter we confront this evolutionary question directly. In what ways might it have been adaptive or advantageous to have either the male or female brain types?[49]

9

Evolution of the Male and Female Brain

Chapter 8 was quite an uphill climb, but now you have got your breath, let's take stock.

Sex differences in empathizing and systemizing are due to both social and biological factors. When one finds biological causes of sex differences in the mind, the obvious thing to consider is whether these differences may have evolved. That is, the genes that ultimately underlie these sex differences may have been selected because they improved the individual's likelihood of surviving and reproducing. Even prior to specific genes being identified, studies of twins suggest that both empathizing and systemizing abilities are likely to have a heritable component.

Some theories suggest that our male and female ancestors occupied quite different niches and had very different roles. If true, the selective pressures are likely to have been very different for each, and could have led to the evolution of different types of cognitive specialization. Naturally, what may have been adaptive for one sex may not have been adaptive for the other.

In this chapter I speculate about why it might have been advantageous for females to have brain type E, and why it might have been advantageous for males to have type S.[1] (Recall from Chapter 1 that brain type E is the description given to those who can empathize with greater skill than they can systemize, and brain type S is the mirror image of this.)

Because empathizing is such a fundamentally human ability that must be as old as the *Homo sapiens* brain itself, you might be prepared to accept that a relative talent in empathizing could characterize the female brain. But you might balk at the idea that a relative talent in systemizing could possibly characterize something as ancient as the male brain, since system-izing resembles the hypothesis-testing of a scientist, and scientific thinking is a recent human development. Let me put you right. Although academic science is relatively recent—a mere few hundred years old—"folk" science is as old as humans themselves. Tribal peoples have been developing their own understandings of natural systems, building their own technologies, formulating their own medical systems, and establishing systems to govern their social groups, for tens of thousands of years.[2]

So what might have been the evolutionary advantages of being a good systemizer or a good empathizer?

The Advantages of the Male Brain

Using and Making Tools

Good systemizers are skilled at understanding, using, and constructing tools, including mechanical systems and weapons. Tools allow you to do such things as hunt, fight, build, fix things, or work more efficiently. Being better at these things could have enabled not only a better chance of sur-vival, but also an increase in wealth and/or social status. And higher social rank can lead to greater reproductive success.

For example, a good systemizer might notice that if an arrow is made too long or too short, its accuracy is affected; or if an axe blade is bound to its handle using a certain kind of knot, it is more durable; or a roof made of palm-tree leaves folded in a very precise pattern is more rainproof.

Being good at systemizing projectile weapons (such as throwing rocks, stones and spears, or shooting arrows) may explain the male superiority in throwing (in terms of accuracy, distance, and velocity), in blocking objects coming toward oneself, and in judging when an object will make contact with another. Using and defending oneself against projectile weapons could have been a major advantage in male–male competition.[3]

Hunting and Tracking

Good systemizers are also skilled at understanding and exploiting natural systems. Put yourself into the shoes of a hunter or tracker. He has to scan the forest for signs of where prey may be. Whereas you or I might look at a clearing in a forest and see only trees and shrubs, a good tracker might notice that the grass is crushed in a pattern indicating that a tiger slept here last night, or that there are certain marks on a particular kind of tree which indicate that an elephant passed by here and rubbed its body against the bark. He might listen to animal cries in order to work out if a predator is approaching: *this* monkey call indicates an eagle is above, or *that* monkey call indicates a tiger is nearby. All of these observations would enable a tracker to predict what kind of animal is where. When a good systemizer is tracking an animal, he might look closely at the feces on the ground because they would tell him not only how long ago the animal was here but also what kind of animal it was, and what other animals it was preying on. He might know the difference between the 900 species of birds in his forest, by sight as well as sound, to determine which produce edible eggs, where they nest, and when each migrates.

Being a hunter or a tracker also requires an excellent spatial memory for routes, so that even if he wanders for hours or days he still knows how to get back home. In the forest, there are no man-made signposts and no maps. Good systemizing allows you to build up a *mental* map of the area rapidly.[4]

In this way, instead of relying solely on landmarks (was this the tree where I turned to follow that deer?), a good systemizer could use geometric and directional cues, such as his or her movement relative to the sun. (If the setting sun is behind me, I know I'm heading east.)

Good systemizers are also able to understand and predict other natural systems—I am thinking of things such as the weather (this cloud formation predicts a storm), the wind (my fishing boat is navigable if I use my sail in this way), and the stars (as a compass system for navigation). In terms of natural selection, a good systemizer could thus have survived physically in harsh conditions. Having a good grasp of the environment could mean the difference between life and death.

Trading

Good systemizing would allow you to spot fluctuations in any marketplace so that you know when to buy and when to sell; for example, if I buy when the price is low (input) and sell when the price is high (operation) then I will make a profit (output). The marketplace, after all, is a system like any other. The system in this case might be a currency, or it might be far less formal than that, such as an exchange of goods. Exchange is not a recent invention of the stock market in New York, but is as old as *Homo sapiens*.[5]

The skill is in detecting when some things are in demand and some things are surplus, and in spotting a good deal. Some things give you excellent returns, and some do not. The pay-off for such careful and accurate systemizing could again be wealth and social rank (and consequently reproductive success).

Naturally, a good trader needs both good systemizing skills and some degree of mindreading (being able to keep quiet about the other person's potential losses if they have not spotted the inequality of the exchange, or even lying to persuade them that they are getting a good deal). The ability to deceive others has little to do with good empathizing, since the good trader cares little about the customer being the loser, or about the customer's emotional state. They care only about their own profits, calculated by understanding the system.

Power

Most primates are social. But what does this social interaction comprise? It turns out that a lot of socializing is about gaining, maintaining, and improving your social rank, and keeping track of everyone else's social rank. And as a general rule of thumb, the higher your social rank, the higher your chances of survival. So if you are good at reading the group as a social hierarchy—a system—you could prosper.

It is not hard to see why your rank, and your skill at negotiating the ranks, determines your survival chances. For one reason, to be socially excluded is to lose the protection of the group. Equally, if you fail to recognize your place in the social system, you risk a conflict with someone higher up who also needs to protect his or her own social rank. Fine if you think you can win in a conflict with a "superior," but if you can't, the costs could be great. Among monkeys, for example, a shocking 50 percent of adolescent males are killed in conflicts over status. So the pressure is on to know your place, and monitor everyone else's place.

Even though in this example we are talking about a *social* system, the same if-then (input–operation–output) conditionality rules are used. If I am number 5 in the pecking order (input), then I can threaten my "inferiors" (numbers 6, 7, and 8) (operation) relatively safely (output). If I threaten my "superiors" (numbers 4, 3, 2, or 1), I risk injury or death. If he is number 3 and challenges number 2 and wins, then he becomes number 2. Social systemizing.

Some actions will cost you rank, other actions will gain you rank, and the good systemizer will be tracking these outcomes. Call it politics. It might be at the level of individual relationships, such as competing in subtle ways so as to be recognized as better than your workmates, and thereby be offered the promotion (the opportunity to climb) when it arises. Or it might be at the level of systemizing whole groups of people, as in tribal or territorial expansion, or warfare over resources. Today's equivalent of systemizing groups of people is seen in local or national politics. Here, a good systemizer can keep track of how big a swing of the votes their party managed, how many seats were won or lost, and so on. A good systemizer could also keep track of how many points a sports team won or lost, and how it affects their position in the rankings.

The other reason that people keep track of social rank is its connection with what Darwin called "sexual selection." Females in many species, but especially among the primates, tend to be the choosy sex (in other words, they play a greater role in selection). This is understandable, because they typically invest more time and energy in producing the offspring. One sexual act may cost a man a few seconds or minutes, but it may cost a woman nine months of pregnancy, and the rest. So how does she make her choice? One way is to use social rank as a cue.

The consequence of this for males is that higher social rank means more access to females. Males of higher social status are attractive because their ascent up the social hierarchy is evidence of both healthy genes and their potential as a provider and defender. As explained earlier, a good systemizer is likely to end up with higher social status.[6]

Women may therefore find a man's strong systemizing abilities attractive. Such a man is seen as independent, as someone who understands things, who knows how to evaluate the relevant information quickly and take decisive action, and who knows how to get ahead and climb socially.

Social Dominance

The combination of low empathizing and high systemizing abilities might mean a rapid ascent of a man to the top of the social pile. This is because men in every culture compete against each other for success in social rank. As we mentioned above, a male's position in the social dominance hierarchy in most species directly affects his fertility. For example, in some species it is only the alpha male that gets to reproduce. And even today, among modern humans, men with higher social status tend to have more children and more wives, compared with men of lower social status. To achieve social dominance, males use physical force, or the threat of force, or other kinds of threat (for example, withdrawing support). That is why, in most species, males are bigger, stronger, and more aggressive than females.[7]

Men compete not just through threat but also through shows of strength and status, and are selected by women for these qualities. These qualities may include not only physical strength but also the ability and drive to climb to the top of the social group. Lower empathizing makes it easier for you to hit or hurt someone, or in less extreme ways, simply to push them aside in a competition, or abandon them when they are no longer useful to you.

As we saw in Chapter 4, in most studies of emotion recognition, men score lower than women. But when it comes to detecting threat from direct eye contact—crucial in anticipating a potential loss of rank in the social system—and sensitivity to dominance hierarchies (key in male–male competition), men actually score better than women. These examples are not signs of high empathizing but high systemizing.[8]

In existing pre-industrial societies, men travel farther than women. They do not do this just in order to hunt, or to find a mate, but also to conduct raids on other groups. Just as in war, conducting raids on other groups brings power. It is presumably easier to use aggression toward others if you are poor at empathizing. Planning how to attack (which tactical maneuver or physical method would be most efficient), and planning your route to and from the attack, would be far easier for someone with good systemizing and low empathizing skills. Even leaving aside direct attacks, low empathizing would result in a person engaging in greater social control with less empathy or guilt.[9]

Expertise

The other trick for gaining a high position in a social hierarchy is cultural success—being the best at something your culture values, and/or controlling valued resources. The drive to systemize is essentially the drive to control or understand a system to the highest level—by definition, since otherwise the system would be suboptimal. Systemizing requires us to understand a system as completely as possible. So competition in systemizing could lead a person to be the best at making a plough or a spear, a musical instrument or a home, thus achieving higher social rank.

Tolerating Solitude

Some tasks that require good systemizing, such as tracking animals or inventing a new tool, take a long time. They might take days, months, or years. Many such tasks benefit from a lack of distraction and lots of hard concentration, preferably in solitude.

So it might be that even if you were good at systemizing you might never accomplish anything great if you were also good at empathizing, since you might then have an equally strong drive to socialize. But supposing you were low on empathizing. You might then be content to lock yourself away for days without much conversation, to focus long and deep on the system that was your current project. In pre-industrial societies this could involve fixing old axe-heads, or perhaps a four-day trek into the forest in search of food for your family (this might be the ancestral equivalent of the modern-day pilot). The pay-off from not needing people as much as others do could be great.

Aggression

In humans and other primates, males typically attempt to control the sexual activities of their partners through the use of threat. Being willing to threaten your female mate with aggression presumes a low level of empathizing. Hurting another person, or putting fear into them, is not a caring act. If it works, a man increases the likelihood that the child he is providing for is indeed genetically his.

Even among human cultures today, monogamy is not the norm. The most common marriage system is polygyny (one man, many wives). Polyandry (one woman, many husbands) is very rare. Polygyny presumably became the most common marriage system as a result of some men becoming dominant in social status, through the accumulation and control of valued material resources. Control of such resources is typically accomplished through the formation of kin-based coalitions between men. Even in monogamous societies in the West, polygynous mating by powerful, high-status men has been the norm.[10]

Aggression is not only a sign of limited empathy. It is also a very efficient strategy for establishing social dominance or resolving social conflict, especially when other social displays or rituals fail. In evolutionary terms, the bravest and most skilled fighters in male–male competition would have earned the highest social status, and thus secured the most wives and offspring.

In studies of pre-industrial societies, aggression has typically been found to take the form of blood revenge (in other words, revenge for the murder of a member of one's kin), economic gain (such as looting and taking people as slaves), capturing women as additional wives, or the maintenance of personal prestige and reputation. All of these routes can lead a man to acquire high social status within the community, which makes him more desirable as a marriage partner.

David Geary gives the following example of the reproductive pay-off for men who take the risk of competing with other men. In a study of the Yanomamo tribe, a present-day pre-industrial people who live in the Amazon rainforests of Brazil and Venezuela, some men were found to have no children at all, while one man (Shinbone) had forty-three children. Shinbone's father had fourteen children (a small family), but these gave him 143 grandchildren, who in turn gave him 335 great-grandchildren and 401 great-great-grandchildren. Shinbone's father had 401 more great-great-grandchildren than his neighbor, who had no great-great-grandchildren at all. If his aim was to spread his genes, Shinbone's father was doing very well. Obviously, such men can sire a large number of children in societies where polygyny is allowed.[11]

Now here is the really scary bit. According to Laura Betzig, in the first civilizations (ancient Mesopotamia, Egypt, the Aztec, the Inca, imperial India, and China), "powerful men mate with hundreds of women, pass their power on to a son by one legitimate wife, and take the lives of men who get in their way."[12] As I explained earlier, these men may have been powerful because they were good systemizers. The fact that they eliminated those who stood up to them implies that they were also low empathizers. And they certainly seemed to have an efficient means of disseminating their genes (polygyny). So we can envision how the genotype for brain type S might have spread widely throughout a male population.

Is aggressive male competition just something of the past? Are we so very different nowadays? Let's look again at the Yanomamo, who can be viewed as a model of pre-industrial society. Here we find that two out of every five men in this tribe have participated in at least one murder. This is astonishing to us. I don't know any men who have committed murder, and I'm guessing that you don't either. So clearly, industrialized societies may make it harder to discern evolutionary pressures.

Worse still, among the Yanomamo, men who kill other men end up with *higher* social status than those who do not. We know that in an industrialized society murderers *lose* their social rank, by being imprisoned. Not so in traditional societies. Consistent with evolutionary theory, those who have committed murder end up with more than double the number of wives, and more than three times the number of children, compared to those who have not. This gloomy picture is not restricted to this present-day tribe but has been found in other pre-industrial societies.[13]

Leadership

Team projects need leaders. The success of the project often depends on the firm hand of the leader. Consider the team leader who keeps a single-minded focus on the overarching goal, whether it be making something, or capturing a new territory. The leader will consider how to achieve this goal in the minimum number of tactical steps and with the most efficient timetable, something that is known in business or technology today as the "critical path."

A leader who is a good systemizer has the advantage of being able to see a group of people as a system. Like cogs in a mechanical system, each person (or group) may have a specific function in the system. Any system, be it a group of people or a tool, needs careful control. A leader with lower empathy will spend less time worrying about how each member of the team feels about having to play their individual part in the project. Instead, such a leader will focus on how the *function* of that individual contributes to the overall goal of the system.

The functions may be indispensable, but the individual workers who carry out these functions may be very dispensable. If a particular person is underproductive, a leader with lower empathy and good systemizing skills would find it easier to identify this individual as a problem and replace them. Sacking this team member involves the ability to cast them to one side, and not worry about the consequences for that individual.

Lower empathizing and high systemizing abilities would thus have been a more adaptive profile for a successful leader. Such a leader would gain access to greater resources, and consequently social rank and reproductive opportunities.

The Advantages of the Female Brain

We can see how high systemizing and lower empathizing abilities (the male brain) might have been adaptive, but what about the opposite profile (the female brain)? How might this have conferred an evolutionary advantage?

Making Friends

Being a good empathizer requires skill in understanding relationships, and not just in terms of power politics. Good empathizers are good communicators who are concerned if a friend takes offense at something they have said, or is being treated unfairly, and they find it easy to anticipate another person's needs, responding rapidly and appropriately to someone else's feelings. Good empathizers are more democratic; they consult others and are more diplomatic in conversation. They do not force their own view on another person or on a group, at the expense of the other person's wishes. Operating in this way is likely to win friends, not make enemies.

The survival advantages of having good friends is that you have social alliances and help when the going gets tough. A high-empathizing female, engaged in childcare, is better equipped to create a community of friends who could watch over her children when she is unable to keep an eye on them all the time. Remember, predators are just waiting to pick off the youngest and most vulnerable members of the group: infants.

There is another advantage to being able to make close friends. Communities of friends make for a more stable community, reducing the risk of aggression between adults. Community instability adversely affects child development, both emotionally and in terms of child mortality. So anything that contributes to community stability can only increase the survival chances for both children and women. Since women are the sex that invests far more time and resources in parenting, one can argue that such benefits of reciprocal relationships will be more relevant to them.[14]

Mothering

Let's face it: infants can be hard to read. They cry, but they can't tell you what they are feeling or wanting. In older children or adults, language serves as a partial printout of their mental states. But when an infant cries, how can you tell what is in his or her mind? You could try to systemize an infant by checking the most likely six options: are they wet, hungry, sleepy, sick, cold, or uncomfortable? Supposing they are none of these, and they still keep on crying. What do you do next?

Good empathizers find it easier to tune in to their child's needs and feelings. It gives them access to a far more subtle set of possibilities; they can imagine their child's mind. Maybe the child feels angry because they thought that you handled them too roughly. Maybe they are feeling resentful because you went away for too long. Maybe they feel ignored because although you were physically present, your mind was preoccupied, rather than connected with theirs. Maybe they just need more love because they are in an unfamiliar place.

If you can imagine all these possibilities, together with hundreds of other feelings your infant might be having, your good empathizing skills would lead your infant to believe that you were in tune with their needs; they would feel cared for and supported, and thus they would develop a more secure attachment. And securely attached infants not only learn faster but they are more easily accepted by their peer group, they are rated as more popular, and they develop more stable relationships throughout their lives.

The infant of a parent who is a good empathizer is likely to grow up with the ability to make stable relationships in adulthood. This itself promotes their own children's physical survival and mental health—a transgenerational cycle that obviously has long-term reproductive pay-offs. And in the short-term, being sensitively attuned to one's infant means that they are less likely to be neglected, and thus less at risk of infant mortality through fatal accident. In this way, a mother with good empathizing skills could end up with greater reproductive success.[15]

This idea has grown into a major theory: some have argued that empathizing co-evolved with primate parental investment.[16] This makes a lot of sense, and it immediately suggests why one finds a female advantage in empathizing. Females—among non-human primates, and therefore presumably among our hominid ancestors—were the principal caregivers.

If an infant monkey is holding tight to its mother's fur on her belly while she walks through the deeper waters, the mother will not check if her baby's face is out of the water. The result is that her offspring is at major risk of drowning. This strongly suggests that female monkeys as mothers cannot take into account the perspective and needs of another animal (in this case, her baby). Among the great apes, such as the chimpanzee, this never occurs. Primatologist Frans De Waal suggests that this is because the great apes have rudimentary empathy. Examples of empathy in apes include "targeted help" (where one animal will provide just the right sort of help that the other needs) and "consolation" (for example, caressing an animal who has suffered a loss).[17]

Gossip

Good empathizing abilities give you access not just to reciprocal communication and the benefits of friendship through talking but also to gossip. The best way to get information about your social group is to be in the loop.

Someone with lower empathizing may make fewer close friends or be less comfortable simply chatting than those with high empathizing abilities, and therefore may hear less gossip. A person with good empathizing skills is likely to have more close friends, or be able to sustain social chit-chat, and will pick up important information about people, such as their trust-worthiness.

Most importantly, anthropologist Robin Dunbar at Liverpool University argues that participating in such social gossip is the human equivalent of primate grooming, providing the social lubricant for getting to know one another and developing dependable alliances. In this way, one could imagine that a good empathizer might have better chances of survival.

Social Mobility

Among humans (and other great apes), males tend to stay in their birth group, while females tend to move to their mate's community. Males therefore are surrounded by their kin more often than females are, and of course they know their kin well, and vice versa. So there may have been less pressure on males to develop good empathy if males typically have had to put far less effort into building and maintaining relationships. Making relationships with individuals you are not genetically related to requires much greater sensitivity to reciprocity and equality, since these are relationships that you cannot take for granted.[18] A woman with low empathy might have had a much harder time being accepted by her in-laws, and earning their support.

Reading Your Partner

Women who had a talent for decoding their male partner's next move would have had greater success in avoiding spousal aggression. Women who were good at detecting deception would have also been more skilled at finding sincere males to mate with, and at judging whether a man would treat them well or just impregnate them. One can see how high empathizing would have been adaptive to females. Being able to empathize with one's partner also makes one more compassionate and tolerant, which can prolong the life of the relationship. In this way, a woman with high empathizing skills might have had a better chance of keeping her relationship stable during her offspring's vulnerable years, thus promoting their survival and the spread of her genes.

Low Systemizing: Any Disadvantages?

In this chapter on evolutionary speculations, we have so far considered how high systemizing, high empathizing and even low empathizing abilities might each have been adaptive. But what about low systemizing?

A low systemizer would find it difficult to use tools or fix things, would be less obsessed with social systems such as status, and would find it tricky to learn spatial routes. It is hard to imagine any scenario in which low systemizing could be adaptive, but a trait could have a genetic basis and remain in the gene pool if it was not truly maladaptive. Low systemizing could be maladaptive if the person was also low at empathizing, and we might think of such an individual as having a general learning disability. They would be impaired at both socializing and understanding their physical environment. They might end up with low social rank on both counts, and carry the lowest chances of reproductive success.

On the other hand, low systemizing in the presence of high empathizing need not have been maladaptive at all. It would not have prevented such an individual from receiving all the benefits of social inclusion, as discussed earlier. And that individual's superior empathizing could even have meant that when a system needed fixing (a tool was broken, a well had dried up), they had all the social skills to persuade a good systemizer to come and help them sort it out. So the profile of lower systemizing in combination with good empathizing (the female brain) was unlikely to have been maladaptive.

Evolution of the Balanced Brain

We can see the clear survival and reproductive advantages of being either a good systemizer (the male brain) or a good empathizer (the female brain), but surely it would have been doubly advantageous to be good at both (in other words, to have the balanced brain)? Although one form of the balanced brain (low systemizing with low empathizing) clearly has no adaptive advantage, what about if you were average to high on both?

Although such a balanced brain would give rise to the best of both worlds (to have a systematic mind and to be an empathic friend), one could imagine that, for a male, this would be slightly less successful than the male brain. For example, in any competition between two leaders, the good systemizer with slightly reduced empathy might be prepared to do what was necessary to win, even if this required the sacrifice of someone's feelings to make it possible. Think of the army general who decides that for the greater good of the regiment, they leave the wounded behind to face certain death but save the healthy members of the unit. Someone with the balanced brain might be a nicer person to have as a boss, but he or she might lack the ruthless edge needed to survive and prosper when the going gets tough. And for a female, such a balanced brain could mean less time spent in relationships, with the risk of less social support.

According to this theory, the male and female brains are perfectly adapted for certain niches. These are specialist niches—one adapted to survival and integration in the social world, and the other adapted to predicting and controlling events.

A different explanation for why we might find the balanced brain to be less common—and this needs proper testing—may be that the development of empathizing and systemizing is a "zero-sum game," in other words, there is a trade-off, so that the better one becomes at empathizing, for example, the worse one becomes at systemizing. While this is clearly not an inevitable trade-off (we all know of people who are good at both), it may be partly true, and needs further exploration.

To summarize, neither brain type E nor S is better or worse than the other. They appear to have been selected as specializations for entirely different goals and niches. So far we have only considered those brain types that are the commonest in the general population. But what about the extremes, those at the margins of this continuum? In the next chapter we make a further specific prediction, that the extreme male brain will also be less common, because it is in some ways maladaptive. Let's have a closer look.

10

Autism:
The Extreme Male Brain

At this point on our journey, we have looked at the evidence for the male brain—slightly lower empathizing skill and slightly better systemizing skill—and for the female brain, which shows the opposite profile. These are normal sex differences. They are small, but real (in the sense of being statistically significant).

But what about individuals who are more extreme? How would those who have a *much lower* ability to empathize, coupled with an average or even *talented* ability to systemize, behave?

These are the people (mostly men) who may talk to others only at work, for the purposes of work alone, or talk only to obtain something they need, or to share factual information. They may reply to a question with the relevant facts only, and they may not ask a question in return because they do not naturally consider what others are thinking. These are the people who are unable to see the point of social chit-chat. They do not mind having a discussion (note, not a chat) on a particular issue in order to establish the truth of the matter (mostly, persuading you to agree with their view). But just a casual, superficial chat? Why bother? And what on earth about? How? For these people it is both too hard and pointless. These are the people who, in the first instance, think of solving tasks *on their own*, by figuring it out for themselves. The object or system in front of them is all that is in their mind, and they do not stop for a moment to consider another person's knowledge of it. These are the people with the extreme male brain.

Present them with a system and they seek to spot the underlying factual regularities. They tune in to the tiny details to such a great degree that, in their fascination with cracking the system, they may become oblivious to all those around them. The spotlight of attention on one tiny variable becomes all that matters, and they might not notice if a person stood next to them with tears rolling down their cheeks. All that they focus on is determining the unvarying if-then rules, which allow them to control and predict the system.

Present them with some speculation about what someone might think or feel, or with a topic that is ultimately not factual, and they switch off or even avoid it because of its unknowability and therefore unpredictability.

When one hits the edge of the range in this way, I suggest that you are meeting autism. Before we look more carefully at this idea, let me remind you what autism is.

Autism

Autism is diagnosed when a person shows abnormalities in social development and communication, and displays unusually strong obsessional interests, from an early age.[1]

When I started researching autism in the early 1980s, only a handful of scientists in the UK were actively investigating it. At that time, autism was thought to be the most severe childhood psychiatric condition, and it was thought to occur rarely.

It was thought to be severe because half of the children diagnosed with autism did not speak, and most (75 percent) had below-average intelligence (IQ). Their poor language ability and low IQ predicted greater difficulties. In addition, they had the core features of autism: poor social skills, limited imagination, and obsessive interests in unusual topics, such as collecting types of stones or traveling to every railway station in Britain just to look at each depot.

They did not learn from others in any social way, and their narrow obsessions often stopped them from picking up broad knowledge. Many of them lived in a world of their own, and were described as unreachable, as if "in a bubble." Others who were socially interested would talk to you without eye contact, or stare at you for too long, or touch you inappropriately, or simply badger you with questions on a topic of their choosing and then walk off without warning. No wonder autism was described as severe.

And autism was thought to be rare because only four children in every 10,000 seemed to be affected in this severe way.[2]

These children attracted the attention of scientists for several reasons. Their social disorder begged for an explanation, since other children of the same IQ seemed appropriately sociable by comparison. Furthermore, some of them also had "islets of ability": even though they were unable to communicate appropriately, some were lightning-fast at mathematical calculation, for example. Some could name which day of the week any date (past or present) falls on (so-called "calendrical calculation"). Some could tell you instantly if a number is a prime number and, if it is not, the factors of that number. Some could recite railway timetable information to a precise degree, from memory. Some could acquire vocabularies and grammars in foreign languages at a tremendous pace, even though they were unable to *chat* in these languages, or even in their native tongue. This is clearly a sign of a different kind of intelligence.[3]

That was the picture of autism then. Children like these are still real enough, and their problems are still regarded as severe and rare. But an interesting shift occurred during the early 1990s.

It had always been known that a small proportion (25 percent) of children with autism have normal, or even above average, intelligence (IQ), but slowly such high-functioning cases started being identified more frequently. By the late 1990s it seemed that high-functioning children with autism were no longer in the minority. It is part of the diagnosis of autism that such children are late to start talking. By late, I mean no single words by two years old, and no phrase speech by three years old. But in these high-functioning cases of autism, the late start in language does not seem to stop them developing good or even talented levels of ability in mathematics, chess, mechanical knowledge and other factual, scientific, technical, or rule-based subjects.

Asperger Syndrome

In the 1990s clinicians and scientists also started talking about a group of children who were just a small step away from high-functioning autism.

They diagnosed these children as suffering from a condition called Asperger Syndrome (AS), which was proposed as a variant of autism. A child with AS has the same difficulties in social and communication skills and has the same obsessional interests. However, such children not only have normal or high IQ (like those with high-functioning autism) but they also start speaking on time. And their problems are not all that rare.

Today, approximately one in 200 children has one of the autism spectrum conditions, which includes AS, and many of them are in mainstream schools. We now have to radically reconceptualize autism. The number of cases has risen from four in 10,000 in the 1970s, to one in 200 at the start of this millennium. That's almost a ten-fold increase in prevalence. This is most likely a reflection of better awareness and broader diagnosis, to include AS.

People with AS do not suffer from problems as obviously severe as are seen in the mute or learning-disabled child with autism. But most children with AS are nevertheless often miserable at school because they can't make friends. It is hard to imagine what this must be like. Most of us just take it for granted that we will fit in well enough to have a mix of friends. But sadly, people with AS are surrounded by acquaintances, or strangers, and often not by friends, as we understand the word. Many of them are teased and bullied because they do not manage to fit in, or have no interest in fitting in. Their lack of social awareness may even result in their not even trying to camouflage their oddities.[4]

The Autism Spectrum

If you put classic autism, high-functioning autism, and AS side by side, you have what is called the "autism spectrum." So, who are these individuals? You can already see that there is a spread of abilities. Compared with someone of the same age and IQ level without autism, all people with autism or AS are seen as socially odd, odd in their communication, and unusually obsessional, to varying degrees; however, some people with autism have little or no language, while others are very verbal. Some have additional learning difficulties, while others can be members of MENSA (the association for gifted people of high intelligence). We will meet one such gifted individual in the next chapter.

But first, a few more facts about the autism spectrum. Autism spectrum conditions are strongly genetic in origin. The evidence for this is derived from studies of twins and families. If an identical twin has autism, the chance of his or her co-twin also having an autism spectrum condition is very high (between 60 and 90 percent). If a non-identical twin has an autism spectrum condition, the equivalent risk for his or her co-twin is much less (about 20 percent). Since a key difference between identical and non-identical twins is that the former share 100 percent of their genes, whereas the latter only share on average 50 percent, this strongly suggests that autism is heritable. And family studies suggest that if there is a child with autism in the family, there is a raised likelihood of their sibling also having an autism spectrum condition.

Autism spectrum conditions also appear to affect males far more often than females. In people diagnosed with high-functioning autism or AS, the sex ratio is at least *ten males to every female*. This too suggests that autism spectrum conditions are heritable. Interestingly, the sex ratio in autism spectrum conditions has not been investigated as much as perhaps it should have been, given that Nature has offered us a big clue about the cause of the condition.[5]

Autism spectrum conditions are also neurodevelopmental. That is, they start early—probably pre-natally—and affect the development and functioning of the brain. There is evidence of brain dysfunction (such as epilepsy) in a proportion of cases. There is also evidence of structural and functional differences in regions of the brain (such as the amygdala being abnormal in size, and less responsive to emotional cues).[6]

Autism is an empathy disorder: those with autism have major difficulties in "mindreading" or putting themselves into someone else's shoes, imagining the world through someone else's eyes and responding appropriately to someone else's feelings. In my earlier book, I called autism a condition of "mindblindness."

People with autism are often the most loyal defenders of someone they perceive to be suffering an injustice. In this way, they are not uncaring, or cold-hearted psychopaths who want to hurt others. On the contrary, when they discover that they have inadvertently hurt another person, perhaps by saying something which has caused offense, they are usually shocked and cannot understand why their actions have had this kind of impact. They typically find it equally puzzling to know how to repair such a hurt. Certainly, they do not set out to upset others. Broadly, they have difficulty making sense of and predicting another's feelings, thoughts, and behavior.[7]

Autism is also a condition where unusual talents abound. These children pay acute attention to detail, and can be the first to spot something that no one else has noticed. They make fine discriminations between things that may be unimportant to, or outside the awareness of, the ordinary person, such as noticing the tiny fibers in the blanket on their bed, and developing a preference for that particular blanket, even though to anyone else the blankets on offer all look and feel the same. They love patterned information, or making patterns, and so will spot the similarities in strings of numbers in otherwise disconnected contexts, or the similarities in the veins of leaves, or the sequence of changes in the weather.

Take one child I came across. At the age of five, he asked his school teacher how computers work. She explained to him that computers store information in a binary code so that every bit of information is either present or not. He immediately said, "But that's how my brain works!" and gave himself the nickname "Binary Boy."

His mother gave me a real example of this extraordinary type of mind in action. Every day they would walk down their street in Fulham, west London, to school. One day the five-year-old boy said to his mother, "We had better tell the woman who lives at number 105 that her parking permit runs out next Tuesday." His mother looked at her son, astonished. "How do you know that?" she asked. "Well," he said, "the parking permit in her windscreen has the date when it runs out. That's her car, the red Landrover, right there." It turned out that this five-year-old boy had first worked out which car in the whole street belonged to which house. This by itself was no mean feat, as there were hundreds of houses on each side of the road. He had then noted the expiration date in every windshield of every car in the street. His mother, flabbergasted, decided to test his knowledge.

> "So, who does that green Saab belong to?" she asked.
> "That would be the old man at number 62," he replied in a monotone voice. He was right.
> "And when does his permit need renewing?" she asked, not quite believing what he was telling her.
> "April 24th next year," he replied, in an equally matter-of-fact tone. She went over and checked. Sure enough, he was correct.

"So are you telling me you know every expiration date of every
car's permit in this street?"
"Yes," he said, in a slightly bored tone.
"Do you know anything else about these permits?"
"I can tell you the serial number for each permit, too. The green
Saab is a Saab 900, and its permit is serial number A473253. The
red Land Rover's permit is serial number Z534221."

People with autism not only notice such small details and sometimes
can retrieve this information in an exact manner, but they also love to predict and control the world. Phenomena that are unpredictable and/or un-
controllable (like people) typically leave them anxious or disinterested, but
the more predictable the phenomenon, the more they are attracted to it.

Some children with autism can look at the spinning of a wheel on a toy
car, over and over again. Others can watch the spinning of the washing machine, for hours. Yet others become engrossed in the pattern created as raw
beans or grains of sand fall through their fingers into a jar, or in strings of
numbers such as dates of birth or phone numbers.

When they are required to join the unpredictable social world, they may
react by trying to impose predictability and "sameness," trying to control
people through tantrums, or insistence on repetition. The pleasure they get
watching a toy train go round and round the same track, something that is
exactly controlled depending on the position of the points, is something
they may try to recreate in the social world, trying to get people to give the
same answers to the same questions, over and over and over again. This
should provide us with a strong clue about the nature of their brain type.

Many people with autism are naturally drawn to the most predictable
things in our world—such as computers. To you and me, computers go
wrong, so they are far from predictable. But unlike people, computers do
follow strict laws. If they go wrong, there is a finite number of reasons for
this, and if you are patient enough, or understand the system well enough,
you will logically track down how to fix the problem.

Computers are a closed system: they are, in theory, knowable, predictable, and controllable. People's feelings and thoughts and behavior are
ultimately unknowable, less predictable and less controllable open systems. Some people with AS will figure out things on the computer at what
to an outsider might seem like an intuitive level but which is the product

of a very exact mind storing rules and patterns and sequences in an orderly and logical way. Others with AS may not make computers their target of understanding, but may latch on to a different, equally closed system (such as bird-migration or trainspotting).[8] A young man with AS who I met had become obsessed with pressure points on the human body, and explained to me that applying pressure to these points with your thumb could kill a person. He had learned (and could demonstrate) the dozens of ways you could kill someone in seconds, using only your thumb as a weapon.

Closed systems can appear superficially very different from each other, but they still share the property of being finite, exact, and predictable. One child might become obsessed with *Harry Potter*, rereading the books and rewatching the videos hundreds of times, able to describe the facts in astonishing precision when asked. Another child might become obsessed with *War Hammer*, the miniature model soldiers that can be arranged and rearranged with total control and precision, his collection becoming ever larger and ever closer to completion.

One young man with AS latched on to juggling as the ultimate closed system. He had tuned in to the mathematics of juggling, the rules that determine whether a juggling trick will succeed or fail. He explained to me that the two key factors are the angle at which the ball leaves your hand and the height of the peak before the ball begins its downwards trajectory. These two factors are totally controllable, especially if you spend (as he did) three hours per day juggling. He could juggle with nine balls in the air at a time.

This attraction in becoming an expert at understanding a closed system is particularly apparent in the high-functioning cases of autism or AS. Here we can see the workings of the autistic mind, without the associated problems of language disorder or developmental delay and learning difficulties that frequently accompany classic autism. People with AS have their greatest difficulties on the playground, in friendship, in intimate relationships, and at work. It is here, where the situation is unstructured and unpredictable, and where relationships, social sensitivity, and reciprocity matter, that people with AS struggle.

In sum, one can think of people with autism and AS as people who are driven by a need to control their environment. Being in a relationship with someone with AS is to have a relationship *on their terms only*. You can play

with a child with AS so long as the game is the game *they* want to play. And
as we will see, a relationship with an adult with AS is only possible when
the other person is able to accommodate in the extreme to their partner's
needs, wishes, and routines. The more controllable an aspect of the environment is, the more people with autism or AS are driven to comb its every
detail, and to master it.

Adults with Asperger Syndrome

I run a clinic in Cambridge for adults who suspect that they may have AS,
but whose problems went undetected in their childhood. AS just wasn't
recognized when they were at school. So they have limped through childhood, adolescence, and young adulthood, and slowly the accumulated difficulties have piled up until they reach a clinic like ours, at which point
they are desperate for a way to make sense of a lifetime of not fitting in, of
being different.

In most cases these patients also suffer from clinical depression, as they
have not found an environment, in terms of a job and a partner, that accepts them as different. They long to be themselves, but instead feel forced
to act a role, desperately trying not to cause offense by saying or doing the
wrong thing, and yet never knowing when someone else is going to react
negatively or judge them as odd.

Many of them struggle to work out a huge set of rules concerning how
to behave in each and every situation, and they expend enormous effort
in consulting a sort of mental table of how to behave and what to say,
from minute to minute. It is as if they are trying to write a manual for social interaction based on if-then rules, or as if they are trying to systemize
social behavior when the natural approach to socializing should be via
empathizing.

Imagine the sort of Victorian books on social etiquette for dinner parties
(which fork to use, how to reply to questions such as "Would you like some
more dessert?", and so on) but writ long, to cover every eventuality in social
discourse. Of course, it is impossible to be fully prepared, and while some
of these individuals do a brilliant job in getting close to this goal, they find
it physically exhausting. By the time they get home from work, where they
have been pretending to interact normally with other people, the last thing

they want to do is socialize. They just want to close the door on the world, and say the words or perform the actions that they have had to censor all day. They do not know why they are not allowed to say what they think, and they wish that others would just speak their mind. It is difficult for them to understand how speaking one's mind could cause offense or lead them into social difficulties.[9]

For example, an employee with AS might say (truthfully) to a prospective client, "Our company produces low quality goods that are unreliable." Or a young man with AS might say to his female office colleague, "You've got big breasts." Or a man with AS might say to someone at a dinner party, "Your voice is too loud and unpleasant." Or a child with AS might say to his teacher, "You're stupid." All of these statements might be true, but it is just self-evident to us that they should not be said. Such things are far from evident to someone with AS.

You might try to advise someone with AS that on certain matters they should just keep quiet to avoid causing offense to the listener. But their low empathizing often leads them to think that it is not their problem if someone is offended. One man with AS put it very clearly to me:

> What I say is what I believe. How someone else perceives what I say is nothing to do with me. If they're hurt or offended, that's not my problem. I just say what is true. I just express myself, and where my words land are nothing to do with me. It's no different to when I use a toilet. Once the feces have left my body, I'm no longer responsible for what happens to them in the toilet, or beyond.

This statement shows that this man (who had an IQ in the superior range) could not appreciate that people are different from toilets and other inanimate objects. He could not see that people have feelings that we have a responsibility not to hurt.

Nevertheless, many people with AS learn to stay silent, rather than make a personal comment about someone. They do this not out of any empathic understanding or concern, but because that way they avoid getting into trouble. Once again, they learn a rule rather than being motivated by empathy.

Another man with AS put it to me very succinctly: "If you don't feel it, fake it." He said this when I asked him what he would do if he saw someone else was a bit tearful. He said he had learned to say, "Would you like some tea?" and sound helpful, but the truth of it was that he did not feel any emotion in response to the other person's tears.

So many adults with AS have to train themselves, through trial and plenty of error, to learn what can be said or done, and what can't. What an effort.

Below I will outline the typical set of characteristics that we see in adults with AS in our clinic, almost all of whom are male.

As Children

When we look back at the childhoods of people with AS, we find a common picture emerging. They almost always tended to be loners. Even though they were aware of other children in the playground, many of the children with AS did not know how to interact with them. Some of them describe the experience as being like "a Martian in the playground"[10] and many of them said that they preferred to talk to adults such as teachers than to the other children.

Sadly, it was the case that as children they were rarely invited to play at other children's houses or to their birthday parties, and if they were invited once, they tended not to be invited back. When we ask their parents what kind of play their child produced, we discover that they did not produce much varied, social pretend play. Instead, they would be far more focused on constructional play (building things), or reading factual books (such as encyclopedias). If other children did come round to play, the child with AS behaved in a way that was often described as "bossy," trying to control the other person. Not just choosing the game, but telling the other child what to say and what to do.

Many of them as children were content to spend long, solitary hours playing with jigsaw puzzles, Legos, and other constructional systems. Some also built houses out of boxes around the home, constructed dens outside, became engrossed in miniature systems such as model-making, or played with armies of tiny figures of knights in armor, soldiers, or fantasy figures.

They all spoke on time (this is part of how their diagnosis is made) but some acquired a precociously exact vocabulary. For example, one mother told me that her (now adult) son's first word was "articulated lorry" (note: not simply "lorry") just after his first birthday.

Because of their unusual interests and lack of normal sociability, many of these adults with AS reported having been bullied or teased by other children at school. This caused depression in some individuals, while others turned bully themselves through the frustration and anger they felt at the unfair treatment they received from their peers.

Typically they pursued their own intellectual interests to high levels, learning books of facts, or studying the movement of the sun and shadows around their bedroom, or attempting to breed tropical fish, becoming very knowledgeable on these subjects. But many also failed to hand in the required schoolwork, so that they were failing in some academic subjects. Having no drive to please the teacher, they simply followed their own interests rather than the whole curriculum.

Throughout childhood there were signs of an obsessional or deep interest in narrow topics, such as collecting a complete set of wildlife picture cards, or carrying around mathematical equations in their pockets, or learning language after language. They were building up collections of knowledge. As for the female patients with AS, many of them recall being described as "tomboys" in their behavior and interests.

As Teenagers

When we asked our patients with AS to recall their adolescence, most recall that they did best at factual subjects such as math, science, history, and geography, or at learning the vocabulary and syntax of foreign languages.

Many (but not all) were weakest at literature, where the task was to *interpret* a fictional text or to write pure fiction or to enter into a character's emotional life. Some learned rules to systemize the analysis of fiction and obtained good grades in this way. In an extreme example, a young woman with AS bought exam-preparation books and learned literary criticisms about texts without actually reading the texts herself.

Many became acutely aware that they were low in social popularity, and they found it difficult to make friends; males with AS found it particularly difficult to establish a girlfriend relationship. Their obsessions continued, and they changed topic only when the last one was fully exhausted—generally every few years. The female patients found their adolescent peer group particularly confusing and impossible to join: "All that giggling in lifts, and talk about fashion and hair. I couldn't understand why they did it."

Some got into trouble for pursuing unusual interests (the chemistry of poisons, the construction of explosives). Most of them at one time or another had said things that had hurt others' feelings, often on a frequent basis, yet they could not understand why the other person took offense if their statement was true. Sometimes the offensive remark was rather blatant: "She's fat," or, at a funeral, "This is boring."

As Adults

Many adults with AS have held a series of jobs, and have experienced social difficulties leading to clashes with colleagues and employers, resulting in their dismissal or resignation. Their work is often considered technically accomplished and thorough, but they may never get promoted because their people skills are so limited.

Some have had a series of short-term sexual relationships. Such relationships usually flounder, in part because their partner feels that they are being over-controlled or used, or because the person with AS is not emotionally supportive or communicative.

Other people recognize that those with AS are socially odd (though this is harder to detect in the female patients), and their few friends are also usually somewhat odd themselves. Typically, their friendships drop away because they do not maintain them.

A significant proportion of adults with AS experience clinical levels of depression and some even feel suicidal because they feel that they are a social failure and do not belong. One woman described her feelings to me very bluntly:

> Do I think that AS should be treated as a disability or simply as
> a difference? Clearly it should be treated as a difference, since
> then the person is accorded all the dignity and respect they de-

serve. But do I wish I hadn't been born with AS? Yes, I hate my
AS, and if I could be rid of it I would.

Another man with AS described his life in a very graphic way:

Every day is like climbing Mount Everest in lead boots, covered
in molasses. Every step in every part of my life is a struggle.

In adulthood, many of them continue to collect hundreds of one type of
object (soccer programs, CDs, and so on). Their books and CD collections
are often organized in highly systematic ways, such as by genre, date last
played or read, sex of author/composer or date of first publication/record-
ing, and they get very upset if one of these is out of place. And even if the
collection is not obviously ordered to the naked eye but instead lies in a
messy heap, the person with AS often knows exactly what they have in
their collection—it is mentally very ordered.

Their life is often governed by "to-do" lists. They may even make lists
of lists. Their domestic lives are frequently full of self-created systems.
For example, one man always had five tubes of toothpaste in the bath-
room, lined up in an exact way alongside the sink. He explained that
when one tube runs out, he brings the next one forward to replace the
empty one. When out shopping, he would then buy a replacement, and
put it into the new empty position (behind tube number four) so that he
was always prepared. Many adults with AS put a huge number of hours
into planning every detail of their lives in order to maintain the systems
that they live by.

Many of them continue to say things that offend others, even though
they do not intend any offense. They may learn to avoid obvious statements
like reference to someone's weight, but instead commit faux pas of a more
subtle kind. For example, one man with AS turned to his sister at her second wedding, as she sat at the reception dinner table with her new husband, and asked, "How's David [the first husband]? Do you see much of
him these days?"

Almost invariably, those with AS are disinterested in small talk and do
not know how to do it, or what it is for. They frequently feel that they cannot say what they think, as people often seem shocked by their independent, extreme, unempathic, and sometimes offensive views. For example,

one man with AS described his politics as "green fascism": the belief that anyone spoiling nature should be shot. Another said he believed in "merito-cratic misogyny": the belief that women have not achieved equally high po-sitions in society because they are less able. Most have no time for political correctness or spin. They believe in saying what they think, seeing no point in sugaring the pill or spin-doctoring.

Many adults with AS hate crowds, or people dropping in. This is proba-bly because they find it anxiety-inducing or annoying when people do things unpredictably. This might include people moving without warning, or a guest moving an object from its customary place on the mantlepiece to a new position on a different shelf. If people are invited over for supper by their partner, the person with AS might just walk into the next room and read a book while the guests are at the table.

Politically or in other ways, their views are often held very strongly, and are black or white. They are typically convinced by the rightness of their beliefs, and given the chance will spend hours relentlessly trying to con-vince the other person to change their view. They do not understand how one's beliefs can be a matter of subjectivity or just one point of view. Rather, they believe that their own beliefs are a true reflection of the world and, as such, that they are correct.

If you sit next to someone with AS at dinner you can begin to feel like you are being pinned to the wall as they will often go too far when explain-ing their views. In response to a polite question about their weekend, the person with AS might go into too much detail about the technicalities of their hobby, not realizing that their listener has long since become bored. Other individuals with AS might converse too briefly and provide only fac-tual responses. It is as if they are unable to judge what another person would like to hear or find interesting.

Their lives are also often governed by routines: going to the same places every weekend or every holiday, eating in the same restaurant, having the same after-work routine each evening. It is often commented that people with AS notice small details that others miss.

Most would not bother to read a novel of pure fiction or watch a human drama on television unless it was based on historical fact, science (science fiction), or an issue (politics). Instead they read factual books or watch documentaries. In this way, their beliefs are in fact like information data-bases, storing up facts. They frequently describe their brains as being just like computers—either containing some piece of information or not. In other words, they think in a way that is binary, digital, and precise; they do not think in approximations in the same way that many other people do. In a recent book about an artist with AS, Sally Wheelwright and I coined a phrase for this: "the exact mind."[11]

Some become obsessed by signs as patterns to causes. For example, some adults with AS are fascinated by crime reports because they enjoy working out basic rules of the following kind: if the victim showed physical signs a, b, and c, then the murder in all likelihood involved techniques x, y, and z. Others become obsessed with natural or man-made disasters such as hurricanes, tornadoes, earthquakes, floods, and bomb attacks, focusing on the physical event rather than the plight of the victim. Some people with AS call this approach to the world "forensic," beautifully epitomized by Sherlock Holmes, and they extend this approach to understanding social situations.

One patient I met watched news reports of buildings collapsing after terrorist bombings, over and over again, in order to understand the differences between types of architecture and the consequences an attack would have for these. He could give me statistics on how many people were killed in each building collapse and the materials that the building was made from, as well as an account of the physics of each type of material; however, he admitted that he did not find himself spontaneously stopping to think about the victims or their families.

People with AS will often also admit they would not know how to comfort someone. They would not notice that someone was upset unless the person told them so, or was showing extreme outward signs of distress, such as tears.

Some of them also end up in trouble with the law, not for acts of dishonesty but for aggression when they don't get their own way. Some become obsessed with role-play games that are tightly scripted and rule-based, such as Dungeons and Dragons.

Some marry, but remain married only if their partner is patient to the point of saintliness, is able to accommodate family life to the rigidity of the autistic routines and systems, and can accept an eccentric, remote, often controlling partner. Some marry a partner of a different ethnicity, possibly because their social oddness and communication abnormality is less apparent to a non-native speaker. Often their partners learn to avoid asking friends around because their spouse with AS is so socially embarrassing. Their social life may be restricted to that which is structured for them (for example, through the church) or by others.[12]

I should stress that the above social difficulties are typical only of those people with AS who are suffering enough that they have sought the help of a clinic. Against this catalog of social difficulties, we must keep in mind that AS involves a different kind of intelligence. The strong drive to systemize means that the person with AS becomes a *specialist* in something, or even in everything they delve into. One man with AS in Denmark who I met put it this way: "You people [without AS] are *generalists*, content to know a little bit about a lot of subjects. We people [with AS] are specialists. Once we start to explore a subject, we do not leave it until we have gathered as much information as we can." In effect, the systemizing drive in AS is often a drive to identify the *underlying structure* in the world.

Now that you have a picture of autism and AS, it is time to relate this to the idea of the extreme male brain.

The Extreme Male Brain Theory of Autism

The extreme male brain (EMB) theory of autism was first informally suggested by Hans Asperger. Here is what he said:

> The autistic personality is an extreme variant of male intelligence. Even within the normal variation, we find typical sex differences in intelligence . . . In the autistic individual, the male pattern is exaggerated to the extreme.[13]

Asperger wrote this statement in 1944, in German. The above is Uta Frith's translation, which did not reach the English-speaking world until 1991. His monumental idea therefore went unnoticed for almost fifty years, and it took until 1997 for anyone to set out to see if there was any truth to his controversial hypothesis.[14]

What did Asperger mean by an extreme of male intelligence? Psychologists usually define intelligence very narrowly as performance on IQ tests. Asperger left this term undefined, but he probably meant it in the widest sense, that there are sex differences in personality, skills, and behavior. In order to make

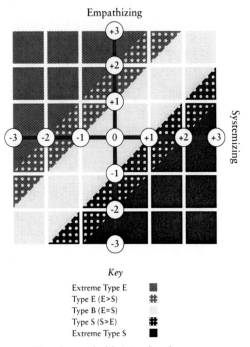

Empathizing

Systemizing

Key

Extreme Type E	▨
Type E (E>S)	✸
Type B (E=S)	░
Type S (S>E)	▦
Extreme Type S	■

*Axes show standard deviations from the mean

A model of the male and female brain, and their extremes
fig 8.

any progress in this area a half-century later, a tight definition of the male and female brain is required so that we can test the EMB theory empirically.

Throughout this book I have defined the female brain as being characterized by the individual's greater ability to empathize than systemize (E>S). If you look at Figure 8, those with the female brain are the grey, dotted zone. The male brain is defined as the opposite of this (S>E). They are the black, dotted zone.

You will notice immediately that many people have neither the male nor the female brain. Their empathizing and systemizing abilities are pretty

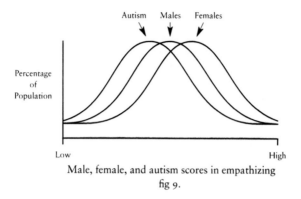

Autism   Males   Females

Percentage
of
Population

Low   High

Male, female, and autism scores in empathizing
fig 9.

much balanced (E=S). They are the people in the pale grey zone. According to the EMB theory, people with autism or AS should always fall in the black zone.[15] For males, it is just a small shift, from type S to extreme type S (from black dotted to black). For females, the shift is bigger, from type E (grey dotted) all the way to extreme type S (black).

So what is the evidence in favor of the extreme male brain theory? I will briefly summarize the different lines of evidence here.

Impaired Empathizing

On the Empathy Quotient (or EQ), females score higher than males, but people with AS or high-functioning-autism score even lower than males (Appendix 2).[16] Moreover, on social tests such as the "Reading the Mind in the Eyes" Test (Appendix 1) or the Facial Expressions Test, females score higher than males, but people with AS score even lower than males.[17]

Females make more eye contact than do males, and people with autism or AS make less eye contact than males.[18] Girls develop vocabulary faster than do boys, and children with autism are even slower than males to develop vocabulary.[19] As we saw in Chapter 4, females tend to be superior to males in terms of chatting and the pragmatics of conversa-

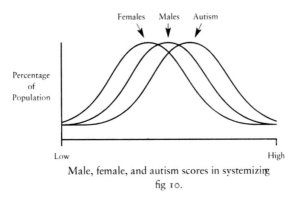

Male, female, and autism scores in systemizing

fig 10.

tion, and it is precisely this aspect of language that people with AS find most difficult.[20]

Females are also better than males at the Faux Pas Test, and people with autism or AS have even lower scores than males do.[21] Girls also tend to be better than boys on standard "theory of mind" tests (tests which involve thinking about others' thoughts and feelings), and people with autism or AS are even worse than normal boys at these tests.[22] Finally, women score higher on the Friendship and Relationship Questionnaire (FQ) that assesses empathic styles of relationships. Adults with AS score even lower than normal males on the FQ.[23]

Superior Systemizing

On tests of intuitive physics, males score higher than females, and people with AS score higher than males.[24] In addition, males are over-represented in departments of mathematics, and math is frequently chosen by people with AS as their favorite subject at school. As we saw in Chapter 2, boys prefer constructional and vehicle toys more than girls do, and children with autism or AS often have this toy preference very strongly. As adults, males prefer mechanics and computing more than females do, and many people with AS pursue mechanics and computing as their major leisure interests.

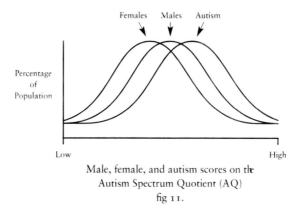

Male, female, and autism scores on the
Autism Spectrum Quotient (AQ)
fig 11.

On the Systemizing Quotient (SQ), males score higher than females, and people with autism score highest of all (Appendix 3).[25] On the Embedded Figures Task (EFT), a test of attention to detail, males score higher than females, and people with AS or HFA score even higher than males. The EFT (see Figure 6) is a measure of detailed local perception, a prerequisite for systemizing, but may also involve systemizing itself because there are rules that govern how the target can fit into the different possible slots (a bit like how to assemble a jigsaw or an engine).[26] On visual search tasks, males have better attention to detail than females do, and people with autism or AS have even faster, more accurate visual search. This, too, is a prerequisite for good systemizing, while not comprising systemizing itself.[27]

Biological and
Family-Genetic Evidence

On the Autism Spectrum Quotient (the AQ), males score higher than females, but people with AS or HFA score highest of all (Appendix 4).[28] When one looks at somatic (bodily) markers such as finger-length ratio, one finds that males tend to have a longer ring finger compared with their index finger; this finding is more pronounced in people with autism or

AS.[29] This finger-length ratio is thought to be determined by one's pre-natal testosterone level. On the Tomboyism Questionnaire (TQ), girls with AS are less interested in female-typical activities.[30] In one small-scale study, men with autism are also reported to show precocious puberty, correlating with increased levels of current testosterone.[31]

When one looks at the wider family as a clue to genetic influences, one finds that fathers and grandfathers of children with autism or AS (on both sides of the family) are over-represented in occupations such as engineering. These occupations require good systemizing, and a mild impairment in empathizing (as has been documented) would not necessarily be an impediment to success.[32] There is a higher rate of autism in the families of those talented in fields such as math, physics, and engineering, when compared with those talented in the humanities. These latter two findings suggest that the extreme male cognitive style is in part inherited.[33]

But enough of data for a moment. I want now to put flesh on the bones, and tell you about a special person with AS who I had the privilege to meet.

11

A Professor of Mathematics[1]

In 1998 Richard Borcherds was awarded the Fields Medal, the equivalent of the Nobel Prize in Mathematics and the highest accolade mathematicians can receive. (There is no Nobel Prize in mathematics, just as in many other fields.) This award was for his work on a topic so obscure that most mathematicians working in his former Cambridge University department are unable to understand what he is doing. His mathematical brilliance is unquestioned by other mathematicians, even if they cannot follow the specifics of his ideas.

Despite his facility with anything mathematical, Richard was puzzled by his sense of alienation from people. He found people to be complex, mysterious beings who were hard to comprehend because they did not conform to the laws of physics or math. Sure, he knew they had emotions and thoughts—in that sense, he wasn't completely mindblind—but he did not know which emotions and thoughts they were having.

The straightforward cases presented no difficulty for him. He could work out that someone might be sad if they got hurt or if they did not get what they wanted, and that they would be happy if they did get what they wanted. He could even appreciate that someone might be sad if they *thought* they were getting something that they did not want. Yet this is no great shakes, since even the average six-year-old child can work that out.[2]

The social world is far more sophisticated than this and moves at a tremendous speed. When people came round to his home, conversation and interaction would become confusing to him, even though it was just

155

the ordinary stuff of everyday chat between a group of friends. Faced with this sea of words and hidden meanings, of exchanges of glances and smiles, of innuendo and double-entendre, of bluff and deception, embarrassment and camouflaged flirtation, it was just all too much. It went over his head. People would tell him later what this or that joke had really meant, or why Michelle had walked off in a huff at that moment. But at the time it was simply beyond him to work out why she had taken offense and at what, or why everyone had suddenly laughed—except him.

In truth, he not only failed to understand all this social stuff but he also did not care much about it. When people came round to his home, he would initially sit with them, but at the earliest opportunity he would withdraw to the corner of the room, pick up his book, and soon lose himself in reading. Meeting him for the first time, you would be forgiven for thinking him rude, but those who knew him just accepted that that was Richard.

I met him in his Cambridge office. The room was relatively bare. He stared at me. After a few minutes it was clear he was not going to offer me a seat, so I said, "I'll sit down here, then," and picked a chair. Basic greetings or social niceties were clearly not part of his routine behavior. He perched several feet above me, on the corner of the desk, put his hands under his thighs, and started to rock back and forth gently. He would stare at the floor, then sporadically steal a glance at me, quickly returning his gaze to the carpet. The silence wasn't going to be broken by him, so I started the conversation.

I explained that I was interested in why he thought he might have Asperger Syndrome (AS), a comment he had made to a newspaper reporter in the *Guardian* that week.[3] He explained that he had been aware all of his life that he did not understand social relationships and had found out about AS on the Web. The descriptions seemed to fit him. He was, however, pleased that I had come to talk to him about it, to explore if this diagnosis was appropriate.

I thought the best way into this unusual situation was to tell him a bit more about AS. I told him that AS was thought by some people to be a form of high-functioning autism. That meant that such individuals had all the signs of autism (I gave him a brief sketch of this, along the lines of the previous chapter in this book), but with normal or even superior intelligence. He nodded. "That's me," he said.

This was a man of few words.

I went on to say that there were degrees of autism, and that you could have a little or a lot of it. He perked up at this point, since it was his view that he might only have it mildly, or that he might be right on the border-line. I told him that we had a way of measuring this now, so that we could, if he was interested, establish precisely where on the autistic spectrum he sat.

Measurement, quantification, statistical means, and distributions—he was hooked. He said that he would be happy to come to the Autism Research Centre in Cambridge and get tested. But that was for another day.

I was interested in his view of himself, but he thought that apart from his mathematical ability, he was in many ways quite ordinary. He could not have been more mistaken.

His own powers of self-reflection, and his judgment of what others might think of his behavior, were quite limited. He was a master of mathematical judgment, but had hardly left first base in relation to social judgment. I asked him, for example, if he thought any of his behavior was socially odd or unusual. Social oddness is the first key symptom of AS. He said that he couldn't think of anything in particular, though other people had told him that it was odd the way he ran down the streets everywhere, even when he wasn't in a hurry. I sat and listened. That did not seem too odd, since maybe he was a man who liked to get a lot done in his day and snatch a bit of exercise wherever possible. I asked him if there was any-thing else that he thought he did differently to others. "No," he said. What about communication, the second of the key symptoms of AS? Was there anything different about that? He could not think of anything, though ad-mitted that he was not much of a conversationalist. From his perspective, talk was for finding out what you needed, and not much beyond that. I thought it was striking that he omitted to mention a major function of lan-guage, which is to communicate your thoughts and feelings to another per-son, and to find out how they might be feeling or thinking. I said as much, but he said that was not really of interest to him.

I asked him if he used email to chat to people, or if he had friends that he liked to spend time with or phone up, but he said that his use of email was restricted to work-related information exchange. He did not really have friends as such, though colleagues would sometimes come round to his apartment. He would often just leave them to chat to his wife, and withdraw into a book. He said that he was able to be with one other person, one to one, for short periods. If he was in a group, he would get confused and withdraw. He said it had always been this way.

As for chatting on the telephone, he admitted that he avoided telephones. I raised an eyebrow. "Why?," I asked. He said that when he was younger, in his twenties and before, he had been afraid of telephones because he couldn't work out how to use them. It wasn't the mechanics of the handset itself. He could give you a lecture on the physics of telephones—how they worked electronically, what sound waves were, and so on. It was the social part that confused him. What you were supposed to say to the other person? When was it your turn to speak? When were you supposed to hang up? How were you to know how to finish or start a conversation? Or where conversation was supposed to go? He was even puzzled about why people phoned, sometimes.

He knew that sometimes other people thought he was rude, though he never intended to be. He had no idea how to work out what was the right or wrong thing to say in different situations. I tried to look as if I were not shocked. Here was a man who could fathom any mathematical problem you could throw at him, but who was unable to work out the basics of friendship or how to have a phone conversation. Was there ever a more dramatic example of dissociation between empathizing and systemizing?

For some years, my colleagues and I had been arguing for the "modularity" of empathizing, by which I mean the independence of empathizing from other processes, and here was Richard, the clearest instance of this that I could imagine.

In retrospect, it struck me that the telephone was a good test of communication skill. On a telephone one does not have access to a wider context, such as the other person's facial expression, to scaffold one's interpretation. Indeed, it occurred to me that many of the adults with AS I had come across had shown a clear abnormality in relation to telephones. Some would talk for far too long, not taking a break for ten minutes or more, even if the listener had not uttered an "Uh-huh" or an "I see" or an "Oh really?" Or they would talk far too minimally, just giving monosyllabic replies, or they would say things which were quite rude but which they did not intend as such. Richard showed a more extreme abnormality in relation to telephone conversation, in his case avoiding it altogether, because he was unable to even work out the basis principles of turn-taking, or what the other person might be interested in.

"So," he asked, "do I have Asperger Syndrome?"

I told him that a diagnosis was not something you could arrive at in a half-hour conversation, but that I would be willing to delve further, to verify if he did have the condition. I told him that I would need to gather information from people who had known him during his life, especially those who had known him in his childhood. He offered me the names of his math tutors who had known him during his undergraduate days, a family friend who had seen him a lot in his teens, and he said that I could visit his parents. I decided to take up this offer, since his parents would be in the best possible position to provide the critical information for a diagnosis. This is because the syndrome—for want of a better word—is developmental, not acquired; in other words, signs of the syndrome are typically present from early in childhood. There were certainly clues in his current adult life that his social behavior and understanding were out of keeping with that expected of a (then) thirty-eight-year-old, highly intelligent man. But it was important to discover whether his parents could provide independent corroboration of his impairment in empathizing alongside his talent for systemizing.

I emailed his father to arrange a visit.

Richard's Parents

Richard's father is a physicist at another university. He had wanted to be a mathematician himself, but had been advised to go into something more useful. He started in engineering, but eventually found himself drawn to physics, and then to the computational, mathematical side of physics. He gave me a picture of the family.

Richard has three brothers, two of whom are math teachers. I joked with Richard's father that it was more than a coincidence to have three sons who are mathematicians, but he did not particularly respond to humor. He simply commented that his own parents, Richard's grandparents, were also of a scientific bent, as were his wife's parents.

Richard's maternal grandmother had been a chemist. Richard's mother chimed in that Richard was similar to the members of both of their families, since he was very independent-minded and did not need people. Both of Richard's parents had moved from South Africa, and they had described their own fathers as the kind of men who could have gone out in the bush for days or weeks alone, without any thought for their families back home, and without missing the company of other human beings. This streak of minimal social interest or involvement, together with talent in mathematics or scientific thinking, seemed to run through this remarkable family.

The bigger surprise came when I heard of Richard's third brother. Another mathematician, I wondered? It transpired that this third brother was quite disabled, and among the range of diagnoses he had was—autism. Since autism is strongly heritable, I was interested to hear that this too might run in the family. But I decided not to let myself be influenced by this fact, since we had not yet gathered a full history of Richard himself. His wider family was, of course, of indirect relevance but was not itself germane to establishing if a diagnosis for Richard was merited.

My questions to Richard's parents soon revealed a set of signs that seemed to fit, however. First, Richard's parents could not recall him having used the pointing gesture when he first started to communicate. This was the first clue, since the absence of the pointing gesture to share interest, at eighteen months of age, is an established risk factor for autism spectrum conditions.

I asked about his language development. Richard's parents recalled that he did not say his first words until he was two and a half years old. They did not think this was particularly late, and had not been concerned enough to seek speech therapy for him. They were aware, though, that he was one of the late developers in relation to language compared with other children in the community. In retrospect, having seen other toddlers more recently, they had realized that Richard had been different. I decided that although the onset of his single word vocabulary was late (the vast majority of children are producing single words by the age of two), the fact that he had some phrase speech by the age of three was significant since it indicated that he did *not* qualify for a diagnosis of language delay.[4]

He had been a quiet little boy, content to play alone. His parents could not recall him playing pretend games, except when he was a schoolboy when he became very interested in the game Battleships. He would play this for hours. The game Battleships does have a pretend dimension to it, since one has to treat the symbols on paper as if they were real battleships. But when I asked about it, the game that Richard played was more about spatial position and mathematical co-ordinates than anything else. Aside from this, he was not particularly interested in dressing up, or in assuming pretend identities, and so on. Again, little interest in imaginative play, with all its creative variability, is another marker of autistic spectrum conditions in toddlerhood.

"Did he have any friends, as a child?" I asked.

"Sure," his mother replied. "He often had one friend round, to play Battleships. It was groups of children that he had no interest in."

That correlated with the picture of Richard as an adult, I thought.

Socially, he had not fitted in at school particularly well. He never stopped to think what others might be feeling. For example, his mother sat worrying one night when, as a teenager, he didn't come home until late. When he finally arrived home she said to him in an anxious state, "Oh Richard. Why didn't you phone me to let me know where you were?" To which he replied, "What for? *I* knew where I was."

It transpired that he had also had some minor obsessions too, such as being very fussy about his food and insisting on wearing the same clothes all the time. By the time he was a teenager, there was a clear obsession: chess. He spent all his free time playing chess or reading every chess book he could lay his hands on. He went out three or four nights a week to play chess tournaments and was in line for becoming a chess master. Then all of a sudden he gave chess up, as he realized that beyond a certain point it was only about competition, not fun.

His other major obsession during his school years was, of course, mathematics. His father said that Richard could have gone to Oxbridge at the age of twelve to read mathematics, but they did not push him in this, believing that it would be better for him to go at the right age. Nevertheless, he won national mathematics competitions and filled his room, and the house, with neatly decorated polyhedra that he had made himself. Each of these polyhedra was unique in terms of its size, shape, and number of protruding structures built on to its core, and his parents showed me some of the collection of these that they still hung from various ceilings around the house. The rest were stored in a glass bookcase at the school where one of Richard's brothers was teaching. There were hundreds of them. This certainly qualified as an unusual, strong, and narrow interest or obsession.

Richard's childhood was clearly consistent with Asperger Syndrome. I emailed Richard to make an appointment to talk through some of the implications of this diagnosis. Diagnostic information is best imparted in person, one to one, in order to handle that person's reaction to the news sensitively. Richard said he was quite happy to have the diagnosis by email. Nevertheless, I went round to his office. He did not seem particularly surprised by the diagnosis, and said that when he was younger the diagnosis would have been useful but that now it did not really make much of a difference to his life.

He asked me and my colleague Sally Wheelwright if we wanted to join him for lunch, and we were pleased to take up the invitation. We walked to the local sandwich shop with two of his colleagues, his regular lunch companions. Richard ran ahead down the road, just as he said he ran everywhere. We followed the towpath along the river, chatting with his colleagues, Richard running ahead. He unexpectedly veered off the path, and I saw him striding across a field.

I started to follow him, thinking that this must be the route to the picnic spot, but his colleague said, "Oh, you don't have to follow him. We'll go along the path. Richard likes to go the muddy way." Sally and I looked at each other, somewhat surprised that Richard had just taken off alone when we had thought that we were his invited guests for lunch, but we then realized that this was all part of the condition. He had little awareness of what the other person might think, of what might confuse the other person or of what the other person might be expecting. I realized that his colleagues just accepted him for the way he is, which was wonderful.

The next week Richard came, as arranged, to our lab. He strode into my office, came right up to my computer and read what happened to be on the screen. In fact it was a confidential reference on a student, but that did not seem to cause Richard any embarrassment. He picked up some papers on my desk and put them down absent-mindedly. I said nothing, interested in his spontaneous behavior.

Sally and I decided it would be good to try to get some quantitative measures of his social understanding and degree of autistic traits, so we asked him to take the "Reading the Mind in the Eyes" Test. Richard scored 25 out of 36. People typically score on average 30 out of 36, so Richard's score was significantly lower than one would have expected. On the Empathy Quotient (EQ) he scored very low (12 out of 80), whereas the average score in the general population is 42 out of 80. On the

Friendship and Relationship Questionnaire (FQ) he scored very low (55 out of 135); most people score 80 out of 135. The FQ measures the extent to which an individual prefers intimate or empathic relationships, as opposed to relationships based around activities. On the Autism Spectrum Quotient (AQ), our questionnaire which measures autistic traits in adults with normal intelligence, he scored 32 out of 50. This is also typical of most people with AS. The average male without autism or AS scores 17 out of 50. He scored 19 out of 20 on the Folk Physics Test, which measures your ability to solve problems dealing with physical causality. He also had a very high score on the Systemizing Quotient (SQ). On this he scored 41 out of 80, which is well above the average score for the population (27 out of 80).

So these tests gave us quantitative evidence for his unusual profile—extremely low empathizing, extremely high systemizing, and a lot of autistic traits.

Richard Borcherds is an example of someone whose AS has not been an obstacle to achievement in his adult life; however, the diagnosis would have been valuable during his school years, as he was not fitting in socially and he admits that he would have found it beneficial to have had this recognized at that time. His talents in mathematics have resulted in his finding a niche where he can excel (to put it mildly), and where his social oddness is tolerated. The fact that he has also found a partner who accepts these qualities means that currently his AS traits do not cause any significant impairment in his functioning. He is thus an example of an adult who in a sense has adapted his AS to an environment where it is no longer a major, or indeed any, obstacle at all.

One might question whether Richard Borcherds really merits a diagnosis at all, given how well adapted he is. Certainly, he is not currently severe enough in his symptoms to warrant a diagnosis in adulthood, as his symptoms are not interfering with his daily functioning. In the jargon of the diagnostic criteria, he is not "suffering any impairment in his daily life." For example, he is not depressed (thankfully), unlike the majority of the patients we see in our clinic.

He is, fortunately, an outstanding example of a man who in a sense has outgrown his diagnosis. But it reminds us how important the environment is, since if you took the same Richard Borcherds and put him in a less understanding environment, in all likelihood his AS would cause him some degree of distress.

Innovation in Silicon Valley

Richard Borcherds' case raises the broader question of whether good systemizing skills (frequently accompanied by reduced empathizing skills) might carry with it the advantage of a talent for innovation. An example might be useful, in case this is becoming too abstract.

William Shockley started a research and development company in Palo Alto, California, in 1955. He had co-invented the transistor just a few years earlier, in 1947, at Bell Laboratories in New Jersey. What better proof of his systemizing talent. He is recognized by some as the man who made an early contribution to Silicon Valley, because he was able to select and attract very talented individuals from around the world. By the end of 1957, eight of Shockley's team had left to form their own company (Fairchild Semiconductor), the company that went on to pioneer the first integrated circuits on silicon (or "chips"). Before long, this technology had mushroomed around the whole area.

Shockley was clearly a high systemizer, and he selected his workers for their unique technical expertise (or systemizing skills). The fact that he was also a low empathizer can be inferred from his crude eugenic proposal of offering $1,000 per IQ point below 100 to individuals with such intelligence scores who volunteered to sterilize themselves.[5]

A number of media reports (*Wired*, Dec 2001) have suggested that the rate of autism and AS (both of which they offensively term "Geek Syndrome") may be unusually high in areas like Silicon Valley. The reports suggest that because such areas attract talented systemizers who then prosper and find a like-minded partner with whom to have children, this increases the risk that their offspring will have autism or AS. Against this view, it should be said that at present there is no evidence at all that the rate of autism and AS is higher in such high-tech environments, compared with other environments: high rates of 1 in 200 children are being reported in many areas, not just in silicon-rich ones. But this does not discount the possibility that there is a link between high systemizing/low empathizing on the one hand, and a talent for innovation, or a risk of AS, on the other.

Physics

The description of high systemizers that I have outlined in this book strikes a chord among some academic physicists today. It is of interest that one study of the personalities of high-achieving physicists reported them to be less sociable than those in the general population.[6]

Helenka Przysiezniak is in that rare minority of female academic physicists—they number less than one in eight of all academic physicists. In 1998 she gave an interview with a reporter from the *Times Higher*, during which she discussed her male colleagues at CERN (European Organization for Nuclear Research):[7]

> They lack basic social skills and some do not take care of themselves . . . there is one characteristic that she says that all physicists have—herself included—and that is "arrogance." "You want to prove that something is right if you believe in it. That's just how it works when you're discussing the 'truth,'" she claims.

Przysiezniak suggests that a psychological analysis of the personalities that physics attracts would reveal that physicists are very focused, one-track-minded, obsessive even. They tend to be just as passionate about their other interests—many of the physicists at CERN are accomplished musicians and concerts are held there almost daily. The mountains and lakes that surround CERN offer the chance for skiing, mountaineering, and sailing, a chance that many of the physicists seize.

Skiing, mountaineering, and sailing—all require good systemizing skills, as does physics. Moreover, an arrogant assumption that you are right and everyone else is wrong suggests low empathizing skills in failing to recognize not only that others might have a valid point of view (there might be several ways of seeing a problem) but also that a dismissal of another's point of view might be hurtful to their feelings.

Paul Dirac

Paul Dirac (1902–84) is another interesting physicist to consider. He held the Lucasian Chair of Mathematics at Cambridge, the professorship that Isaac Newton had held and that is now held by Stephen Hawking. Between the ages of twenty-three and thirty-one, Dirac worked on his own interpretation of quantum mechanics, and formulated a quantum theory of the emission and absorption of radiation by atoms, the relativistic wave equation of the electron, the idea of anti-particles and even a theory of magnetic monopoles. By the age of thirty-one Dirac had been awarded the Nobel Prize.

The German physicist and biologist Walter Elsasser described Dirac as "a man . . . of towering magnitude in one field, but with little interest or competence left for other human activities." Dirac himself confirmed this statement when he recalled his time as a Ph.D. student at Cambridge:

> [I] confined myself entirely to the scientific work, and continued at it pretty well day after day, except on Sundays when I relaxed and, if the weather was fine, I took a long solitary walk out in the country.

Furthermore, a Fellow at Cambridge described Dirac as someone who was "quite incapable of pretending to think anything that he did not really think."

Around 1950, Dirac was supervising Dennis Sciama's graduate studies at Cambridge. One day, Sciama burst in to Dirac's office, and said, "Professor Dirac, I've just thought of a way of relating the formation of stars to cosmological questions. Shall I tell you about it?" Dirac replied, "No." He did not seem to realize that his brevity could be thought rude. If someone in the audience of one of Dirac's lectures had not understood a point and asked Dirac to repeat it, Dirac would repeat it exactly. Dirac could not appreciate that he was being asked to rephrase his words differently in order to help the listener understand.

Paul Dirac's father was described as a rigid disciplinarian, who ran the household like a regiment and who was emotionally detached from his children. Paul later married Margit, a widow and the sister of a Hungarian physicist. He had two children with her, but he, too, remained detached from family life. Margit declared, "Paul, although not domineering like his father, kept himself too aloof from his children." The picture suggested by the Dirac family is one of extremely high systemizing abilities, with low empathizing.[8]

Isaac Newton and Albert Einstein

What have these two physicists got in common? Apart from being two of the greatest physicists that the world has seen, there is one other feature that they share: they had not only high systemizing skills but also rather low empathizing skills. Indeed, their social difficulties were probably severe enough to warrant a diagnosis of AS. Despite this, it didn't stop them achieving the highest levels in their chosen fields.[9]

An observer of Newton wrote that he

> always kept close to his studies, very rarely went a-visiting & had as few visiters . . . I never knew him take any recreation or pastime, either in riding out to take the air, a-walking, bowling or any other exercise whatever, thinking all hours lost that were not spent in his studies.

We have an account of Einstein's childhood from his son Hans Albert:

> He was a very well-behaved child. He was shy, lonely and withdrawn from the world even then. He was even considered backward by his teachers. He told me that his teachers reported to his father that he was mentally slow, unsociable and adrift forever in his foolish dreams.

Einstein was described as "lonely and dreamy" as a child, with a difficulty in making friends. He was said to prefer "solitary and taxing" games, such as complex constructional play with blocks or making houses of cards up to fourteen storeys high. He would "softly repeat every sentence he uttered—a habit he continued until the age of seven." He was still not considered fluent in speech at the age of nine. He was also a loner: "I'm not much with people," he would say. "I do not socialize because social encounters would distract me from my work and I really only live for that, and it would shorten even further my very limited lifespan."

These two world-class physicists certainly showed many of the signs of AS, though whether they would have warranted a diagnosis is questionable, since they had found a niche in which they could blossom.

Michael Ventris: Arch Code-Breaker

A final character to mention briefly is Michael Ventris (1922–56), the man who cracked Linear B.[10] As a fourteen-year-old child he was exposed to this ancient hieroglyphic language that had been found by archaeologists, and for the next sixteen years he worked obsessively to make sense of what this ancient language might be. All he had were squiggles to go on, but Ventris, a talented linguist (he could speak English, French, German, Polish, Latin, Danish, and Greek, among others), was determined to work out the meanings of every squiggle, together with how they were pronounced and spoken.

His breakthrough came when he realized that Linear B was in fact Greek. He became the first person on the planet to be able to read and speak Linear B for 4000 years. His motivation was to crack the system—to systemize.

Ventris is described by his family and by colleagues as someone who was emotionally remote, a man who wanted to remain apart from people, and who became obsessed with cracking the code. He designed his home in Hampstead in London so that the children lived downstairs while he and his wife lived upstairs; he did not want his children to intrude into his adult space. Eventually he stopped talking to his wife, since he said that there was nothing left to talk about. His daughter said that he was never really interested in spending time with them.[11]

These are people with the extreme male brain. Sometimes one finds them in academia (and typically in the "hard" sciences or mathematics), sometimes in practical pursuits (such as carpentry), or socially isolated occupations (working as a librarian or a gardener, for example). Sometimes they are the technical wizards in a company, or the innovator in a business. They are not invariably as distinguished as Richard Borcherds, but there is a red thread that runs through their lives that binds them all together: high systemizing and low empathizing.

Consider the words of Hans Asperger:

> To our own amazement, we have seen that autistic individuals, as long as they are intellectually intact, can almost always achieve professional success, usually in highly specialised academic professions, with a preference for abstract content. We found a large

number of people whose mathematical ability determines their professions: mathematicians, technologists, industrial chemists, and high ranking civil servants . . . A good professional attitude involves single-mindedness as well as a decision to give up a large number of other interests . . . It seems that for success in science or art, a dash of autism is essential.

Some people with the extreme male brain end up with a diagnosis of AS because this profile leads to secondary problems, such as loneliness, unemployment, bullying, depression, and divorce. But happily, some never need a diagnosis because, despite having the same profile of strengths and difficulties, they find a niche for themselves among a group of people (or just one saint of a partner) who find their oddities somewhat charming and eccentric, and value their difference from others.

12

The Extreme Female Brain:
Back to the Future

By now we are almost at the end of our journey, at least in terms of the known terrain. We have seen that, according to the model in Figure 8, about 95 percent of the population have one of the following three brain types: the balanced brain (type B), the male brain (type S), or the female brain (type E). A small percentage (about 2.5 percent) have the extreme male brain.

And then we get to the unknown terrain. There is a small percentage (another 2.5 percent) who presumably have the extreme female brain. The what? This is something that I have barely mentioned until this point. But this is the place to discuss it, as it is a topic for future exploration.

The Extreme Female Brain

All scientists know about the extreme female brain is that it is predicted to arise, as we can see from the model in Figure 8. Scientists have never got close up to these individuals. It is a bit like positing the existence of a new animal on theoretical grounds, and then setting out to discover if it is really found in nature.

The existence of chronic pain suggests to neurologists that there might be people in nature who experience no pain. The existence of phobias suggests to psychiatrists that there might be people in nature who experience no anxiety. Neither of these is the sort of problem that turns up in clinics—maybe because people with these problems do not survive very long. Someone who experiences no pain would not learn about things that could burn them, or falls that could injure them, and might not avoid such hazards in the environment. Someone who experiences no anxiety would not learn about other kinds of dangers, and might comfortably stand on a cliff edge or go into a dark alley alone. In evolutionary terms, these individuals may not have survived long enough to pass on their genes, and therefore at this time they may only exist in theory, or at most very rarely. But they might still exist.

Similarly, the map we used to find the extreme male brain suggests that there should be a mirror opposite: the extreme female brain. So what would such people look like?

People with the extreme female brain would fall in the upper left-hand quadrant of the graph in Figure 8, the dark grey area. Their empathizing ability would be average or significantly better than that of other people in the general population, but their systemizing would be impaired. So these would be people who have difficulty understanding math or physics or machines or chemistry, *as systems*. But they could be extremely accurate at tuning in to others' feelings and thoughts.

Would such a profile carry any necessary disability? Hyperempathizing could be a great asset, and poor systemizing may not be too crippling. It is possible that the extreme female brain is not seen in clinics because it is not maladaptive.

We saw that those with the extreme male brain do experience a disability, but only when the person is expected to be socially able. Remove this expectation, and the person can flourish. Unfortunately, in our society this social expectation is pervasive: at school, in the workplace and in the home. So it is hard to avoid.

But for those with the extreme female brain, the disability might only show up in circumstances where the person is expected to be systematic or technical. The person with the extreme female brain would be *systemblind*. Fortunately, in our society there is considerable tolerance for such individuals. For example, if you were a child who was systemblind, your teachers at school might simply allow you to drop mathematics and science at the earliest possible stage, and encourage you to pursue your stronger subjects. If you were a systemblind adult and your car didn't work, you could just call the mechanic (who is likely to be at least type S). If your computer needs putting together, and you can't work out which lead goes into which socket, there are phone numbers that you can ring for technical support. And in evolutionary terms, there were in all likelihood equivalent people that a systemblind person could turn to for help when that person's home was destroyed in strong winds, or when their spear broke.

But what about hyperempathy? Is this invariably a good thing to have, or might it be a problem?

Candidates for the Extreme Female Brain

You might think that being hyperempathic could lead to difficulties. For example, if you are constantly trying to ascertain the mental states of others, you could attribute intentions to people that they do not have; you might verge on the paranoid, or certainly display an oversensitivity. Could it be that oversensitive or paranoid individuals have the extreme female brain?

Other contenders might be people with hysterical personality disorder, a diagnosis given to individuals who are overwhelmed by emotions (their own and others) to such an extent that they can no longer reason clearly. So are individuals with these psychiatric conditions (for that is what paranoia and personality disorders are) revealing the extreme female brain?

This cannot be the case. If someone is over-attributing intentions, or has become preoccupied by their own emotions, then by definition they are not exhibiting hyperempathy. Hyperempathy is the ability to ascertain the mental states of others to an unusually accurate and sensitive degree, and it can only occur if one is appropriately tuned in to the other person's feelings. A paranoid person, or someone who is easily inflamed into aggression by suspecting that others are hostile, has a problem. But their problem is not hyperempathy.

Equally, a psychopath may be exceptionally good at figuring out other people's thoughts and how to dupe them, but this is not hyperempathy because the psychopath does not also have the appropriate emotional response to someone else's emotional state (recall our original definition of empathy). They might even feel pleasure at someone else's pain, which is hardly empathic.

Nor would any of the personality disorders easily qualify for the privileged status of an extreme female brain, since a characteristic of the personality disorders is that they are profoundly self-centered. If anything, empathy deficits are also likely to characterize these groups.[1]

Finally, some people have wondered whether Williams' Syndrome might be an example of the extreme female brain, as individuals with this syndrome demonstrate good or even superior attention to faces, and can chat easily, despite other aspects of their learning and cognition being impaired. But such sociability can be quite superficial—they may be good at keeping a conversation going, but not really pick up with any special sensitivity what you are feeling and thinking—so again this may not qualify as the extreme of brain type E.[2]

So we have a good idea what the extreme female brain (or extreme type E) is *not*. We can draw such conclusions because Williams' Syndrome, personality disorders, psychopaths and paranoia are all part of the known terrain. But to say what the extreme female brain *is* requires a best guess about what we might find in the unknown terrain ahead.

New Contenders

One suggestion is that people who are more prone to believe in telepathy might qualify as having the extreme female brain.[3] These are not individuals who are prone to believe in any old parapsychological phenomenon (such as ghosts or telekinesis), nor do they have some mild variant of psychosis or schizotypy. Rather, these individuals would need to be healthy and normal in every way except for having this remarkable belief that others' minds are more transparent to them. And critically, their accuracy in such mindreading would need to be very good, since otherwise their belief in their own telepathy could simply be a delusion.

A second, and to my mind more likely, contender for who might have the extreme female brain would be a wonderfully caring person who can rapidly make you feel fully understood. For example, an endlessly patient psychotherapist who is excellent at rapidly tuning in to your feelings and your situation, who not only says he or she feels a great sadness at your sadness or great pleasure at your pleasure but also actually experiences these emotions as vividly as if your feelings were theirs.

However, the contender for the extreme female brain would also need to be someone who was virtually technically disabled. Someone for whom math, or computers, or political schisms, or do-it-yourself projects held no interest. Indeed, someone who found activities requiring systemizing hard to follow. We may all know people like this, but it is likely that they do not find their way into clinics, except perhaps as staff in the caring professions.

Throughout this book I have explored these two dimensions, empathizing and systemizing, and yet there is still much to be discovered. What are some of the questions and issues that I hope we will have answers to in the next few years? They tend to fall into three key areas: the model, the autistic mind, and society's options and responsibilities. Let's briefly look at each of these.

The Model

Are there are some essential sex differences in the mind that are not encompassed by the model shown in Figure 8? Is it really the case that the only important differences between the brains of the average man or woman can be reduced to these two dimensions of empathizing and systemizing? The more familiar examples of sex differences, such as aggression or language skills, have already been discussed in Chapter 4, where we concluded that reduced empathizing in men could give rise to increased aggression, and better empathizing in women could give rise to better communication skills. A challenge for the future will be to identify psychological sex differences that are not easily accommodated by this model.

For example, some people suggest that fear is another sex difference (men being less fearful). But this could still boil down to better systemizing skills in men (in other words, a careful and detached analysis of the risks of flying a plane, or a logical analysis of how to track and trap and kill a predator).

One might also wonder what the two processes of empathizing and systemizing are really like. Are they separate modules in the brain? Are they really independent dimensions? As I mentioned earlier, there seems to be a trade-off for many people, so that a higher ability in one process tends to be accompanied by a lower ability in the other process. Why?

It could be that these two processes reduce to something more general. We can glimpse this possibility by stepping back and reflecting on the nature of the two processes. Systemizing involves exactness, excellent attention to local detail, an attraction to phenomena that are in principle treated as lawful, and context-independence. In other words, what one discovers about the laws relating to buoyancy or temperature should hold true from one context to another. Empathizing, on the other hand, involves inexactness (one can only ever approximate when one ascertains another's mental state), attention to the larger picture (what one thinks he thinks or feels about other people, for example), context (a person's face, voice, actions and history are all essential information in determining that person's mental state), with no expectation of lawfulness (what made her happy yesterday may not make her happy tomorrow). Future research will need to examine the possibility that these two processes are not defined by their topic, but instead by these more general features.

The Autistic Mind

In this book you have come across one model of autism, that of empathizing and systemizing. But it would be improper of me not to refer to other models that have also attempted to explain the riddle of autism. Future work will entail the use of critical scientific experiments to test these competing models against each other, but let's have a brief look at these alternative models.

It is said that people with autism have "executive function" deficits, for example deficits in planning skills.[4] Executive function is shorthand for the control centers of the brain that allow not just planning but also attention-switching and the inhibition of impulsive action. It is certainly true that individuals with autism with some degree of learning disability (or below average IQ) have executive function difficulties, but it is not yet clear if this extends to what might be considered as "pure" cases of autism, such as those with completely normal or above average IQ.

Executive dysfunction has been found in individuals who are said to have "high-functioning autism" (HFA) but this term can be very misleading. HFA is used to describe any individual with autism whose IQ is higher than 70, since this is the accepted point at which one is able to diagnose general learning difficulties (mental retardation) and average intelligence. In fact, an IQ of around 70 is still likely to lead to considerable educational problems.

It is often said, for example, that someone with an IQ of 70 would be unlikely to pass the exams required to complete mainstream secondary-school education, or that someone with an IQ of much less than 100 would be unlikely to be selected for a place at a university.[5] So an individual with an IQ of around 70 is only "high-functioning" *relative* to the other individuals with autism whose IQ is even lower than this, and who have clearly recognized learning difficulties or mental retardation. To discover that such individuals have some executive dysfunction may be no surprise, and may be linked to their relatively low IQ.

Indeed, if autism involves an intact or superior systemizing ability, and if systemizing requires an ability to predict that input X causes output Y in a system, then this suggests that those with autism are capable of some executive function (planning). Richard Borcherds, who we met in the last chapter, has terrific systemizing skills (when it comes to math), considerable difficulties in empathizing, but not a trace of any executive dysfunction. So it may be that executive dysfunction is not a necessary or universal feature of autism.

It is also said that people with autism have "central coherence" deficits, such that they spend more time processing local detail, rather than getting the larger picture. But if autism involves an intact or superior systemizing ability, then those with autism must be able to see the larger picture, at least where systems are involved. Input X may be quite distant from output Y, and yet they can keep track of these contingencies. Again, how are these two accounts related?[6] Indeed, it may even be that good systemizing would resemble weak central coherence. Good systemizing would lead the individual to focus on one possible domain as a system, and that individual would start with very local details in case these turned out to be variables that followed laws. At the point when the individual had worked (systematically) through all the local details in that domain, that individual would end up with a good picture of the larger system, which is not what the weak-central-coherence theory would predict.

Are there facts about autism that are inconsistent with the extreme male brain theory? For example, if there is reduced lateralization for language in the left hemisphere of the autistic brain, as has been suggested by some studies, is this what would be expected of the extreme male brain? Further work is needed to understand the relationship between sex and laterality at the extremes.[7]

A potential criticism of the extreme male brain theory of autism is that the sex ratio of many conditions (not just autism) is biased toward males, so the account may lack specificity. For example, stuttering affects boys more than girls, and attention deficit with hyperactivity disorder (ADHD) is also more common among boys. So is conduct disorder. Are we just witnessing some biological vulnerability among males that puts them at increased risk for everything going?

This is unlikely. There are some developmental conditions (such as anorexia, or teenage depression) that affect girls more often than boys. For this reason we need specific explanations for the sex ratios in each condition. Moreover, the sex ratio in Asperger Syndrome—estimated to occur in at least ten males for every female—far outnumbers the sex ratio seen in other developmental conditions (these are usually of the order of two or three males to every female). Note that the extreme male brain theory does not specify that the sex ratio in autism should be of a particular magnitude. It may be that the sex ratio in autism is lower than 10:1, but that females with AS get by more often without requiring a diagnosis because of better acting skills, or because they are more accepted by society.

It is also possible that there are important associations between the autism spectrum conditions and some of the other developmental conditions that affect males more often than they do females. Language delay and disorder may well involve a similar neurobiological mechanism to autism. Some genetic studies have already found that they may share an abnormality on the long arm of chromosome 7, though these results are very new and will need independent replication.[8] Other studies have also shown that levels of pre-natal testosterone affect not only social development but also language development.[9] Therefore, common mechanisms are a possibility. One must also take into account the fact that similar psychological processes may cut across different diagnoses. For example, reduced empathizing is not an exclusive feature of autism spectrum conditions but is also seen in conduct disorder. So far from the existence of these other conditions creating a problem for the model, they may actually help us understand things more clearly, and add new twists and complexity.

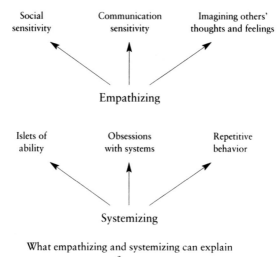

What empathizing and systemizing can explain
fig 12.

The attraction of the empathizing-systemizing model of autism is that it has the power to explain the *cluster* of symptoms seen in this condition (both the social and the non-social). The model can also make sense of some symptoms in autism that were previously neglected, such as repetitive behavior—also sometimes described as "purposeless"—for example, spinning a bottle over and over again. These relationships are shown in Figure 12.

The Nobel Prize-winning physicist Richard Feynman is said to have spent his afternoons during his Ph.D. in the university canteen spinning plates, but nobody described this as purposeless repetitive behavior. Feynman was behaving in a way that he couldn't resist, like a spider that can't help but spin a web. He was systemizing. Whether he did it on paper with equations or with a plate in the canteen, he was captivated and engrossed by the pattern of information—the laws, the regularities—that one can test and retest when one plays with variables systematically.

We should be wary of saying that a child with autism who shows echolalia (repeating everything you say in your exact intonation) or who plays a musical sequence over and over again, or who puts his eyes inches away from a spinning fan, is engaged in purposeless behavior. Such a child may be trying to systemize human behavior (speech) or mechanical motion, or auditory strings of input, at a level that is consistent with or higher than you would expect from their overall IQ.

A case in point is the art of Lisa Perini, an Italian artist who had classic autism as a child. As a five-year-old girl she filled every page with the identical, repetitive shape of the letter "W." It was as if she had isolated this variable as a feature or input to the writing or drawing process. She then operated on this in a highly systematic way, varying only the angle of this shape, until she had mastered her motor control and achieved the pleasing effect she was striving for. Later she did the same thing with the repeating motif of flowers, producing thousands of superficially similar flowers, in reality each comprising a mini-experiment in manipulating one tiny variable. As an adult, her technical skill as an artist is outstanding, and she retains this systematic approach to creativity. Sabina Maffei, the Italian graphologist who introduced me to Lisa's work, told me that if Lisa sees some broken red indicator-light glass from a car accident lying in the street she will pick up the pieces, study the shapes, and ask other people to send her similar fragments of colored glass that they might come across, so that she can find the perfect shapes for her art. Systemizing creatively.

The systemizing-empathizing model of autism can also encompass the "islets of ability" that previously were studied as if separate from the other aspects of autism itself. Calendrical calculation, or gifted drawing ability, or a facility to calculate prime numbers, or an excellent musical memory, was seen as an oddity that occurred in autism more often than in other conditions, but defied explanation. In the model presented in this book such islets of ability are simply well-developed examples of what all people with autism do without trying. They systemize.

The model can also explain the unusual attention to detail seen in autism. Why does the child notice those tiny numbers on the backs of lamp posts? Or remember the number of the seat in the theater they visited eight years ago? Or spot that an ornament on the mantlepiece has moved? Or that Auntie Becky has new earrings? Or that Mr. Hackett lives in house number 106? This unusual attention to detail is a prerequisite for good systemizing, and the brain in these examples is taking any feature and treating it as an anchor point, to see if this could be the basis of a new law or rule. Is seat 1124 the same or different to seat 1123 in this theater? Are the silver and red earrings a reliable way to recognize that this is Auntie Becky? Do the light bulbs in the lamp posts in our street tend to burn out in a particular order? Who else goes into house number 106, and since it is an even number, is it necessarily on the left-hand side of the street?

Finally, other models paint an essentially negative view of autism by concluding that the brains of those with autism suffer from executive dysfunction. It is true that damage to your frontal lobes can produce executive dysfunction, and that this is not uncommon in those individuals with autism who have a below-average IQ. Indeed, low IQ might even be a marker for such executive dysfunction. But a model of autism has to be able to explain not just those who have such pervasive problems but also those—like Richard Borcherds—who have reached supreme heights of achievement, despite their difficulties in empathy, with no trace of executive dysfunction. The empathizing-systemizing model bestows some dignity on those with the diagnosis of autism by identifying both their talents (at systemizing) as well as difficulties (in empathizing), suggesting that people on the autistic spectrum are simply different from others in their abilities. As one young man with AS said to me in Denmark:

> People with AS are like salt-water fish who are forced to live in fresh water. We're fine if you just put us into the right environment. When the person with AS and the environment *match*, the problems go away and we even thrive. When they don't match, we seem disabled.

Keep the salt- and fresh-water metaphor in mind. I think it is very powerful.

Society's Responsibilities: To Intervene or Not to Intervene?

One upshot of this book might be that teachers need worry less about boys when it comes to the development of systemizing, and need worry less about girls when it comes to the development of empathizing. Rather, they could target their teaching on areas where each sex is likely to need more direction and support. This may come as welcome news to some readers, who might have assumed that if there is evidence that biology partly determines an individual's profile, there is nothing teachers or parents can do to change that individual. Such a conclusion would be a mistake. In all likelihood, biology may be pushing an individual down one track in development, but there is plenty of evidence that the brain can be resculptured by experience.[10] But should we really attempt intervention at all? Should society strive to make an average male more empathic, or an average female more focused on systemizing?

We should recall that although the sexes do differ, these individual differences in most people are at a level that do not cause either them or anyone else any distress. In which case, the grounds for any intervention are weak. Rather, the hope is that laying out what we understand about essential differences in the minds of men and women may lead to greater acceptance and respect of difference. Targeted teaching is, of course, still desirable, but this should always be based on an assessment of each individual's strengths and weaknesses.

But then there is the specter of medical intervention, with all the ethical issues this raises. If autism is linked to high levels of fetal testosterone (and this has not yet been shown), would a form of estrogen therapy in the womb reduce the risks of autism? Or is there some other kind of pharmacological treatment that could mediate the effects of high testosterone? Certainly, as we saw in Chapter 8, a few less drops of this precious stuff can lead you to make more eye-contact and to have better communication abilities. But, ethically, would one really wish to intervene? To do so might be to lose what is special and valuable about the extreme male brain. As one person with autism put it in a recent email to me: "Without autism, we might not have fire and the wheel." Certainly, if good systemizing leads to innovation, as we hinted at in Chapter 11, we might be losing something priceless if the medical profession tried to alter fetal brain development through biochemical treatment.

Issues relating to pre-natal screening for autism are unlikely to arise for a good while yet, as biological markers for autism have not yet been reliably demonstrated. All we have are clues. But even when such markers are available, it is likely that the autism community will be divided on the issue of prevention or intervention. Some will say:

> If I could have been helped as an infant so that I could have had
> my autism taken away, I would have wanted that. My autism has
> been an enormous daily struggle.

These are the words of Ros Blackburn, a woman with autism who gives talks publicly about what it is like to live with the condition. Yet other people with the condition advocate the opposite view. A Web page asserts with dignity: http://groups.yahoo.com/group/AS-and-Proud-of-it.

Equally, parents of children with an autism spectrum condition, and who are at risk of having another child with autism for genetic reasons, may be divided on the issue. Some parents will (and do) say:

> The idea of having to cope with another child with severe autism is just too much for us to bear. The difficult behavior, the lack of any acknowledgement, the disinterest in other people's feelings, and the extremely limited life that autism has forced on the family is overwhelming. Since he was born, neither he nor we have had more than two hours of sleep a night. And the way he bites his own hand and hits his head against the wall is overwhelmingly distressing. If we were offered a cure, or if prevention had been available, we would have taken it.

Yet other parents, while acknowledging the difficulties, assert their child's right to be different, and would not want to force them to be like everyone else. They admire their child's independence of mind, their lack of conformity, their unusual intellect, and protect them fiercely from any suggestion that this should be medicalized, treated, or prevented.

Clearly, individuals with the condition, and their parents, deserve the freedom to make their own choices if and when the time comes for medical science to face these big societal decisions.

Misconceptions

I would weep with disappointment if a reader took home from this book the message that "all men have lower empathy" or "all women have lower systemizing skills." Hopefully, I have made clear that when we talk about the female brain or the male brain, these terms are shorthand for psychological profiles based upon the average scores obtained when testing women as a group, or the average scores obtained when testing men as a group.

Such group statistics say nothing about individuals. I am fortunate enough in my research group at Cambridge University to work with women who have far more systemizing skill than I will ever have, and as a result they do wonderful science. Equally, I am fortunate enough to have some male friends who go against the norm, and have what we have been calling the female brain. It may be no coincidence that they work in the caring professions, and their clients appreciate how emotionally connected they are to their needs. However, the model in the book still stands: in order to explain why these particular women have a gift for systemizing, or why these particular men are talented at empathizing, we must refer to their particular biology and experience.

Some may think that the small but real differences between men and women (on average) mean that there is never going to be any hope for relationships working well. Again, I think this worry is overstated. In the majority of opposite-sex couples or friendships, there is sufficiently good communication to enable people not only to understand each other but also to respect each other's differences. And, after all, the age-old solution to the need for a like-minded companion has always been to have same-sex friends outside of any primary relationship involving someone of the opposite sex. A girls' night out, or a night out with the guys, has always been a need for most people.

Some may worry that the view of the male and female brain offered in this book risks portraying the male brain as more intelligent than the female brain. Systemizing sounds like the sort of thing that might come in useful on an IQ test, while empathizing may not figure in such a test at all. I do not think this risk is real, however, because both processes give rise to different patterns of "intelligence." Systemizing may be useful for parts of the non-verbal ("performance") IQ test, while empathizing might be useful for the more verbal aspects of the IQ test.

Some may worry that portraying autism as hyper-male will trigger associations of people with autism as super-macho. Again, this would be a misconception, as machismo does not overlap with any exactness with the dimensions of empathizing and systemizing. Indeed, the negative connotations of being macho, such as aggression, are far from a good characterization of many people with autism spectrum conditions. Aggression is determined by many factors, and reduced empathy may be just one of them. And even then, reduced empathy does not invariably lead to aggression. It may not even lead to this in the majority of cases. Many people with autism spectrum conditions are gentle, kind people, who are struggling to fit in socially and care passionately about social justice: not the stereotype of a macho male at all.

Respect

When we find someone with the extreme female brain, my guess is that we will also find that society has made it easy for them to find a niche and a value, without that person having to feel that they must in some way hide their systemblindness. I hope that at least one benefit of this book is that society might become more accepting of essential sex differences in the mind, and make it easier for someone with the extreme male brain to find their niche and for us to acknowledge their value. They should not feel the need to hide their mindblindness (as many currently do).[11]

A central tenet of this book is that the male and female brain differ from each other, but that *overall* one is not better or worse than the other. Hopefully, in reading this book, men will also experience a resurgence of pride at the things they can do well, things like being able to work out confidently how to program a new appliance in the home, being able quickly to discover how to use a new piece of software, or how to fix something with whatever available tools and materials are around. All these need good systemizing skills.

Society needs both of the main brain types. People with the female brain make the most wonderful counselors, primary-school teachers, nurses, carers, therapists, social workers, mediators, group facilitators, or personnel staff. Each of these professions requires excellent empathizing skills. People with the male brain make the most wonderful scientists, engineers, mechanics, technicians, musicians, architects, electricians, plumbers, taxonomists, catalogists, bankers, toolmakers, programmers, or even lawyers. Each of these professions requires excellent systemizing skills. (People with low systemizing but good empathizing could apply for the public relations and communication aspects of these jobs.) And people with the balanced brain make the most wonderful medical doctors, as comfortable with the details of the biological system as with the feelings of the patient. Or they can be skilled as communicators of science, not just understanding systems but being able to describe them to others in ways that do not presume the same degree of knowledge—that is, adapting language to the needs of the listener. People with the balanced brain can be excellent architects if they not only understand buildings but also understand their client's feelings, and the needs and feelings of the people who will be inhabiting the space they are designing. Or talented company directors, grasping the mathematical details of economics and financial planning while building a strong team around them based on their sensitive way of including each and every individual in the team.

Society at present is likely to be biased toward accepting the extreme female brain and stigmatizes the extreme male brain. Fortunately, the modern age of electronics, science, engineering, and gadgets means that there are more openings now for the extreme male brain to flourish and be valued. My hope is that the stigmatizing will soon be history.

Appendix 1

THE "READING THE MIND IN THE EYES" TEST[1]

Instructions

For each set of eyes, choose which word best describes what the person in the picture is thinking or feeling.

playful   comforting

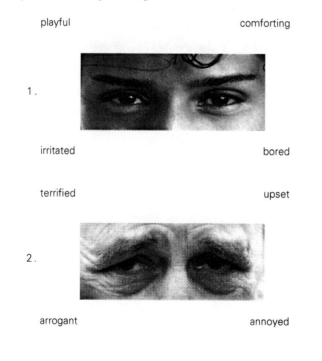

1.

irritated   bored

terrified   upset

2.

arrogant   annoyed

joking   flustered

3.

desire   convinced

joking   insisting

4.

amused   relaxed

irritated   sarcastic

5.

worried   friendly

aghast   fantasizing

6.

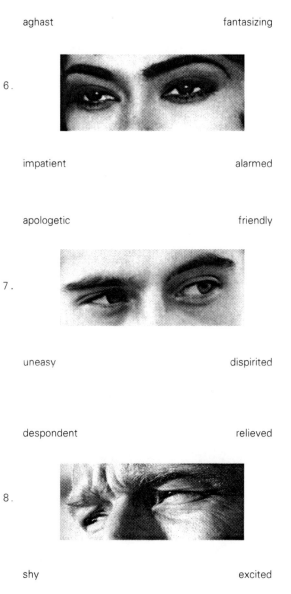

impatient   alarmed

apologetic   friendly

7.

uneasy   dispirited

despondent   relieved

8.

shy   excited

annoyed   hostile

9.

horrified   preoccupied

cautious   insisting

10.

bored   aghast

terrified   amused

11.

regretful   flirtatious

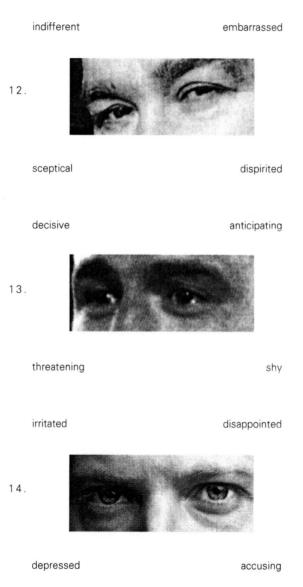

indifferent   embarrassed

12.

sceptical   dispirited

decisive   anticipating

13.

threatening   shy

irritated   disappointed

14.

depressed   accusing

contemplative   flustered

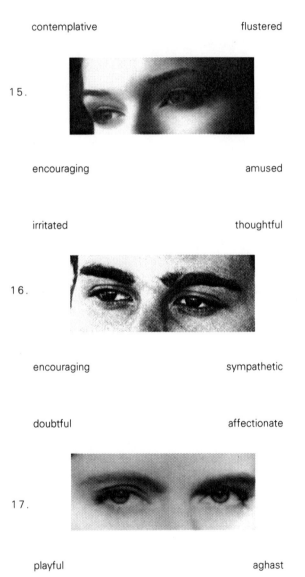

15.

encouraging   amused

irritated   thoughtful

16.

encouraging   sympathetic

doubtful   affectionate

17.

playful   aghast

decisive   amused

18.

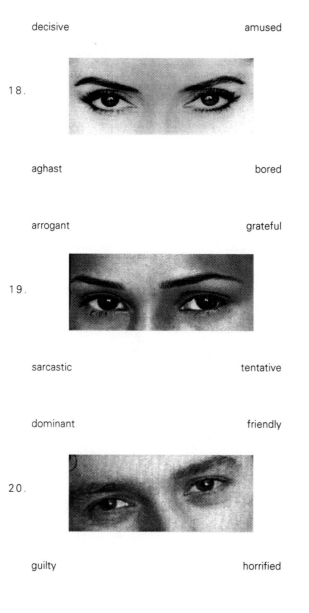

aghast   bored

arrogant   grateful

19.

sarcastic   tentative

dominant   friendly

20.

guilty   horrified

embarrassed   fantasizing

21.

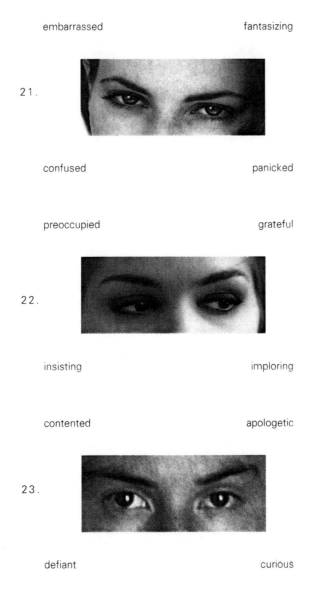

confused   panicked

preoccupied   grateful

22.

insisting   imploring

contented   apologetic

23.

defiant   curious

pensive   irritated

24.

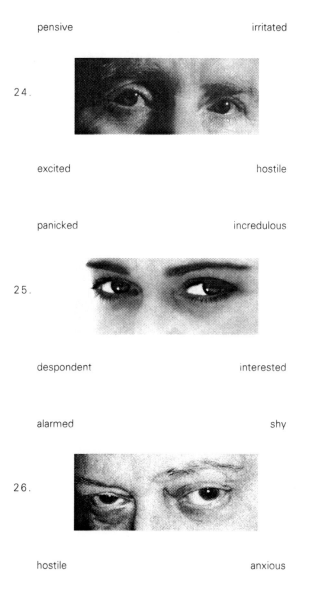

excited   hostile

panicked   incredulous

25.

despondent   interested

alarmed   shy

26.

hostile   anxious

joking   cautious

27.

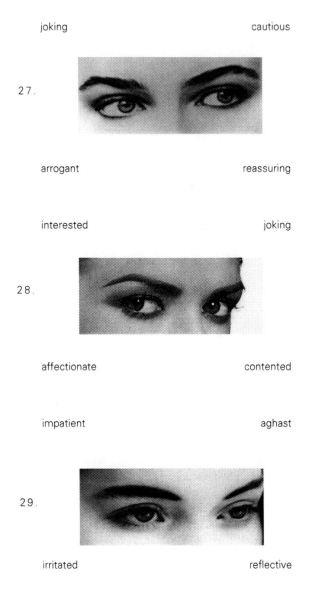

arrogant   reassuring

interested   joking

28.

affectionate   contented

impatient   aghast

29.

irritated   reflective

grateful   flirtatious

30.

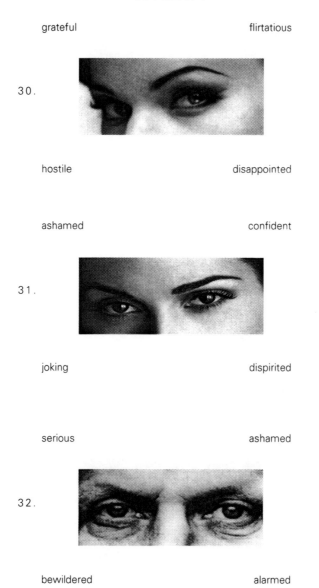

hostile   disappointed

ashamed   confident

31.

joking   dispirited

serious   ashamed

32.

bewildered   alarmed

embarrassed   guilty

33.

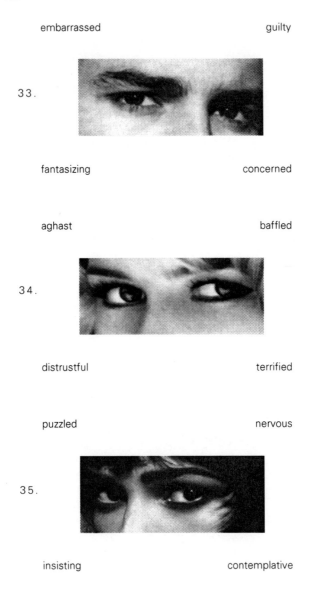

fantasizing   concerned

aghast   baffled

34.

distrustful   terrified

puzzled   nervous

35.

insisting   contemplative

ashamed   nervous

36.

suspicious   indecisive

Answers

1. playful	19. tentative
2. upset	20. friendly
3. desire	21. fantasizing
4. insisting	22. preoccupied
5. worried	23. defiant
6. fantasizing	24. pensive
7. uneasy	25. interested
8. despondent	26. hostile
9. preoccupied	27. cautious
10. cautious	28. interested
11. regretful	29. reflective
12. skeptical	30. flirtatious
13. anticipating	31. confident
14. accusing	32. serious
15. contemplative	33. concerned
16. thoughtful	34. distrustful
17. doubtful	35. nervous
18. decisive	36. suspicious

How to Interpret Your Score

Count how many correct words you identified. A typical score is in the range 22–30. If you scored over 30 you are very accurate at decoding a person's facial expressions around their eyes. If you scored less than 22 this indicates that you find this task quite difficult.

Appendix 2

THE EMPATHY QUOTIENT (EQ)[1]

Read each statement very carefully and rate how strongly you agree or disagree with it.

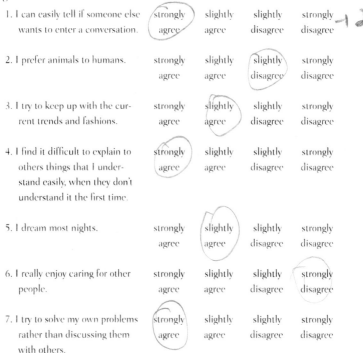

1. I can easily tell if someone else wants to enter a conversation.	**strongly agree** ⟲	slightly agree	slightly disagree	strongly disagree
2. I prefer animals to humans.	strongly agree	slightly agree	**slightly disagree** ⟲	strongly disagree
3. I try to keep up with the current trends and fashions.	strongly agree	**slightly agree** ⟲	slightly disagree	strongly disagree
4. I find it difficult to explain to others things that I understand easily, when they don't understand it the first time.	**strongly agree** ⟲	slightly agree	slightly disagree	strongly disagree
5. I dream most nights.	strongly agree	**slightly agree** ⟲	slightly disagree	strongly disagree
6. I really enjoy caring for other people.	strongly agree	slightly agree	slightly disagree	**strongly disagree** ⟲
7. I try to solve my own problems rather than discussing them with others.	**strongly agree** ⟲	slightly agree	slightly disagree	strongly disagree

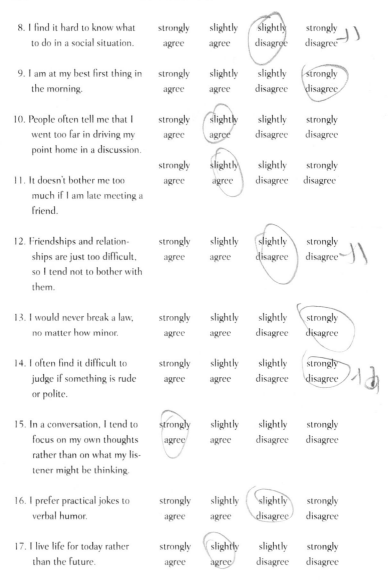

8. I find it hard to know what to do in a social situation.

strongly agree   slightly agree   slightly disagree   strongly disagree

9. I am at my best first thing in the morning.

strongly agree   slightly agree   slightly disagree   strongly disagree

10. People often tell me that I went too far in driving my point home in a discussion.

strongly agree   slightly agree   slightly disagree   strongly disagree

11. It doesn't bother me too much if I am late meeting a friend.

strongly agree   slightly agree   slightly disagree   strongly disagree

12. Friendships and relationships are just too difficult, so I tend not to bother with them.

strongly agree   slightly agree   slightly disagree   strongly disagree

13. I would never break a law, no matter how minor.

strongly agree   slightly agree   slightly disagree   strongly disagree

14. I often find it difficult to judge if something is rude or polite.

strongly agree   slightly agree   slightly disagree   strongly disagree

15. In a conversation, I tend to focus on my own thoughts rather than on what my listener might be thinking.

strongly agree   slightly agree   slightly disagree   strongly disagree

16. I prefer practical jokes to verbal humor.

strongly agree   slightly agree   slightly disagree   strongly disagree

17. I live life for today rather than the future.

strongly agree   slightly agree   slightly disagree   strongly disagree

18. When I was a child, I en-   strongly   slightly   slightly   strongly
    joyed cutting up worms to   agree   agree   disagree   disagree
    see what would happen.

19. I can pick up quickly if   strongly   slightly   slightly   strongly
    someone says one thing but   agree   agree   disagree   disagree
    means another.

20. I tend to have very strong   strongly   slightly   slightly   strongly
    opinions about morality.   agree   agree   disagree   disagree

21. It is hard for me to see why   strongly   slightly   slightly   strongly
    some things upset people so   agree   agree   disagree   disagree
    much.

                                    strongly   slightly   slightly   strongly
22. I find it easy to put myself in agree   agree   disagree   disagree
    somebody else's shoes.

23. I think that good manners   strongly   slightly   slightly   strongly
    are the most important   agree   agree   disagree   disagree
    thing a parent can teach
    their child.

24. I like to do things on the   strongly   slightly   slightly   strongly
    spur of the moment.   agree   agree   disagree   disagree

25. I am good at predicting how   strongly   slightly   slightly   strongly
    someone will feel.   agree   agree   disagree   disagree

26. I am quick to spot when   strongly   slightly   slightly   strongly
    someone in a group is feeling   agree   agree   disagree   disagree
    awkward or uncomfortable.

27. If I say something that   strongly   slightly   slightly   strongly
    someone else is offended   agree   agree   disagree   disagree
    by, I think that that's their
    problem, not mine.

28. If anyone asked me if I liked their haircut, I would reply truthfully, even if I didn't like it.

    strongly agree   slightly agree   slightly disagree   strongly disagree

    strongly agree   slightly agree   slightly disagree   strongly disagree

29. I can't always see why someone should have felt offended by a remark.

    strongly agree   slightly agree   slightly disagree   strongly disagree

30. People often tell me that I am very unpredictable.

    strongly agree   slightly agree   slightly disagree   strongly disagree

31. I enjoy being the center of attention at any social gathering.

    strongly agree   slightly agree   slightly disagree   strongly disagree

32. Seeing people cry doesn't really upset me.

    strongly agree   slightly agree   slightly disagree   strongly disagree

33. I enjoy having discussions about politics.

    strongly agree   slightly agree   slightly disagree   strongly disagree

34. I am very blunt, which some people take to be rudeness, even though this is unintentional.

    strongly agree   slightly agree   slightly disagree   strongly disagree

35. I don't tend to find social situations confusing.

    strongly agree   slightly agree   slightly disagree   strongly disagree

36. Other people tell me I am good at understanding how they are feeling and what they are thinking.

    strongly agree   slightly agree   slightly disagree   strongly disagree

37. When I talk to people, I tend to talk about their experiences rather than my own.

    strongly agree   slightly agree   slightly disagree   strongly disagree

38. It upsets me to see an animal in pain.

strongly agree   slightly agree   slightly disagree   strongly disagree

39. I am able to make decisions without being influenced by people's feelings.

strongly agree   **slightly agree**   slightly disagree   strongly disagree

40. I can't relax until I have done everything I had planned to do that day.

strongly agree   slightly agree   slightly disagree   **strongly disagree**

41. I can easily tell if someone else is interested or bored with what I am saying.

strongly agree   slightly agree   slightly disagree   **strongly disagree**

42. I get upset if I see people suffering on news programs.

strongly agree   slightly agree   slightly disagree   **strongly disagree**

43. Friends usually talk to me about their problems as they say that I am very understanding.

strongly agree   slightly agree   **slightly disagree**   strongly disagree

44. I can sense if I am intruding, even if the other person doesn't tell me.

strongly agree   slightly agree   slightly disagree   strongly disagree

45. I often start new hobbies but quickly become bored with them and move on to something else.

strongly agree   slightly agree   **slightly disagree**   strongly disagree

46. People sometimes tell me that I have gone too far with teasing.

strongly agree   **slightly agree**   slightly disagree   strongly disagree

47. I would be too nervous to go on a big rollercoaster.

strongly agree   slightly agree   slightly disagree   **strongly disagree**

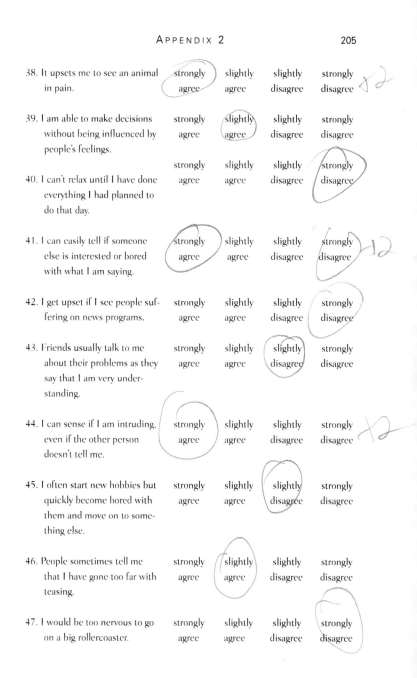

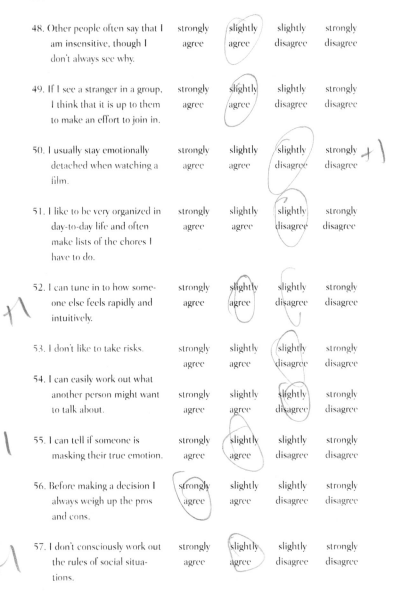

48. Other people often say that I am insensitive, though I don't always see why.
    strongly agree / (slightly agree) / slightly disagree / strongly disagree

49. If I see a stranger in a group, I think that it is up to them to make an effort to join in.
    strongly agree / (slightly agree) / slightly disagree / strongly disagree

50. I usually stay emotionally detached when watching a film.
    strongly agree / slightly agree / (slightly disagree) / strongly disagree   +)

51. I like to be very organized in day-to-day life and often make lists of the chores I have to do.
    strongly agree / slightly agree / (slightly disagree) / strongly disagree

52. I can tune in to how someone else feels rapidly and intuitively.
    strongly agree / (slightly agree) / slightly disagree / strongly disagree

53. I don't like to take risks.
    strongly agree / slightly agree / (slightly disagree) / strongly disagree

54. I can easily work out what another person might want to talk about.
    strongly agree / slightly agree / (slightly disagree) / strongly disagree

55. I can tell if someone is masking their true emotion.
    strongly agree / (slightly agree) / slightly disagree / strongly disagree

56. Before making a decision I always weigh up the pros and cons.
    (strongly agree) / slightly agree / slightly disagree / strongly disagree

57. I don't consciously work out the rules of social situations.
    strongly agree / (slightly agree) / slightly disagree / strongly disagree

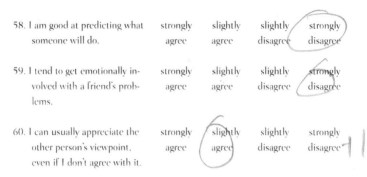

58. I am good at predicting what someone will do.	strongly agree	slightly agree	slightly disagree	strongly disagree
59. I tend to get emotionally involved with a friend's problems.	strongly agree	slightly agree	slightly disagree	strongly disagree
60. I can usually appreciate the other person's viewpoint, even if I don't agree with it.	strongly agree	slightly agree	slightly disagree	strongly disagree

How to Score Your EQ

Score two points for each of the following items if you answered "definitely agree," or one point if you answered "slightly agree": 1, 6, 19, 22, 25, 26, 35, 36, 37, 38, 41, 42, 43, 44, 52, 54, 55, 57, 58, 59, 60.

Score two points for each of the following items if you answered "definitely disagree" or one point if you answered "slightly disagree": 4, 8, 10, 11, 12, 14, 15, 18, 21, 27, 28, 29, 32, 34, 39, 46, 48, 49, 50.

The following items are not scored: 2, 3, 5, 7, 9, 13, 16, 17, 20, 23, 24, 30, 31, 33, 40, 45, 47, 51, 53, 56.

Simply add up all the points you have scored and obtain your total EQ score.

How to Interpret Your EQ Score

• 0–32 = **low** (*most people with Asperger Syndrome or high-functioning autism score about 20*)
• 33–52 = **average** (*most women score about 47, and most men score about 42*)
• 53–63 **above average**
• 64–80 **very high**
• 80 = **maximum**

Appendix 3

THE SYSTEMIZING
QUOTIENT (SQ)[1]

Read each statement very carefully and rate how strongly you agree or disagree with it.

1. When I listen to a piece of music, I always notice the way it's structured.	strongly agree	slightly agree	slightly disagree	strongly disagree
2. I adhere to common superstitions.	strongly agree	slightly agree	slightly disagree	strongly disagree
3. I often make resolutions, but find it hard to stick to them.	strongly agree	slightly agree	slightly disagree	strongly disagree
4. I prefer to read non-fiction than fiction.	strongly agree	slightly agree	slightly disagree	strongly disagree
5. If I were buying a car, I would want to obtain specific information about its engine capacity.	strongly agree	slightly agree	slightly disagree	strongly disagree

6.	When I look at a painting, I do not usually think about the technique involved in making it.	strongly agree	slightly agree	slightly disagree	strongly disagree
7.	If there was a problem with the electrical wiring in my home, I'd be able to fix it myself.	strongly agree	slightly agree	slightly disagree	strongly disagree
8.	When I have a dream, I find it difficult to remember pre- cise details about the dream the next day.	strongly agree	slightly agree	slightly disagree	strongly disagree
9.	When I watch a film, I pre- fer to be with a group of friends, rather than alone.	strongly agree	slightly agree	slightly disagree	strongly disagree
10.	I am interested in learning about different religions.	strongly agree	slightly agree	slightly disagree	strongly disagree
11.	I rarely read articles or Web pages about new technology.	strongly agree	slightly agree	slightly disagree	strongly disagree
12.	I do not enjoy games that involve a high degree of strategy.	strongly agree	slightly agree	slightly disagree	strongly disagree
13.	I am fascinated by how ma- chines work.	strongly agree	slightly agree	slightly disagree	strongly disagree.
14.	I make a point of listening to the news each morning.	strongly agree	slightly agree	slightly disagree	strongly disagree
15.	In math, I am intrigued by the rules and patterns gov- erning numbers.	strongly agree	slightly agree	slightly disagree	strongly disagree

16.	I am bad about keeping in touch with old friends.	strongly agree	slightly agree	slightly disagree	strongly disagree
17.	When I am relating a story, I often leave out details and just give the gist of what happened.	strongly agree	slightly agree	slightly disagree	strongly disagree
18.	I find it difficult to understand instruction manuals for putting appliances together.	strongly agree	slightly agree	slightly disagree	strongly disagree
19.	When I look at an animal, I like to know the precise species it belongs to.	strongly agree	slightly agree	slightly disagree	strongly disagree
20.	If I were buying a computer, I would want to know exact details about its hard drive capacity and processor speed.	strongly agree	slightly agree	slightly disagree	strongly disagree
21.	I enjoy participating in sports.	strongly agree	slightly agree	slightly disagree	strongly disagree
22.	I try to avoid doing household chores if I can.	strongly agree	slightly agree	slightly disagree	strongly disagree
23.	When I cook, I do not think about exactly how different methods and ingredients contribute to the final product.	strongly agree	slightly agree	slightly disagree	strongly disagree
		strongly agree	slightly agree	slightly disagree	strongly disagree
24.	I find it difficult to read and understand maps.	strongly agree	slightly agree	slightly disagree	strongly disagree

25. If I had a collection (e.g., CDs, coins, stamps), it would be highly organized.	strongly agree	slightly agree	slightly disagree	strongly disagree
26. When I look at a piece of furniture, I do not notice the details of how it was constructed.	strongly agree	slightly agree	slightly disagree	strongly disagree
27. The idea of engaging in "risk-taking" activities appeals to me.	strongly agree	slightly agree	slightly disagree	strongly disagree
28. When I learn about historical events, I do not focus on exact dates.	strongly agree	slightly agree	slightly disagree	strongly disagree
29. When I read the newspaper, I am drawn to tables of information, such as football scores or stock market indices.	strongly agree	slightly agree	slightly disagree	strongly disagree
30. When I learn a language, I become intrigued by its grammatical rules.	strongly agree	slightly agree	slightly disagree	strongly disagree
31. I find it difficult to learn my way around a new city.	strongly agree	slightly agree	slightly disagree	strongly disagree
32. I do not tend to watch science documentaries on television or read articles about science and nature.	strongly agree	slightly agree	slightly disagree	strongly disagree
33. If I were buying a stereo, I would want to know about its precise technical features.	strongly agree	slightly agree	slightly disagree	strongly disagree

34.	I find it easy to grasp exactly how odds work in betting.	strongly agree	slightly agree	slightly disagree	strongly disagree
35.	I am not very meticulous when I carry out do-it-your-self projects.	strongly agree	slightly agree	slightly disagree	strongly disagree
36.	I find it easy to carry on a conversation with someone I've just met.	strongly agree	slightly agree	slightly disagree	strongly disagree
37.	When I look at a building, I am curious about the pre-cise way it was constructed.	strongly agree	slightly agree	slightly disagree	strongly disagree
38.	When an election is being held, I am not interested in the results for each con-stituency.	strongly agree	slightly agree	slightly disagree	strongly disagree
39.	When I lend someone money, I expect them to pay me back exactly what they owe me.	strongly agree	slightly agree	slightly disagree	strongly disagree
40.	I find it difficult to under-stand information the bank sends me on different invest-ment and saving systems.	strongly agree	slightly agree	slightly disagree	strongly disagree
41.	When traveling by train, I of-ten wonder exactly how the rail networks are coordinated.	strongly agree	slightly agree	slightly disagree	strongly disagree
42.	When I buy a new appliance, I do not read the instruction manual very thoroughly.	strongly agree	slightly agree	slightly disagree	strongly disagree

43. If I were buying a camera, I would not look carefully into the quality of the lens.

   strongly agree   slightly agree   slightly disagree   strongly disagree

44. When I read something, I always notice whether it is grammatically correct.

   strongly agree   slightly agree   slightly disagree   strongly disagree

45. When I hear the weather forecast, I am not very interested in the meteorological patterns.

   strongly agree   slightly agree   slightly disagree   strongly disagree

46. I often wonder what it would be like to be someone else.

   strongly agree   slightly agree   slightly disagree   strongly disagree

47. I find it difficult to do two things at once.

   strongly agree   slightly agree   slightly disagree   strongly disagree

48. When I look at a mountain, I think about how precisely it was formed.

   strongly agree   slightly agree   slightly disagree   strongly disagree

49. I can easily visualize how the freeways in my region link up.

   strongly agree   slightly agree   slightly disagree   strongly disagree

50. When I'm in a restaurant, I often have a hard time deciding what to order.

   strongly agree   slightly agree   slightly disagree   strongly disagree

   strongly agree   slightly agree   slightly disagree   strongly disagree

51. When I'm in a plane, I do not think about the aerodynamics.

52. I often forget the precise details of conversations I've had.

   strongly agree   slightly agree   slightly disagree   strongly disagree

53. When I am walking in the country, I am curious about how the various kinds of trees differ.	strongly agree	slightly agree	slightly disagree	strongly disagree
54. After meeting someone just once or twice, I find it difficult to remember precisely what they look like.	strongly agree	slightly agree	slightly disagree	strongly disagree
55. I am interested in knowing the path a river takes from its source to the sea.	strongly agree	slightly agree	slightly disagree	strongly disagree
56. I do not read legal documents very carefully.	strongly agree	slightly agree	slightly disagree	strongly disagree
57. I am not interested in understanding how wireless communication works.	strongly agree	slightly agree	slightly disagree	strongly disagree
58. I am curious about life on other planets.	strongly agree	slightly agree	slightly disagree	strongly disagree
59. When I travel, I like to learn specific details about the culture of the place I am visiting.	strongly agree	slightly agree	slightly disagree	strongly disagree
60. I do not care to know the names of the plants I see.	strongly agree	slightly agree	slightly disagree	strongly disagree

How to Score Your SQ

Score two points for each of the following items if you answered "definitely agree" and one point if you answered "slightly agree": 1, 4, 5, 7, 13, 15, 19, 20, 25, 29, 30, 33, 34, 37, 41, 44, 48, 49, 53, 55.

Score two points for each of the following items if you answered "definitely disagree" or one point if you answered "slightly disagree": 6, 11, 12, 18, 23, 24, 26, 28, 31, 32, 35, 38, 40, 42, 43, 45, 51, 56, 57, 60.

The following items are not scored: 2, 3, 8, 9, 10, 14, 16, 17, 21, 22, 27, 36, 39, 46, 47, 50, 52, 54, 58, 59.

Simply add up all the points you have scored and obtain your total SQ score.

How to Interpret Your SQ Score

*0–19 = **low***

*20–39 = **average** (most women score about 24, and most men score about 30)*

*40–50 = **above average** (most people with Asperger Syndrome or high functioning autism score in this range)*

*51–80 = **very high** (three times as many people with Asperger Syndrome score in this range, as compared to typical men, and almost no women score in this range)*

*80 = **maximum***

Appendix 4

THE AUTISM SPECTRUM QUOTIENT (AQ)[1]

Read each statement very carefully and rate how strongly you agree or disagree with it.

1.	I prefer to do things with others rather than on my own.	strongly agree	slightly agree	slightly disagree	strongly disagree
2.	I prefer to do things the same way over and over again.	strongly agree	slightly agree	slightly disagree	strongly disagree
3.	If I try to imagine something, I find it very easy to create a picture in my mind.	strongly agree	slightly agree	slightly disagree	strongly disagree
4.	I frequently get so strongly absorbed in one thing that I lose sight of other things.	strongly agree	slightly agree	slightly disagree	strongly disagree
5.	I often notice small sounds when others do not.	strongly agree	slightly agree	slightly disagree	strongly disagree
6.	I usually notice car number plates or similar strings of information.	strongly agree	slightly agree	slightly disagree	strongly disagree

7.	Other people frequently tell me that what I've said is impolite, even though I think it is polite.	strongly agree	slightly agree	slightly disagree	strongly disagree
8.	When I'm reading a story, I can easily imagine what the characters might look like.	strongly agree	slightly agree	slightly disagree	strongly disagree
9.	I am fascinated by dates.	strongly agree	slightly agree	slightly disagree	strongly disagree
10.	In a social group, I can easily keep track of several different people's conversations.	strongly agree	slightly agree	slightly disagree	strongly disagree
11.	I find social situations easy.	strongly agree	slightly agree	slightly disagree	strongly disagree
12.	I tend to notice details that others do not.	strongly agree	slightly agree	slightly disagree	strongly disagree
13.	I would rather go to a library than a party.	strongly agree	slightly agree	slightly disagree	strongly disagree
14.	I find making up stories easy.	strongly agree	slightly agree	slightly disagree	strongly disagree
15.	I find myself drawn more strongly to people than to things.	strongly agree	slightly agree	slightly disagree	strongly disagree
16.	I tend to have very strong interests which I get upset about if I can't pursue.	strongly agree	slightly agree	slightly disagree	strongly disagree

17. I enjoy social chit-chat.	strongly agree	slightly agree	slightly disagree	strongly disagree
18. When I talk, it isn't always easy for others to get a word in edgewise.	strongly agree	slightly agree	slightly disagree	strongly disagree
19. I am fascinated by numbers.	strongly agree	slightly agree	slightly disagree	strongly disagree
20. When I'm reading a story, I find it difficult to work out the characters' intentions.	strongly agree	slightly agree	slightly disagree	strongly disagree
21. I don't particularly enjoy reading fiction.	strongly agree	slightly agree	slightly disagree	strongly disagree
22. I find it hard to make new friends.	strongly agree	slightly agree	slightly disagree	strongly disagree
23. I notice patterns in things all the time.	strongly agree	slightly agree	slightly disagree	strongly disagree
24. I would rather go to the theater than a museum.	strongly agree	slightly agree	slightly disagree	strongly disagree
25. It does not upset me if my daily routine is disturbed.	strongly agree	slightly agree	slightly disagree	strongly disagree
26. I frequently find that I don't know how to keep a conversation going.	strongly agree	slightly agree	slightly disagree	strongly disagree
27. I find it easy to "read between the lines" when someone is talking to me.	strongly agree	slightly agree	slightly disagree	strongly disagree

28. I usually concentrate more on the whole picture, rather than the small details.	strongly agree	slightly agree	slightly disagree	strongly disagree
29. I am not very good at re-membering phone numbers.	strongly agree	slightly agree	slightly disagree	strongly disagree
30. I don't usually notice small changes in a situation, or a person's appearance.	strongly agree	slightly agree	slightly disagree	strongly disagree
31. I know how to tell if some-one listening to me is get-ting bored.	strongly agree	slightly agree	slightly disagree	strongly disagree
32. I find it easy to do more than one thing at once.	strongly agree	slightly agree	slightly disagree	strongly disagree
33. When I talk on the phone, I'm not sure when it's my turn to speak.	strongly agree	slightly agree	slightly disagree	strongly disagree
34. I enjoy doing things sponta-neously.	strongly agree	slightly agree	slightly disagree	strongly disagree
35. I am often the last to under-stand the point of a joke.	strongly agree	slightly agree	slightly disagree	strongly disagree
36. I find it easy to work out what someone is thinking or feeling just by looking at their face.	strongly agree	slightly agree	slightly disagree	strongly disagree
37. If there is an interruption, I can switch back to what I was doing very quickly.	strongly agree	slightly agree	slightly disagree	strongly disagree

38.	I am good at social chit-chat.	strongly agree	slightly agree	slightly disagree	strongly disagree
39.	People often tell me that I keep going on and on about the same thing.	strongly agree	slightly agree	slightly disagree	strongly disagree
40.	When I was young, I used to enjoy playing games involving pretending with other children.	strongly agree	slightly agree	slightly disagree	strongly disagree
41.	I like to collect information about categories of things (e.g. types of car, types of bird, types of train, types of plant, etc.).	strongly agree	slightly agree	slightly disagree	strongly disagree
42.	I find it difficult to imagine what it would be like to be someone else.	strongly agree	slightly agree	slightly disagree	strongly disagree
43.	I like to plan any activities I participate in carefully.	strongly agree	slightly agree	slightly disagree	strongly disagree
44.	I enjoy social occasions.	strongly agree	slightly agree	slightly disagree	strongly disagree
45.	I find it difficult to work out people's intentions.	strongly agree	slightly agree	slightly disagree	strongly disagree
46.	New situations make me anxious.	strongly agree	slightly agree	slightly disagree	strongly disagree
47.	I enjoy meeting new people.	strongly agree	slightly agree	slightly disagree	strongly disagree

48. I am a good diplomat.	strongly agree	slightly agree	slightly disagree	strongly disagree

49. I am not very good at remembering people's dates of birth.	strongly agree	slightly agree	slightly disagree	strongly disagree

	strongly agree	slightly agree	slightly disagree	strongly disagree
50. I find it very easy to play games with children that involve pretending.				

How to Score Your AQ

Score one point for each of the following items if you answered "definitely agree" or "slightly agree": 2, 4, 5, 6, 7, 9, 12, 13, 16, 18, 19, 20, 21, 22, 23, 26, 33, 35, 39, 41, 42, 43, 45, 46.

Score one point for each of the following items if you answered "definitely disagree" or "slightly disagree": 1, 3, 8, 10, 11, 14, 15, 17, 24, 25, 27, 28, 29, 30, 31, 32, 34, 36, 37, 38, 40, 44, 47, 48, 49, 50.

Simply add up all the points you have scored and obtain your total AQ score.

How to Interpret Your AQ Score

- *0–10 = **low***
- *11–22 = **average** (most women score about 15, and most men score about 17)*
- *23–31 = **above average***
- *32–50 = **very high** (most people with Asperger Syndrome or high functioning autism score about 35)*
- *50 = **maximum***

If You Are Worried

None of the tests included in the Appendixes are diagnostic. If you have concerns that you might have AS or any other medical condition, and your concerns predate you filling out these tests, you should contact your GP or family doctor.

REFERENCES

Acknowledgments

1. Baron-Cohen and Hammer (1997b).
2. Baron-Cohen (1999).
3. Baron-Cohen (2002); Baron-Cohen, Wheelwright, Griffin *et al*.

Chapter 1
The Male and Female Brain

1. Kimura (1987).
2. Baron-Cohen (1995).
3. Greenblatt (1963).
4. Gray (1993).
5. Widener (1979).

Chapter 3
What Is Empathizing?

1. Baron-Cohen (1995).
2. *Mind Reading: the interactive guide to emotions*, Jessica Kingsley Publishers, London (2003). (*www.human-emotions.com*).
3. De Waal (2001).
4. *Ibid*.
5. Davis (1994); Wellman (1990).
6. Leslie (1987).

Chapter 4
The Female Brain as Empathizer

1. Lloyd and Smith (1986); Whiting and Edwards (1988).
2. Pitcher and Schultz (1983).

3. Charlesworth and Dzur (1987).

4. Maccoby and Jacklin (1974); Maccoby (1998); Maccoby (1966).

5. Crombie and Desjardins (1993); Crick and Ladd (1990); Cairns, Cairns, Neckerman et al. (1989); Howes (1988).

6. Dodge (1980); Dodge and Frame (1982); Dodge, Murphy and Buchsbaum (1984); Happe and Frith (1996).

7. Hoffman (1977); Zahn-Waxler, Radke-Yarrow, Wagner et al. (1992).

8. Baron-Cohen, O'Riordan, Jones et al. (1999); Bosacki (1998); Happe (1995).

9. Buck, Savin, Miller et al. (1972); Wagner, Buck and Winterbotham (1993); Hall (1978); Hall (1984); Rosenthal, Hall, DiMatteo et al. (1979).

10. Baron-Cohen, Wheelwright and Hill (2001); Baron-Cohen, Jolliffe, Mortimore et al. (1997).

11. De Waal (1993); Eibl-Eibesfeldt (1989); Ahlgren and Johnson (1979); Jarvinen and Bucgikksm (1996).

12. Knight, Fabes and Higgins (1989); Baumeister and Leary (1995); Willingham and Cole (1997).

13. Baron-Cohen and Wheelwright (in press); Wright (1998).

14. Ellis and Symons (1990); Buss et al. (1992).

15. Blair (1995); Independent, 12th July, 2003, p. 13.

16. Cairns, Cairns, Neckerman et al. (1989).

17. Crick and Wellman (1997); Crick, Casas and Mosher (1997); Crick and Grotpeter (1995).

18. Daly and Wilson (1988).

19. Daly and Wilson (1983).

20. Strayer (1980).

21. Savin-Williams (1987).

22. Borja-Alvarez, Zarbatany and Pepper (1991); Maccoby (1998).

23. Golombok and Fivush (1994); Benenson, Apostoleris and Parnass (1997).

24. Maccoby (1998); Maccoby (1998).

25. Sandberg and Meyer-Bahlburg (1994); Sutton-Smith, Rosenberg and Morgan (1963); Lever (1978).

26. Leaper (1991); Maccoby (1998).

27. Campbell (1995).

28. Maccoby (1990); Maltz and Borker (1983).

29. Maccoby (1966).

30. Smith (1985); Hartup, French, Laursen et al. (1993); Sheldon (1992); Miller, Danaher and Forbes (1986).

31. Leaper and Gleason (1996).

32. Tannen (1994); Tannen (1990).

33. Mannle and Tomasello (1987); Field (1978); Lamb, Frodi, Frodi et al. (1982); Power (1985); Huang (1986).

34. Haviland and Malatesta (1981); Garai and Scheinfeld (1968); Eibl-Eibesfeldt (1989); Goodenough (1957); McGuinness and Morley (1991); McGuinness and Symonds (1977).

35. Lutchmaya and Baron-Cohen (2002).

36. Connellan, Baron-Cohen, Wheelwright et al. (2001).

37. Hall (1978).

38. Baron-Cohen, Richler, Bisarya et al. (2003); Hoffman (1977); Davis (1994); Eisenberg and Lennon (1983).

39. Halpern (1988); Hunt, Lunneborg and Lewis (1975).

40. Huttonlocher, Haights, Bryk et al. (1991); Fagot (1978); Leaper (1991); Lutchmaya, Baron-Cohen and Raggatt (2002a); Denckla and Rudel (1974); DuBois (1939); Kimura (1999); Kimura, Saucier and Matuk (1996); Nicholson and Kimura (1996); Duggan (1950); McGuinness, Olson and Chapman (1990); Bleecker, Bolla-Wilson and Meyers (1988); Jensen and Reynolds (1983); Grossi, Orsini, Monetti et al. (1979); Stumpf and Jackson (1994); Kramer, Delis and Daniel (1988); Mann, Sasanuma, Sakuma et al. (1990).

41. Shaywitz, Shaywitz, Pugh et al. (1995); Frost, Binder, Springer et al. (1999); Pugh, Shaywitz, Shaywitz et al. (1996); Pugh, Fletcher, Skudlarski et al. (1997).

42. Feingold (1988).

43. Willingham and Cole (1997); Hedges and Nowell (1995).

Chapter 5
What Is Systemizing?

1. Premack (1995).

2. Baron-Cohen, Wheelwright, Griffin et al. (2002); Myers, Baron-Cohen and Wheelwright (2003).

Chapter 6
The Male Brain as Systemizer

1. Christie and Johnsen (1987); Jennings (1977); Rubin, Fein and Vandenberg (1983); Garai and Scheinfeld (1968); Hutt (1972); Eibl-Eibesfeldt (1989).

2. Connellan, Baron-Cohen, Wheelwright et al. (2001); Lutchmaya and Baron-Cohen (2002).

3. Daly and Wilson (1983).

4. McGuinness and Symonds (1977).

5. *Times Higher*, 3 December 1999, p.32.

6. Vetter (1979); Mitchell (1999).

7. Benbow (1988); Benbow and Stanley (1983); Kolata (1980); Benditt (1994); "Biennial survey of the National Science Foundation" (1991); Brush (1991); Lubinski and Benbow (1992).

8. Lawson, Baron-Cohen and Wheelwright (in press).

9. Hyde, Fennema and Lamon (1990); Hyde, Geiringer and Yen (1975); Kimball (1989); Mills, Ablard and Stumpf (1993); Wentzel (1988); Kimura (1999).

10. *NAE 1989 almanac of higher education* (1989); Geary (1996); Geary, Saults, Liu *et al.* (2000); Engelhard (1990); Lummis and Stevenson (1990).

11. Stanley (1990); Hausman (unpublished Ph.D. dissertation).

12. Kalichman (1989); Thomas, Jamison and Hummel (1973); Wittig and Allen (1984); De Lisi, Parameswaran and McGillicuddy-De Lisi (1989); Robert and Chaperon (1989); Piaget and Inhelder (1956); Robert and Ohlmann (1994).

13. Witkin, Dyk, Faterson *et al.* (1962); McGee (1979).

14. Witkin, Dyk, Faterson *et al.* (1962); Elliot (1961); Sherman (1967).

15. Linn and Petersen (1985); Voyer, Voyer and Bryden (1995); Cohen and Gelber (1975); McGuinness and Morley (1991); Geary (1998); Velle (1987).

16. Mayes and Jahoda (1988); Collins and Kimura (1997); Mann, Sasanuma, Sakuma *et al.* (1990); Linn and Petersen (1985); Pearson and Ferguson (1989); Shephard and Metzler (1971); Sanders, Soares and D'Aguila (1982); Rosser, Ensing, Glider *et al.* (1984); Delgado and Prieto (1997); Halpern (1992); Johnson and Meade (1987); Masters and Sanders (1993); Vandenberg and Kuse (1978); Geary (1995).

17. Galea and Kimura (1993); Beatty and Troster (1987); Maccoby (1966); Silverman and Eals (1992); Matthews (1987); Matthews (1992); Just and Carpenter (1985).

18. Silverman and Eals (1992); Herlitz, Nilsson and Backman (1997); Collins and Kimura (1997); Stumpf and Eliot (1995); James and Kimura (1997).

19. Holding and Holding (1989); Miller and Santoni (1986); Dabbs, Chang, Strong *et al.* (1998).

20. Willis and Schaie (1988); Robert and Tanguay (1990); Kerns and Berenbaum (1991); Johnson and Meade (1987); McGuinness and Morley (1991); Kimura (1999).

21. Rammsayer and Lustnauer (1989); Schiff and Oldak (1990); Smith and McPhee (1987); Law, Pellegrino and Hunt (1993).

22. Watson and Kimura (1991); Nicholson and Kimura (1996); Thomas and French (1985); Jardine and Martin (1983); Kolakowski and Malina (1974).

23. Atran (1994); Berlin, Boster and O'Neill (1981).

24. *Guardian*, 30 November 1999, p.7.

25. Baron-Cohen, Richler, Bisarya *et al.* (2003).

26. Connellan, Baron-Cohen, Wheelwright *et al.* (2001); Cohen and Gelber (1975).

27. Lutchmaya and Baron-Cohen (2002).

Chapter 7
Culture

1. Connellan, Baron-Cohen, Wheelwright *et al.* (2001).

2. Condry and Condry (1976); Stern and Karraker (1989); Seavey, Katz and Zalk (1975); Sidorowicz and Lunney (1980).

3. Whiting and Edwards (1988).

4. Snow, Jacklin and Maccoby (1983); Block (1978).

5. Haviland and Malatesta (1981); Tronick and Cohn (1989); Maccoby and Jacklin (1974); Maccoby, Snow and Jacklin (1984); Lytton and Romney (1991); Huston (ed.) (1983).

6. Dunn, Bretherton and Munn (1987); Langlois and Downs (1980); Russell and Russell (1987); Fivush (1989).

7. Perry, White and Perry (1984).

8. Maccoby (1998); Perry and Bussey (1979); Barkley, Ullman, Otto *et al.* (1977).

9. Geary (1998).

10. Pratto (1996); Eagly (1987); Valian (1999).

11. Daly and Wilson (1983); Whitten (1987); Andersson (1994).

Chapter 8
Biology

1. De Waal (2001); Povinelli (2000).

2. Meaney, Stewart and Beatty (1985); Lovejoy and Wallen (1988).

3. Watson (2001).

4. Bixo, Backstrom, Winblad *et al.* (1995); Michael and Zumpe (1998).

5. Geschwind and Galaburda (1987); Geschwind and Galaburda (1985); Martino and Winner (1995); McManus and Bryden (1991); Bryden, McManus and Bulman-Fleming (1994).

6. Reinisch (1981).

7. Reinisch and Saunders (1984); Reinisch (1977); Saunders and Reinisch (1985); Stern (1989); Goy, Bercovitch and McBrair (1988).

8. Van Goozen, Cohen-Kettenis, Gooren *et al.* (1995).

9. Lutchmaya, Baron-Cohen and Raggatt (2002a); Lutchmaya, Baron-Cohen, and Raggatt (2002b); Finegan, Niccols and Sitarenios (1992).

10. Knickmeyer, Baron-Cohen and Raggatt (unpublished MS).

11. Diamond, Dowling and Johnson (1981); De Lacoste-Utamsin and Holloway (1982).

12. Williams, Barnett and Meck (1990).

13. Janowsky, Oviatt and Orwoll (1994).

14. Gouchie and Kimura (1991); Hampson (1990); Hampson, Rovet and Altmann (1998); Resnick, Berenbaum, Gottesman et al. (1986); Shute, Pellegrino, Hubert et al. (1983); Grimshaw, Sitarenios and Finegan (1995).

15. Hier and Crowley (1982).

16. Masica, Money, Erhardt et al. (1968).

17. Hines and Kaufman (1994); Collaer and Hines (1995); Berenbaum and Snyder (1995).

18. Van Goozen, Cohen-Kettenis, Gooren et al. (1995).

19. Shucard, Shucard and Thomas (1987); Lutchmaya, Baron-Cohen and Raggatt (2002a).

20. Kimura (1966); Kimura (1961).

21. McGlone (1980).

22. Kimura and Harshman (1984); Lake and Bryden (1976); Weekes, Zaidel and Zaidel (1995); Basso, Capitani and Moraschini (1982); Pizzamiglio and Mammucari (1985).

23. McGlone and Fox (1982).

24. Geschwind and Galaburda (1985); Levy and Levy (1978); Chang, Hsu, Chan et al. (1960); Kimura (1994).

25. Holt (1968).

26. Kimura (1994); Sanders, Aubert and Kadam (1995).

27. Kimura and Carson (1995); Everhart, Shucard, Quatrin et al. (2001).

28. Cabeza and Nyberg (1997); Gur, Mozley, Mozley et al. (1995); Maguire, Frackowiak and Frith (1997).

29. Witelson (1976).

30. Kimura (1996); George, Ketter, Parekh et al. (1996).

31. Hines (1982).

32. Kimball (1989); Peterson and Lansky (1974); Peterson (1978); Benbow (1986); Benbow and Lubinski (1992).

33. Tanner (1970); Tanner (1990); Bayley (1965).

34. Fitch and Denenberg (1995).

35. Brothers (1990).

36. Le Doux (2000); Garavan, Pendergrass, Ross et al. (2001); Fine and Blair

(2000); MacLusky and Naftolin (1981); Baron-Cohen, Ring, Wheelwright et al. (1999); Meaney and McEwen (1986); Killgore, Oki and Yurgelun-Todd (2001); Vinader-Caerols, Collado, Segovia et al. (2000); Rasia-Filho, Londero and Achaval (1999); Cooke, Tabibnia and Breedlove (1999); Stefanova (1998); Siddiqui and Shah (1997); Hines, Allen and Gorski (1992); Wolterink, Daenen, Dubbeldam et al. (2001).

37. Goel, Graffman, Sadato et al. (1995); Happe, Ehlers, Fletcher et al. (1996); Fletcher, Happe, Frith et al. (1995); Baron-Cohen, Ring, Moriarty et al. (1994); Stone, Baron-Cohen and Knight (1999); Rowe, Bullock, Polkey et al. (2001); Eslinger and Damasio (1985); Adolphs (2001); Farrow, Zheng, Wilkinson et al. (2001).

38. Baron-Cohen, Ring, Wheelwright et al. (1999); Perrett, Smith, Potter et al. (1985).

39. Hines (1992); Aboitiz, Scheibel, Fisher et al. (1992); Bishop and Wahlsten (1997); Allen and Gorski (1991); Allen, Richey, Chai et al. (1991); Allen, Hines, Shryne et al. (1989); De Lacoste-Utamsin and Holloway (1982); Dreisen and Raz (1995); Holloway, Anderson, Defendini et al. (1993); Witelson (1985); Witelson (1989); Bleier, Houston and Byne (1986).

40. Kochanska, Murray, Jacques et al. (1996); Diamond (1985); Diamond (1988).

41. Ankney (1992); Pakkenberg and Gundersen (1997).

42. Jancke, Schlaug, Huang et al. (1994).

43. Lucas, Lombardino, Roper et al. (1996); Sherry, Vaccarino, Buckenham et al. (1989); Sherry, Jacobs and Gaulin (1992); Roof and Havens (1992).

44. Jacobson, Csernus, Shryne et al. (1981); Allen and Gorski (1991); Swaab and Hofman (1995); LeVay (1991).

45. Maxson (1997).

46. Skuse, James, Bisop et al. (1997); Skuse (2000).

47. Hughes and Cutting (1999); Scourfield, Martin, Lewis et al. (1999); Matthews, Batson, Horn et al. (1981); Rushton, Fulker, Neale et al. (1986).

48. DeFries, Vandenberg and McClearn (1976); Butterworth (1999); Lewis, Hitch and Walker (1994).

49. Darwin (1871).

Chapter 9
Evolution of the Male and Female Brain

1. Gaulin (1995); Buss (1995); Symons (1979).
2. Mithen (1996).

3. Keely (1996); Tanner (1970); Thomas and French (1985).

4. McBurney, Gaulin, Devineni et al. (1997); Eals and Silverman (1994).

5. Tooby and Cosmides (1990).

6. Betzig (1986); Casimir and Rao (1995).

7. Hrdy (1997); Altmann, Alberts, Haines et al. (1996); Andersson (1994); Chagnon (1979); Irons (1979).

8. Erwin, Gur, Gur et al. (1992); Rosenthal, Hall, DiMatteo et al. (1979); Rotter and Rotter (1988); Wagner, Buck and Winterbotham (1993); Dimberg and Ohman (1996).

9. Betzig (1986); Mealey (1995); Chagnon (1979); Keely (1996).

10. Betzig (1981); Flinn and Low (1986).

11. Chagnon (1979).

12. Betzig (1993).

13. Hill and Hurtado (1996); Knauft (1987); Daly and Wilson (1988); Chagnon (1988).

14. Tucker, Friedman, Schwartz et al. (1997).

15. Bowlby (1969); Harlow and Harlow (1962).

16. MacLean (1985).

17. De Waal (2002); Cheyney and Seyfarth (1992).

18. Foley and Lee (1989); Hartup and Stevens (1997).

Chapter 10
Autism: The Extreme Male Brain

1. APA (1994).

2. Rutter (1978).

3. Baron-Cohen and Bolton (1993); Wing (1976); Frith (1989).

4. Attwood (1999); Gillberg (1991); Wing (1981a); Wing (1988); Frith (1991); Sainsbury (2000); Ozonoff, South and Miller (2001).

5. Folstein and Rutter (1988); Bailey, Bolton and Rutter (1998); Bailey, Le Couteur, Gottesman et al. (1995); Tsai and Beisler (1983); Wing (1981b); Szatmari (1999); Tsai, Stewart and August (1981); Lord and Schopler (1985).

6. Baron-Cohen, Ring, Wheelwright et al. (1999); Abell, Krams, Ashburner et al. (1999); Baron-Cohen, Ring, Bullmore et al. (2000); Baumann and Kemper (1988); Howard, Cowell, Boucher et al. (2000).

7. Baron-Cohen (1995); Baron-Cohen, Jolliffe, Mortimore et al. (1997); Baron-Cohen, Wheelwright and Hill (2001); Baron-Cohen, Leslie and Frith (1985); Baron-Cohen, Wheelwright, Stone et al. (1999); Baron-Cohen, Richler, Bisarya et al. (2003); Happe (1994).

8. Baron-Cohen and Wheelwright (1999); Baron-Cohen, Wheelwright, Stone, et al. (1999); Baron-Cohen, Wheelwright, Scahill et al. (2001); O'Riordan, Plaisted, Driver et al. (2001); Plaisted, O'Riordan and Baron-Cohen (1998a); Scheuffgen, Happe, Anderson et al. (2000); Plaisted, O'Riordan and Baron-Cohen (1998b); Shah and Frith (1983); Shah and Frith (1993); Happe (1996).

9. Willey (1999).

10. Sainsbury (2000).

11. Myers, Baron-Cohen and Wheelwright (2003).

12. Howlin (2001); Tantam (2001).

13. Asperger (1944).

14. Baron-Cohen and Hammer (1997b).

15. Baron-Cohen and Hammer (1997b); Baron-Cohen, Wheelwright, Stone et al. (1999); Baron-Cohen (2000); Baron-Cohen and Wheelwright (2002); Baron-Cohen, Richler, et al. (2003); Baron-Cohen, Jolliffe, Mortimore et al. (1997); Baron-Cohen, Wheelwright and Hill (2001); Baron-Cohen, Wheelwright and Jolliffe (1997); Lutchmaya, Baron-Cohen and Raggatt (2002b); Swettenham et al. (1998); Phillips et al.(1992); Lutchmaya, Baron-Cohen and Raggatt (2002a); ICD–10 (1994); Baron-Cohen (1988); Surian et al. (1996); Baron-Cohen, O'Riordan, Jones et al. (1999).

16. Baron-Cohen, Richler, Bisarya et al. (2003).

17. Baron-Cohen, Jolliffe, Mortimore et al. (1997); Baron-Cohen, Wheelwright and Hill (2001); Baron-Cohen, Wheelwright and Jolliffe (1997).

18. Lutchmaya, Baron-Cohen and Raggatt (2002b); Swettenham et al. (1998); Phillips et al. (1992).

19. Lutchmaya, Baron-Cohen and Raggatt (2002a); ICD–10 (1994).

20. Baron-Cohen (1988); Surian et al. (1996).

21. Baron-Cohen, O'Riordan, Jones et al. (1999).

22. Baron-Cohen, Jolliffe, Mortimore et al. (1997); Happe (1995); Charman, Ruffman and Clements (1999).

23. Baron-Cohen and Wheelwright (in press).

24. Baron-Cohen, Wheelwright, Scahill et al. (2001); Lawson, Baron-Cohen and Wheelwright (in press).

25. Baron-Cohen, Richler, Bisarya et al. (2003).

26. Jolliffe and Baron-Cohen (1997).

27. O'Riordan et al. (2001); Plaisted, O'Riordan and Baron-Cohen (1998a); Plaisted, O'Riordan and Baron-Cohen (1998b).

28. Baron-Cohen, Wheelwright, Skinner et al. (2001).

29. Manning, Baron-Cohen, Wheelwright et al. (2001).

30. Knickmeyer, Baron-Cohen and Wheelwright (unpublished MS).

31. Tordjman, Ferrari, Sulmont *et al.* (1997).

32. Baron-Cohen, Wheelwright, Stott *et al.* (1997).

33. Baron-Cohen, Bolton, Wheelwright *et al.* (1998); Baron-Cohen and Hammer (1997a).

Chapter 11: A Professor of Mathematics

1. Baron-Cohen, Wheelwright, Stone *et al.* (1999).

2. Harris *et al.* (1989); Baron-Cohen (1991).

3. *Guardian*, 31 August 1998, p.5.

4. APA (1994); Baron-Cohen, Allen and Gillberg (1992); Baron-Cohen, Wheelwright, Cox *et al.* (2000).

5. Caddes (1986); Blyth (1994).

6. Wilson and Jackson (1994).

7. *Times Higher*, 24 April 1998, p.19.

8. Hovis and Kragh (1993).

9. Chadwick (1990).

10. BBC4, 22 July 2002: *A very English genius*.

Chapter 12: The Extreme Female Brain: Back to the Future

1. Fonagy (1989).

2. Tager-Flusberg and Sullivan (2000); Karmiloff-Smith, Grant, Belluji *et al.* (1995).

3. Donovan (1997).

4. Russell (ed.) (1997).

5. Mackintosh (1998).

6. Frith (1989); Frith and Happe (1994); Happe (1996a); Happe (1997).

7. Dawson, Warrenburg and Fuller (1982); Chiron, Leboyer, Leon *et al.* (1995).

8. Bailey, Bolton, Rutter *et al.* (1998).

9. Lutchmaya, Baron-Cohen and Raggatt (2002a); Lutchmaya, Baron-Cohen and Raggatt (2002b).

10. Robertson (1999).

11. Willey (1999).

Appendix 1

1. Baron-Cohen, Wheelwright and Hill (2001). A child version of this test is also available; see Baron-Cohen, Wheelwright, Scahill *et al.* (2001).

Appendix 2

1. Baron-Cohen, Richler, Bisarya *et al*. (2003).

Appendix 3

1. Baron-Cohen, Richler, Bisarya *et al*. (2003).

Appendix 4

1. Baron-Cohen, Wheelwright, Skinner, *et al.* (2001).

BIBLIOGRAPHY

Abell, F., Krams, M., Ashburner, J., Passingham, R., Friston, K., Frackowiak, R., Happe, F., Frith, C. and Frith, U. (1999), "The neuroanatomy of autism: a voxel-based whole brain analysis of structural scans," *Cognitive Neuroscience* 10, pp. 1647–51.

Aboitiz, F., Scheibel, A.B., Fisher, R.S. and Zaidel, E. (1992), "Fiber composition of the human corpus callosum," *Brain Research* 598, pp. 143–53.

Adolphs, R. (2001), "The neurobiology of social cognition," *Current Opinions in Neurobiology* 11, pp. 231–9.

Ahlgren, A. and Johnson, D.W. (1979), "Sex differences in cooperative and competitive attitudes from the 2nd to the 12th grades," *Developmental Psychology* 15, pp. 45–9.

Allen, L.S. and Gorski, R.A. (1991), "Sexual dimorphism of the anterior commissure and massa intermedia of the human brain," *Journal of Comparative Neurology* 312, pp. 97–104.

Allen, L.S., Hines, M., Shryne, J.E. and Gorski, R.A. (1989), "Two sexually dimorphic cell groups in the human brain," *Journal of Neuroscience* 9, pp. 497–506.

Allen, L.S., Richey, M.F., Chai, Y.M. and Gorski, R.A. (1991), "Sex differences in the corpus callosum of the living human being," *Journal of Neuroscience* 11, pp.933–42.

Altmann, J., Alberts, S.C., Haines, S.A., Dubach, J., Muruthi, P., Coote, T. and Andersson, M. (1994), *Sexual Selection*, Princeton University Press.

Ankney, C.D. (1992), "Sex differences in relative brain size: the mismeasure of woman, too?" *Intelligence* 16, pp.329–36.

APA (1994), *DSM-IV Diagnostic and Statistical Manual of Mental Disorders*, 4th edn, Washington DC, American Psychiatric Association.

Asperger, H. (1944), "Die 'Autistischen Psychopathen' im Kindesalter," *Archiv für Psychiatrie und Nervenkrankheiten* 117, pp.76–136.

Atran, S. (1994), "Core domains versus scientific theories: evidence from systematics and Itza-Maya folkbiology" in L.A. Hirschfeld and S.A. Gelman (eds.), *Map-*

ping the Mind: Domain Specificity in Cognition and Culture, New York, Cambridge University Press.

Attwood, A. (1999), Asperger Syndrome, London, Jessica Kingsley Publishers.

Bailey, A., Bolton, P., Rutter, M. and the International Molecular Genetic Consortium (1998), "A full genome screen for autism with evidence for linkage to a region on chromosome 7q," Human Molecular Genetics 7, pp.571–8.

Bailey, T., Le Couteur, A., Gottesman, I., Bolton, P., Simonoff, E., Yuzda, E. and Rutter, M. (1995), "Autism as a strongly genetic disorder: evidence from a British twin study," Psychological Medicine 25, pp.63–77.

Barkley, A., Ullman, G., Otto, L. and Brecht, M. (1977), "The effects of sex-typing and sex-appropriateness of modeled behavior on children's imitation," Child Development 48, pp.721–5.

Baron-Cohen, S. (1988), "Social and pragmatic deficits in autism: cognitive or affective?" Journal of Autism and Developmental Disorders 18, pp.379–402.

_____(1991), "Do people with autism understand what causes emotion?" Child Development 62, pp.385–95.

_____(1995), Mindblindness: An Essay on Autism and Theory of Mind, Cambridge, Mass., MIT Press/Bradford Books.

_____(1999), "The extreme male brain theory of autism" in H. Tager-Flusberg (ed.), Neurodevelopmental Disorders, Cambridge, Mass., MIT Press.

_____(2000), "The cognitive neuroscience of autism: implications for the evolution of the male brain" in M. Gazzaniga (ed.), The Cognitive Neurosciences, 2nd edn, Cambridge, Mass., MIT Press.

_____(2002), "The extreme male brain theory of autism," Trends in Cognitive Sciences 6, pp.248–54.

Baron-Cohen, S., Allen, J. and Gillberg, C. (1992), "Can autism be detected at 18 months? The needle, the haystack, and the CHAT," British Journal of Psychiatry 161, pp.839–43.

Baron-Cohen, S. and Bolton, P. (1993), Autism: The Facts, Oxford University Press.

Baron-Cohen, S., Bolton, P., Wheelwright, S., Scahill, V., Short, L., Mead, G. and Smith, A. (1998), "Does autism occur more often in families of physicists, engineers, and mathematicians?," Autism 2, pp.296–301.

Baron-Cohen, S. and Hammer, J. (1997a), "Parents of children with Asperger Syndrome: what is the broader phenotype?," Journal of Cognitive Neuroscience 9, pp.548–54.

_____(1997b), "Is autism an extreme form of the male brain?," Advances in Infancy Research 11, pp.193–217.

Baron-Cohen, S., Jolliffe, T., Mortimore, C. and Robertson, M. (1997), "Another advanced test of theory of mind: evidence from very high functioning adults with autism or Asperger Syndrome," *Journal of Child Psychology and Psychiatry* 38, pp.813–22.

Baron-Cohen, S., Leslie, A.M. and Frith, U., "Does the autistic child have a 'theory of mind?'" *Cognition* 21, pp.37–46.

Baron-Cohen, S., O'Riordan, M., Jones, R., Stone, V. and Plaisted, K. (1999), "Recognition of faux pas by normally developing children and children with Asperger Syndrome or high-functioning autism," *Journal of Autism and Developmental Disorders* 29, pp.407–18.

Baron-Cohen, S., Richler, J., Bisarya, D., Gurunathan, N. and Wheelwright, S. (2003), "The systemising quotient (SQ): an investigation of adults with Asperger Syndrome or high-functioning autism, and normal sex differences," *Philosophical Transactions of the Royal Society, Series B*, special issue on "Autism: Mind and Brain," 358, (1430), 361–740.

Baron-Cohen, S., Ring, H., Bullmore, E., Wheelwright, S., Ashwin, C. and Williams, S. (2000), "The amygdala theory of autism," *Neuroscience and Behavioural Reviews* 24, pp.355–64.

Baron-Cohen, S., Ring, H., Moriarty, J., Schmitz, B., Costa, D. and Ell, P. (1994), "Recognition of mental state terms: a clinical study of autism, and a functional neuroimaging study of normal adults," *British Journal of Psychiatry* 165, pp.640–49.

Baron-Cohen, S., Ring, H., Wheelwright, S., Bullmore, E., Brammer, M., Simmons, A. and Williams, S. (1999), "Social intelligence in the normal and autistic brain: an fMRI study," *European Journal of Neuroscience* 11, pp.1891–8.

Baron-Cohen, S. and Wheelwright, S. (1999), "Obsessions in children with autism or Asperger Syndrome: a content analysis in terms of core domains of cognition," *British Journal of Psychiatry* 175, pp.484–90.

_____(in press), "The friendship and relationship questionnaire (FQ): An investigation of adults with Asperger syndrome or high-functioning autism, and normal sex differences," *Journal of Autism and Developmental Disorders.*

Baron-Cohen, S., Wheelwright, S., Cox, A., Baird, G., Charman, T., Swettenham, J., Drew, A. and Doehring, P. (2000), "The early identification of autism: the checklist for autism in toddlers (CHAT)," *Journal of the Royal Society of Medicine* 93, pp.521–5.

Baron-Cohen, S., Wheelwright, S., Griffin, R., Lawson, J. and Hill, J. (2002) "The exact mind: empathising and systemising in autism spectrum conditions," in U. Goswami (ed.), *Handbook of Cognitive Development*, Oxford, Blackwell.

Baron-Cohen, S., Wheelwright, S. and Hill, J. (2001) "The 'reading the mind in the eyes' test, revised version: a study with normal adults, and adults with

Asperger Syndrome or high-functioning autism," *Journal of Child Psychology and Psychiatry* 42, pp.241–52.

Baron-Cohen, S., Wheelwright, S. and Jolliffe, T. (1997), "Is there a "language of the eyes"? Evidence from normal adults and adults with autism or Asperger Syndrome," *Visual Cognition* 4, pp.311–31.

Baron-Cohen, S., Wheelwright, S., Scahill, V., Spong, A. and Lawson, J. (2001), "Are intuitive physics and intuitive psychology independent? A test with children with Asperger Syndrome," *Journal of Developmental and Learning Disorders* 5, pp.47–78.

Baron-Cohen, S., Wheelwright, S., Skinner, R., Martin, J. and Clubley, E. (2001), "The autism-spectrum quotient (AQ): evidence from Asperger Syndrome or high-functioning autism, males and females, scientists and mathematicians," *Journal of Autism and Developmental Disorders* 31, pp.5–17.

Baron-Cohen, S., Wheelwright, S., Stone, V. and Rutherford, M. (1999), "A mathematician, a physicist, and a computer scientist with Asperger Syndrome: performance on folk psychology and folk physics test," *Neurocase* 5, pp.475–83.

Baron-Cohen, S., Wheelwright, S., Stott, C., Bolton, P. and Goodyer, I. (1997), "Is there a link between engineering and autism?" *Autism* 1, pp.101–8.

Basso, A., Capitani, E. and Moraschini, S. (1982), "Sex differences in recovery from aphasia," *Cortex* 18, pp.469–75.

Bauman, M. and Kemper, T. (1988) "Limbic and cerebellar abnormalities: consistent findings in infantile autism," *Journal of Neuropathology and Experimental Neurology* 47, p.369.

Baumeister, R.F. and Leary, M.R. (1995), "The need to belong: desire for interpersonal attachments as a fundamental human motivation," *Psychological Bulletin* 117, pp.497–529.

Bayley, N. (1965), "Comparisons of mental and motor test scores for ages 1–15 months by sex, birth order, race, geographical location, and education of parents," *Child Development* 36, pp.380–411.

Beatty, W.W. and Troster, A.I. (1987), "Gender differences in geographical knowledge," *Sex Roles* 16, pp.565–90.

Benbow, C. (1986), "Physiological correlates of extreme intellectual precocity," *Neuropsychologia* 24, pp.719–25.

———(1988), "Sex differences in mathematical reasoning ability in intellectually talented preadolescents: their nature, effects, and possible causes," *Behavioral and Brain Sciences* 11, pp.169–232.

Benbow, C. and Lubinski, D. (1992), "Psychological profiles of the mathematically talented: some sex differences and evidence supporting their biological basis" in *Origins and Development of High Ability*, CIBA Foundation Symposium, New York, John Wiley & Sons Inc.

Benbow, C. and Stanley, J. (1983), "Sex differences in mathematical reasoning ability: more facts," *Science* 222, pp.1029–31.

Benditt, J. (1994), "Women in science. Comparisons across cultures," *Science* 263, pp.1391–1496.

Benenson, J.F., Apostoleris, N.H. and Parnass, J. (1997), "Age and sex differences in dyadic and group interaction," *Developmental Psychology* 33, pp.538–43.

Berenbaum, S.A. and Snyder, E. (1995), "Early hormonal influences on childhood sex-typed activity and playmate preferences: implications for the development of sexual orientation," *Developmental Psychology* 31, pp.31–42.

Berlin, B., Boster, J.S. and O"Neill, J.P. (1981), "The perceptual bases of ethnobiological classification: evidence from Aguaruna Jívaro ornithology," *Journal of Ethnobiology* 1, pp.95–108.

Betzig, L. (1986), *Despotism and Differential Reproduction: A Darwinian View of History*, New York, Aldine de Gruyter.

——(1981), "Medieval monogamy," *Journal of Family History* 20, pp.181–216.

——(1993), "Sex, succession, and stratification in the first six civilizations: how powerful men reproduced, passed power on to their sons, and used power to defend their wealth, women, and children" in L. Ellis (ed.), *Social Stratification and Socioeconomic Inequality: A Comparative Biosocial Analysis*, vol. 1, Westport, Conn., Praeger.

"Biennial survey of the National Science Foundation" (1991), *Science* 252, pp.1112–17.

Bishop, K.M. and Wahlsten, D. (1997), "Sex differences in the human corpus callosum: myth or reality?," *Neuroscience and Biobehavioral Reviews* 21, pp.581–601.

Bixo, M., Backstrom, T., Winblad, B. and Andersson, A., "Estradiol and testosterone in specific regions of the human female brain in different endocrine states," *Journal of Steroid Biochemistry & Molecular Biology* 55, pp.297–303.

Blair, R.J. (1995), "A cognitive developmental approach to morality: investigating the psychopath," *Cognition* 57, pp.1–29.

Bleecker, M.L., Bolla-Wilson, K. and Meyers, D.A. (1988), "Age-related sex differences in verbal memory," *Journal of Clinical Psychology* 44, pp.403–11.

Bleier, R., Houston, L. and Byne, W. (1986), "Can the corpus callosum predict gender, age, handedness, or cognitive differences?" *Trends in Neuroscience*, September, pp.391–4.

Block, J.H. (1978), "Another look at sex differentiation in the socialization behaviors of mothers and fathers" in J. Sherman and F.L. Denmark (eds.), *The Psychology of Women: Future Directions of Research*, New York, Psychological Dimensions.

Blyth, J. (1994), "Our jobs and our super-extended phenotypes," *Journal of Social and Evolutionary Systems* 17, pp.1–8.

Borja-Alvarez, Zarbatany T.L. and Pepper, S. (1991), "Contributions of male and female guests and hosts to peer group entry," *Child Development* 62, pp.1079–90.

Bosacki, S. (unpublished Ph.D. dissertation), "Theory of mind in preadolescents: relationships among social understanding, self-concept and social relations," University of Toronto.

Bowlby, J. (1969), *Attachment*, London, The Hogarth Press.

Brothers, L. (1990), "The social brain: a project for integrating primate behaviour and neurophysiology in a new domain," *Concepts in Neuroscience* 1, pp.27–51.

Brush, S.G. (1991), "Women in science and engineering," *American Scientist* 79, pp.404–19.

Bryden, M., McManus, I. and Bulman-Fleming, M. (1994), "Evaluating the empirical support for the Geschwind-Behan-Galaburda model of cerebral lateralization," *Brain and Cognition* 26, pp.103–67.

Buck, R.W., Savin, V.J., Miller, R.E. and Caul, W.F. (1972), "Communication of affect through facial expression in humans," *Journal of Personality and Social Psychology* 23, pp.362–71.

Buss, D.M. (1995), "Psychological sex differences," *American Psychologist* 50, pp.164–8.

Buss, D.M., Larsen, R.J., Westen, D. and Semmelroth, J. (1992), "Sex differences in jealousy: evolution, physiology, and psychology," *Psychological Science* 3, pp.251–5.

Butterworth, B. (1999), *The Mathematical Brain*, London, Macmillan.

Cabeza, R. and Nyberg, L. (1997), "Imaging cognition: an empirical review of PET studies with normal subjects," *Journal of Cognitive Neuroscience* 9, pp.1–26.

Caddes, C. (1986), *Portraits of Success*, Palo Alto, Ca., Tioga Press.

Cairns, R.B., Cairns, B.D., Neckerman, H.J., Ferguson, L.L. and Gariepy, J. (1989), "Growth and aggression: 1. Childhood to early adolescence," *Developmental Psychology* 25, pp.320–33.

Campbell, A. (1995), "A few good men: evolutionary psychology and female adolescent aggression," *Ethology and Sociobiology* 16, pp.99–123.

Casimir, M.J. and Rao, A. (1995), "Prestige, possessions, and progeny: cultural goals and reproductive success among the Bakkarwal," *Human Nature* 6, pp.241–72.

Chadwick, J. (1990), *The Decipherment of Linear B*, Cambridge, Cambridge University Press.

Chagnon, N.A. (1979), "Is reproductive success equal in egalitarian societies?" in N.A. Chagnon, and W. Irons (eds.), *Evolutionary Biology and Human Social Behavior: An Anthropological Perspective*, North Scituate, Mass., Duxbury Press.

———(1988), "Life histories, blood revenge, and warfare in a tribal population," *Science* 239, pp.985–92.

Chang, K.S.F., Hsu, F.K., Chan, S.T. and Chan, Y.B. (1960), "Scrotal asymmetry and handedness," *Journal of Anatomy* 94, pp.543–8.

Charlesworth, W.R. and Dzur, C. (1987), "Gender comparisons of preschoolers' behavior and resource utilization in group problem-solving," *Child Development* 58, pp.191–200.

Charman, T., Ruffman, T. and Clements, W. (2002), "Is there a gender difference in false belief?," *Social Development* 11, pp.1–10.

Cheyney, D. and Seyfarth, R. (1992), *How Monkeys See the World: Inside the Mind of Another Species*, Chicago, University of Chicago Press.

Chiron, C., Leboyer, M., Leon, F., Jambaque, I., Nuttin, C. and Syrota, A. (1995), "SPECT of the brain in childhood autism: evidence for a lack of normal hemispheric asymmetry," *Developmental Medicine and Childhood Neurology* 37, pp.849–60.

Christie, J.F. and Johnsen, E.P. (1987), "Reconceptualizing constructive play: a review of the empirical literature," *Merrill-Palmer Quarterly* 33, pp.439–52.

Cohen, L.B. and Gelber, E.R. (1975), "Infant visual memory" in L.B. Cohen and P. Salapatek (eds.), *Infant Perception: From Sensation to Cognition*, New York, Academic Press.

Collaer, M. and Hines, M. (1995), "Human behavioural sex differences: a role for gonadal hormones during early development?" *Psychological Bulletin* 118, pp.55–107.

Collins, D.W. and Kimura, D. (1997), "A large sex difference on a two-dimensional mental rotation task," *Behavioral Neuroscience* 111, pp.845–9.

Condry, J. and Condry, S. (1976), "Sex differences: a study in the eye of the beholder," *Child Development* 47, pp.812–19.

Connellan, J., Baron-Cohen, S., Wheelwright, S., Ba'tki, A. and Ahluwalia, J. (2001), "Sex differences in human neonatal social perception," *Infant Behavior and Development* 23, pp.113–18.

Cooke, B., Tabibnia, G. and Breedlove, S. (1999), "A brain sexual dimorphism controlled by adult circulating androgens," *Proceeding of the National Academy of Sciences* (USA) 96, pp.7538–40.

Cosmides, L. (1989), "The logic of social exchange: has natural selection shaped how humans reason? Studies with the Wason selection task," *Cognition* 31, pp.187–276.

Crick, N.R., Casas, J.F. and Mosher, M. (1997), "Relational and overt aggression in pre-school," *Developmental Psychology* 33, pp.579–88.

Crick, N.R. and Grotpeter, J.K. (1995), "Relational aggression, gender, and social-psychological adjustment," *Child Development* 66, pp.710–22.

Crick, N.R. and Ladd, G.W. (1990), "Children's perceptions of the outcomes of social strategies: do the ends justify being mean?" *Developmental Psychology* 26, pp.612–26.

Crick, N.R. and Wellman, N.E. (1997), "Social information-processing mechanisms in relational and overt aggression," Biennial Meeting of the Society for Research in Child Development, Washington DC.

Crombie, G. and Desjardins, M.J. (1993), "Predictors of gender: the relative importance of children's play, games and personality characteristics?," New Orleans, conference paper, Society for Research in Child Development (SRCD).

Dabbs, J., Chang, E., Strong, R. and Milun, R. (1998), "Spatial ability, navigation strategy, and geographic knowledge among men and women," *Evolution and Human Behaviour* 19, pp.89–98.

Daly, M. and Wilson, M. (1983), *Sex, Evolution and Behavior*, Boston, Willard Grant Press.

———(1988), *Homicide*, New York, Aldine de Gruyter.

Darwin, C. (1871), *The Descent of Man, and Selection in Relation to Sex*, London, John Murray.

Davis, M.H. (1994), *Empathy: A Social Psychological Approach*, Social Psychology Series, Colorado, Westview Press.

Dawson, G., Warrenburg, S. and Fuller, P. (1982), "Cerebral lateralization in individuals diagnosed as autistic in early childhood," *Brain and Language* 15, pp.353–68.

De Lacoste-Utamsin, M.C. and Holloway, R.L. (1982), "Sexual dimorphism in the human corpus callosum," *Science* 216, pp.1431–2.

De Lisi, R., Parameswaran, G. and McGillicuddy-De Lisi, A. (1989), "Age and sex differences in representation of horizontality among children in India," *Perceptual and Motor Skills* 68, pp.739–46.

De Waal, F. (1993), "Sex differences in chimpanzee (and human) behavior: a matter of social values?" in M. Hechter, L. Nadel and R.E. Michod (eds.), *The Origin of Values*, New York, Aldine de Gruyter, pp.285–303.

De Waal, F. (2001), *The Ape and the Sushi Master*, Harmondsworth, Penguin Books.

DeFries, J., Vandenberg, S. and McClearn, G. (1976), "Genetics of specific cognitive abilities," *Annual Review of Genetics* 10, pp.179–207.

Delgado, A.R. and Prieto, G. (1997), "Mental rotation as a mediator for sex-differences in visualization," *Intelligence* 24, pp.405–16.

Denckla, M.B. and Rudel, R. (1974), "Rapid 'automatized' naming of pictured objects, colors, letters and numbers by normal children," *Cortex* 10, pp.186–202.

Diamond, A. (1985), "Development of the ability to use recall to guide actions, as indicated by infants' performance on AB," *Child Development* 56, pp.868–83.

———(1988), "Abilities and neural mechanisms underlying AB performance," *Child Development* 59, pp.523–7.

Diamond, M.C., Dowling, G.A. and Johnson, R.E. (1981), "Morphological cerebral cortical asymmetry in male and female rats," *Experimental Neurology* 71, pp.261–8.

Dimberg, U. and Ohman, A. (1996), "Behold the wrath – psychophysiological responses to facial stimuli," *Motivation and Emotion* 20, pp.149–82.

Dodge, K. (1980), "Social cognition and children's aggressive behaviour," *Child Development* 51, pp.162–70.

Dodge, K. and Frame, C. (1982), "Social cognitive biases and deficits in aggressive boys," *Child Development* 53, pp.620–35.

Dodge, K., Murphy, R. and Buchsbaum, K. (1984), "The assessment of intention-cue detection skills in children: implications for developmental psychology," *Child Development* 55, pp.163–73.

Donovan, J. (1997), "Towards a model relating empathy, charisma, and telepathy," *Journal of Scientific Exploration* 11, pp.455–71.

Dreisen, N.R. and Raz, N. (1995), "The influence of sex, age, and handedness on corpus callosum morphology: a meta-analysis," *Psychobiology* 23, pp.240–47.

DuBois, P.H. (1939), "The sex difference on the color naming test," *American Journal of Psychology* 52, pp.380–82.

Duggan, L. (1950), "An experiment on immediate recall in secondary school children," *British Journal of Psychology* 40, pp.149–54.

Dunn, J., Bretherton, I. and Munn, P. (1987), "Conversations about feeling states between mothers and their young children," *Developmental Psychology* 23, pp.132–9.

Eagly, A.H. (1987), *Sex Differences in Social Behavior: A Social-role Interpretation*, Hillsdale, N.J., Erlbaum.

Eals, M. and Silverman, I. (1994), "The hunter-gatherer theory of spatial sex differences: proximate factors mediating the female advantage in recall of object arrays," *Ethology & Sociobiology* 15, pp.95–105.

Eibl-Eibesfeldt, J. (1989), *Human Ethology*, New York, Aldine de Gruyter.

Eisenberg, N. and Lennon, R. (1983), "Sex differences in empathy and related capacities," *Psychological Bulletin* 94, pp.100–131.

Elliot, R. (1961), "Interrelationship among measures of field dependence, ability, and personality traits," *Journal of Abnormal and Social Psychology* 63, pp.27–36.

244 BIBLIOGRAPHY

Ellis, B.J. and Symons, D. (1990), "Sex differences in sexual fantasy: an evolutionary psychological approach," *Journal of Sex Research* 27, pp.527–55.

Engelhard, G. (1990), "Gender differences in performance on mathematics items: evidence from USA and Thailand," *Contemporary Educational Psychology* 15, pp.13–16.

Erwin, R.J., Gur, R.C., Gur, R.E., Skolnick, B., Mawhinney-Hee M. and Smailis, J. (1992), "Facial emotion discrimination: I. Task construction and behavioral findings in normal subjects," *Psychiatry Research* 42, pp.231–40.

Eslinger, P. and Damasio, A. (1985), "Severe disturbance of higher cognition after bilateral frontal lobe ablation: patient EVR," *Neurology* 35, pp.1731–41.

Everhart, D., Shucard, J., Quatrin, T. and Shucard, D. (2001), "Sex-related differences in event-related potentials, face recognition, and facial affect processing in prepubertal children," *Neuropsychology*, 15, 329–41.

Fagot, B.I. (1978), "The influence of sex of child on parental reactions to toddler children," *Child Development* 49, pp.459–65.

Farrow, T., Zheng, Y., Wilkinson, I., Spence, S., Deakin, J., Tarrier, N., Griffiths, P. and Woodruff, P. (2001), "Investigating the functional anatomy of empathy and forgiveness," *NeuroReport* 12, pp.2433–8.

Feingold, A. (1988), "Cognitive gender differences are disappearing," *American Psychologist* 43 (2), pp.95–103.

Field, T.M. (1978), "Interaction patterns of primary versus secondary caretaker fathers," *Developmental Psychology* 14, pp.183–84.

Fine, C. and Blair, J. (2000), "The cognitive and emotional effects of amygdala damage" *Neurocase* 6, pp.435–50.

Finegan, J, Niccols, G. and Sitarenios, G. (1992) "Relations between prenatal testosterone levels and cognitive abilities at 4 years," *Developmental Psychology* 28, pp.1075–89.

Fitch, R. and Denenberg, V. (1995), "The role for ovarian hormones in sexual differentiation of the brain," *Psychology* 6, pp.1–12.

Fitzgerald, M. (2002), "Did Isaac Newton have Asperger Syndrome or Disorder?," *European Journal of Child and Adolescent Psychiatry*.

Fivush, R. (1989), "Exploring sex differences in the emotional content of mother-child conversations about the past," *Sex Roles* 11/12, pp.675–91.

Fletcher, P.C., Happe, F., Frith, U., Baker, S.C., Dolan, R.J., Frackowiak R.S.J. and Frith, C.D. (1995), "Other minds in the brain: a functional imaging study of 'theory of mind' in story comprehension," *Cognition* 57, pp.109–28.

Flinn, M.V. and Low, B.S. (1986), "Resource distribution, social competition, and mating patterns in human societies" in D.I. Rubenstein and R.W. Wrangham (eds.), *Ecological Aspects of Social Evolution: Birds and Mammals*, Princeton University Press.

Foley, R.A. and Lee, P.C. (1989), "Finite social space, evolutionary pathways, and reconstructing hominid behavior," *Science* 243, pp.901–6.

Folstein, S. and Rutter, M. (1988), "Autism: familial aggregation and genetic implications," *Journal of Autism and Developmental Disorders* 18, pp.3–30.

Fonagy, P. (1989), "On tolerating mental states: theory of mind in borderline personality syndrome," *Bulletin of the Anna Freud Centre* 12, pp.91–115.

Frith, U. (1989), *Autism: Explaining the Enigma*, Oxford, Basil Blackwell.

———(1991), *Autism and Asperger's Syndrome*, Cambridge University Press.

Frith, U. and Happe, F. (1994), "Autism: beyond 'theory of mind,'" *Cognition* 50 pp.115–32.

Frost, J., Binder, J., Springer, J., Hammeke, T., Bellgowan, P., Rao, S. and Cox, R. (1999), "Language processing is strongly left lateralized in both sexes. Evidence from fMRI," *Brain* 122, pp.199–208.

Galea, L.A.M. and Kimura, D. (1993), "Sex differences in route learning," *Personality & Individual Differences* 14, pp.53–65.

Garai, J.E. and Scheinfeld, A. (1968), "Sex differences in mental and behavioral traits," *Genetic Psychology Monographs* 77, pp.169–299.

Garavan, H., Pendergrass, J., Ross, T., Stein, E. and Risinger, R. (2001), "Amygdala response to both positively and negatively valenced stimuli," *NeuroReport* 12, pp.2779–83.

Gaulin, S.J.C. (1995), "Does evolutionary theory predict sex differences in the brain?" in M.S. Gazzaniga (ed.), *The Cognitive Neurosciences*, Cambridge, Mass., MIT Press/Bradford Books.

Geary, D. (1995), "Sexual selection and sex differences in spatial cognition," *Learning and Individual Differences* 7, pp.289–301.

———(1996), "Sexual selection and sex differences in mathematical abilities," *Behavioural and Brain Sciences* 19, pp.229–84.

———(1998), *Male, Female*, Washington DC, American Psychological Association.

Geary, D., Saults, S., Liu, F. and Hoard, M. (2000), "Sex differences in spatial cognition, computational fluency, and arithmetical reasoning," *Journal of Experimental Child Psychology* 77, pp.337–53.

Geffen, E., Chessman, D.J., Mututua, R.S., Saiyalel, S.N., Wayne, R.K., Lacy, R.C. and Bruford, M.W. (1996), "Behavior predicts genetic structure in a wild primate group," *Proceedings of the National Academy of Sciences* 93, pp.5797–5801.

George, M.S., Ketter, T.A., Parekh, P.I., Herscovitch, P. and Post, R.M. (1996), "Gender differences in regional cerebral blood flow during transient self-induced sadness or happiness," *Biological Psychiatry* 40, pp.859–71.

Geschwind, N. and Galaburda, A.M. (1985), "Cerebral lateralization, biological mechanisms, associations, and pathology: I. A hypothesis and a program for research," *Archive of Neurology* 42, pp.428–59.

————(1987), *Cerebral Lateralization*, Cambridge, Mass., MIT Press.

Gillberg, C. (1991), "Clinical and neurobiological aspects of Asperger syndrome in six family studies" in U. Frith, *Autism and Asperger Syndrome*, Cambridge University Press.

Goel, V., Graffman, J., Sadato, N. and Hallett, M. (1995), "Modeling other minds," *NeuroReport* 6, pp.1741–6.

Golombok, S. and Fivush, S. (1994), *Gender Development*, New York, Cambridge University Press.

Goodenough, E. (1957), "Interest in persons as an aspect of sex difference in the early years," *Genetic Psychology Monographs* 55, pp.287–323.

Gouchie, C. and Kimura, D. (1991), "The relationship between testosterone levels and cognitive ability patterns," *Psychoneuroendocrinology* 16, pp.323–34.

Goy, R.W., Bercovitch, F.B. and McBrair, M.C. (1988), "Behavioral masculinization is independent of genital masculinization in pre-natally androgenized female rhesus macaques," *Hormones and Behavior* 22, pp.552–71.

Gray, J. (1993), *Men Are From Mars, Women Are From Venus*, New York, Harper-Collins.

Greenblatt, R. (1963), *The Hirsute Female*. Springfield, Ill., Charles Thomas.

Grimshaw, G., Sitarenios, G. and Finegan, J. (1995), "Mental rotation at 7 years: relations with pre-natal testosterone levels and spatial play experiences," *Brain and Cognition* 29, pp.85–100.

Grossi, D., Orsini, A., Monetti, C. and DeMichele, G. (1979), "Sex differences in children's spatial and verbal memory span," *Cortex* 15, pp.667–70.

Gur, R.C., Mozley, L.H., Mozley, P.D., Resnick, S.M., Karp, J.S., Alavi, A., Arnold, S.E. and Gur, R.E. (1995), "Sex differences in regional cerebral glucose metabolism during a resting state," *Science* 267, pp.528–31.

Hall, J. (1984), *Nonverbal sex differences: communication accuracy and expressive style*, Baltimore, Johns Hopkins University Press.

Hall, J.A. (1978), "Gender effects in decoding nonverbal cues," *Psychological Bulletin* 85, pp.845–58.

Halpern, D. (1992), *Sex differences in cognitive ability*, Hillsdale, NJ, Laurence Erlbaum Assoc.

Hampson, E. (1990), "Estrogen-related variations in human spatial and articulatory-motor skills," *Psychoneuroendocrinology* 15, pp.97–111.

Hampson, E., Rovet, J.F. and Altmann, D. (1998), "Spatial reasoning in children with congenital adrenal hyperplasia due to 21-hydroxylase deficiency," *Developmental Neuropsychology* 14, pp.299–320.

Happe, F. (1994), "An advanced test of theory of mind: understanding of story characters" thoughts and feelings by able autistic, mentally handicapped, and normal children and adults," *Journal of Autism and Development Disorders* 24, pp.129–54.

———(1995), "The role of age and verbal ability in the theory of mind task performance of subjects with autism," *Child Development* 66, pp.843–55.

———(1996a), "Studying weak central coherence at low levels: children with autism do not succumb to visual illusions. A research note," *Journal of Child Psychology and Psychiatry* 37, pp.873–7.

———(1996b), *Autism*, University College London Press.

———(1997), "Central coherence and theory of mind in autism: reading homographs in context," *British Journal of Developmental Psychology* 15, pp.1–12.

Happe, F. and Frith, U. (1996), "Theory of mind and social impairment in children with conduct disorder," *British Journal of Developmental Psychology* 14, pp.385–98.

Happe, F., Ehlers, S., Fletcher, P., Frith, U., Johansson, M., Gillberg, C., Dolan, R., Frackowiak, R. and Frith, C. (1996), "Theory of mind in the brain. Evidence from a PET scan study of Asperger Syndrome," *NeuroReport*, 8, pp.197–201.

Harlow, H. and Harlow, M. (1962), "Social deprivation in monkeys," *Scientific American* 207, pp.136ff.

Harris, P., Johnson, C., Hutton, N., Andrews, D. and Cooke, G. (1989), "Young children's theory of mind and emotion," *Cognition and Emotion* 3, pp.379–400.

Hartup, W.W., French, D.C., Laursen, B., Johnston, M.K. and Ogawa, J.R. (1993), "Conflict and friendship relations in middle childhood: behavior in a closed-field situation," *Child Development* 64, pp.445–54.

Hartup, W.W., and Stevens, N. (1997), "Friendships and adaptation in the life course," *Psychological Bulletin* 121, pp.817–18.

Hausman, P. (unpublished Ph.D. dissertation), "*On the rarity of mathematically and mechanically gifted females*," cited in J. Kleinfeld (1999), http://www.uaf.edu/northern/mitstudy.

Haviland, J.J. and Malatesta, C.Z. (1981), "The development of sex differences in nonverbal signals: fallacies, facts, and fantasies" in C. Mayo and N.M. Henley (eds.), *Gender and Nonverbal Behavior*, New York, Springer-Verlag, pp.183–208.

Hedges, L.V. and Nowell, A. (1995), "Sex differences in mental scores, variability, and numbers of high-scoring individuals," *Science* 269, pp.41–5.

Herlitz, A., Nilsson, L.-G. and Backman, L. (1997), "Gender differences in episodic memory," *Memory and Cognition* 25, pp.801–11.

Hier, D.B. and Crowley, W.F. (1982), "Spatial ability in androgen-deficient men," *New England Journal of Medicine* 306, pp.1202–5.

Hill, K. and Hurtado, A.M. (1996), *Ache Life History: The Ecology and Demography of a Foraging People*, New York, Aldine de Gruyter.

Hines, M. (1982), "Pre-natal gonadal hormones and sex differences in human behaviour," *Psychological Bulletin* 92, pp.56–80.

_____(1992), "Cognition and the corpus callosum: verbal fluency, visuospatial ability and language lateralization related to midsagittal surface areas of callosal subregions," *Behavioral Neuroscience* 106, pp.3–14.

Hines, M., Allen, L. and Gorski, R. (1992), "Sex differences in subregions of the medial nucleus of the amygdala and the bed nucleus of the stria terminalis of the rat," *Brain Research* 579, pp.321–6.

Hines, M. and Kaufman, F.R. (1994), "Androgens and the development of human sex-typical behavior: Rough-and-tumble play and sex of preferred playmates in children with congenital adrenal hyperplasia (CAH)," *Child Development* 65, pp.1042–53.

Hoffman, M.L. (1977), "Sex differences in empathy and related behaviors," *Psychological Bulletin* 84, pp.712–22.

Holding, C.S. and Holding, D.H. (1989), "Acquisition of route network knowledge by males and females," *Journal of Genetic Psychology* 116, pp.29–41.

Holloway, R.L., Anderson, P.J., Defendini, R., Harper, C. (1993), "Sexual dimorphism of the human corpus callosum from three interdependent samples: relative size of the corpus callosum," *American Journal of Physical Anthropology* 92, pp.481–98.

Holt, S. (1968), *The Genetics of Dermal Ridges*, Springfield, Ill., Charles C. Thomas.

Hovis, R. and Kragh, H. (1993), "P.A.M. Dirac and the beauty of physics," *Scientific American*, May, pp.62–7.

Howard, M., Cowell, P., Boucher, J., Broks, P., Mayes, A., Farrant, A. and Roberts, N. (2000), "Convergent neuroanatomical and behavioural evidence of an amygdala hypothesis of autism," *NeuroReport* 11, pp.2931–5.

Howes, C. (1988), "Same- and cross-sex friends: implications for interaction and social skills," *Early Childhood Research Quarterly* 3, pp.21–37.

Howlin, P. (2001), "Outcome in adult life for more able individuals with autism or Asperger Syndrome," *Autism* 4, pp.63–83.

Hrdy, S. (1997), "Raising Darwin's consciousness: female sexuality and the prehominid origins of patriarchy," *Human Nature* 8, pp.1–49.

Huang, C.P. (1986), "Behavior of Swedish primary and secondary caretaking fathers in relation to mother's presence," *Developmental Psychology* 22, pp.749–51.

Hughes, C. and Cutting, A. (1999), "Nature, nurture, and individual differences in early understanding of mind," *Psychological Science* 10, pp.429–33.

Hunt, E., Lunneborg C. and Lewis, J. (1975), "What does it mean to be high verbal?," *Cognitive Psychology* 7, pp.194–227.

Huston, A.C. (1983), "Sex Typing," in P. Mussen (ed.) *Socialization, personality, and social development*. Vol.4, New York, John Wiley.

Hutt, C. (1972), "Sex differences in human development," *Human Development* 15, pp.153–70.

Huttonlocher, J., Haights, W., Bryk, A., Seltzer, M. and Lyons, T. (1991), "Early vocabulary growth: relation to language input and gender," *Developmental Psychology* 27, pp.236–48.

Hyde, J.S., Fennema, E. and Lamon, S.J. (1990) "Gender differences in mathematics performance: a meta-analysis," *Psychological Bulletin* 107, pp.139–55.

Hyde, J.S., Geiringer, E.R. and Yen, M.W. (1975), "On the empirical relation between spatial ability and sex differences in other aspects of cognitive performance," *Multivariate Behavioural Research* 10, pp.289–309.

Hyde, J.S. and Linn, M.C. (1988), "Gender differences in verbal ability: a meta-analysis," *Psychological Bulletin* 104, pp.53–69.

ICD–10 (1994), *International Classification of Diseases*, 10th edn, Geneva Switzerland, World Health Organization.

Irons, W. (1979), "Cultural and biological success" in N.A. Chagnon and W. Irons (eds.), *Natural Selection and Social Behavior*, North Scituate, Mass., Duxbury Press.

Jacobson, C.D., Csernus, V.J., Shryne, J.E. and Gorski, R.A. (1981), "The influence of gonadectomy, androgen exposure, or a gonadal graft in the neonatal rat on the volume of the sexually dimorphic nucleus of the preoptic area," *Journal of Neuroscience* 1, pp.1142–7.

James, I. (2003), "Six singular scientists: Newton, Cavendish, Einstein, Curie, Dirac, Yukama," *Journal of the Royal Society of Medicine*, 96, pp. 36–9.

James, T.W. and Kimura, D. (1997), "Sex differences in remembering the locations of objects in an array: location-shifts versus local exchanges," *Evolution and Human Behavior* 18, pp.155–63.

Jancke, L., Schlaug, G., Huang, Y. and Steinmetz, H. (1994), "Asymmetry of the planum parietale," *NeuroReport* 5, pp.1161–3.

Janowsky, J.S., Oviatt, S.K. and Orwoll, E.S. (1994), "Testosterone influences spatial cognition in older men," *Behavioral Neuroscience* 108, pp.325–32.

Jardine, R. and Martin, N.G. (1983), "Spatial ability and throwing accuracy," *Behavior Genetics* 13, pp.331–40.

Jarvinen, D.W. and Buegikksm, G.H., (1996), "Adolescents' social goals, beliefs about the causes of social success, and satisfaction in peer relations," *Developmental Psychology* 32, pp.435–41.

Jennings, K.D. (1977), "People versus object orientation in preschool children: do sex differences really occur?," *Journal of Genetic Psychology* 131, pp.65–73.

Jensen, A.R. and Reynolds, C.R. (1983), "Sex differences on the WISC-R," *Personality and Individual Differences* 4, pp.223–6.

Johnson, E.S. and Meade, A.C. (1987), "Developmental patterns of spatial ability: an early sex difference," *Child Development* 58, pp.725–40.

Jolliffe, T. and Baron-Cohen, S. (1997), "Are people with autism or Asperger's Syndrome faster than normal on the Embedded Figures Task?," *Journal of Child Psychology and Psychiatry* 38, pp.527–34.

Just, M.A. and Carpenter, P.A. (1985), "Cognitive coordinate system: accounts of mental rotation and individual differences in spatial ability," *Psychological Review* 92, pp.137–72.

Kalichman, S.C. (1989), "The effects of stimulus context on paper-and-pencil spatial task performance," *Journal of General Psychology* 116, pp.133–9.

Karmiloff-Smith, A., Grant, J., Belluji, U. and Baron-Cohen, S. (1995), "Is there a social module? Language, face-processing, and theory of mind in Williams' Syndrome and autism," *Journal of Cognitive Neuroscience* 7, pp.196–208.

Keely, L.H. (1996), *War Before Civilization: The Myth of the Peaceful Savage*, New York, Oxford University Press.

Kerns, K.A. and Berenbaum, S.A. (1991), "Sex differences in spatial ability in children," *Behavior Genetics* 21, pp.383–96.

Killgore, W., Oki, M. and Yurgelun-Todd, D. (2001), "Sex-specific developmental changes in amygdala responses to affective faces," *NeuroReport* 12, pp.427–33.

Kimball, M.M. (1989), "A new perspective on women's math achievement," *Psychological Bulletin* 105, pp.198–214.

Kimura, D. (1961), "Cerebral dominance and the perception of verbal stimuli," *Canadian Journal of Psychology* 15, pp.166–71.

———(1966), "Dual functional asymmetry of the brain in visual perception," *Neuropsychologia* 4, pp.275–85.

———(1987), "Are men's and women's brains really different?" *Canadian Psychology* 28, pp.133–47.

———(1994), "Body asymmetry and intellectual pattern," *Personality & Individual Differences* 17, pp.53–60.

———(1996), "Sex, sexual orientation and sex hormones influence human cognitive function," *Current Opinion in Neurobiology* 6, pp.259–63.

———(1999), *Sex and Cognition*, Cambridge, Mass., MIT Press.

Kimura, D. and Carson, M. (1995), "Dermatoglyphic asymmetry: relation to sex, handedness, and cognitive pattern," *Personality and Individual Differences* 19, pp.471–8.

Kimura, D. and Harshman, R.A. (1984), "Sex differences in brain organization for verbal and non-verbal functions" in G.J. DeVries, J.P.C. DeBruin, H.B.M. Uylings and M.A. Corner (eds.), Sex Differences in the Brain. Progress in Brain Research, Amsterdam, Elsevier.

Kimura, D., Saucier, D.M. and Matuk, R. (1996), "Women name both colors and forms faster than men," Society for Neuroscience Abstracts 22, pp.1860ff.

Knauft, B.M. (1987), "Reconsidering violence in simple human societies: homicide among the Debusi of New Guinea," Current Anthropology 28, pp.457–500.

Knickmeyer, R., Baron-Cohen, S. and Raggatt, P. (unpublished MS), "Foetal Testosterone, Social Cognition, and Restricted Interests in Children," University of Cambridge.

Knickmeyer, R., Baron-Cohen, S. and Wheelwright, S. (unpublished MS), "The tomboyism quotient (TQ)," University of Cambridge.

Knight, G.P., Fabes, R.A. and Higgins, D.A. (1989), "Gender differences in the co-operative, competitive, and individualistic social values of children," Motivation and Emotion 13, pp.125–41.

Kochanska, G., Murray, K., Jacques, T.Y., Koenig, A.L. and Vandegeest, K.A. (1996), "Inhibitory control in young children and its role in emerging internalization," Child Development 67, pp.490–507.

Kolakowski, D. and Malina, R.M. (1974), "Spatial ability, throwing accuracy and man's hunting heritage," Nature 251, pp.410–12.

Kolata, G. (1980), "Math and sex: are girls born with less ability?," Science 210, pp.1234–5.

Kramer, J.H., Delis, D.C. and Daniel, M. (1988), "Sex differences in verbal learning," Journal of Clinical Psychology 44, pp.907–15.

Lake, D.A. and Bryden, M.P. (1976), "Handedness and sex differences in hemispheric asymmetry," Brain & Language 3, pp.266–82.

Lamb, M.E., Frodi, A.M., Frodi, M. and Huang, C.P. (1982), "Characteristics of maternal and paternal behavior in traditional and non-traditional Swedish families," International Journal of Behavioral Development 5, pp.131–41.

Langlois, J.H. and Downs, A.C. (1980), "Mothers, fathers, and peers as socialization agents of sex-typed play behaviors in young children," Child Development 51, pp.1217–47.

Law, D.J., Pellegrino, J.W. and Hunt, E.B. (1993), "Comparing the tortoise and the hare: gender differences and experience in dynamic spatial reasoning tasks," Psychological Sciences 4, pp.35–40.

Lawson, J., Baron-Cohen, S. and Wheelwright, S. (in press), "Empathising and systemising in males and females with and without Asperger Syndrome," Journal of Autism and Developmental Disorders.

Le Doux, J. (2000), "Emotion circuits in the brain," *Annual Review of Neuroscience* 23, pp.155–184.

Leaper, C. (1991), "Influence and involvement in children's discourse: age, gender, and partner effects," *Child Development* 62, pp.797–811.

Leaper, C. and Gleason, J.B. (1996), "The relationship of play activity and gender to parent and child sex-typed communication," *International Journal of Behavioral Development* 19, pp.689–703.

Leslie, A. (1987), "Pretence and representation: the origins of theory of mind," *Psychological Review* 94, pp.412–26.

LeVay, S. (1991), "A difference in hypothalamic structure between heterosexual and homosexual men," *Science* 253, pp.1034–7.

Lever, J. (1978), "Sex differences in the complexity of children's play and games," *American Sociological Review* 43, pp.471–83.

Levy, J. and Levy, J.M. (1978), "Human lateralization from head to foot: sex-related factors," *Science* 200, pp.1291–2.

Lewis, C., Hitch, G. and Walker, P. (1994), "The prevalence of specific arithmetic difficulties and specific reading difficulties in 9- and 10-year-old boys and girls," *Journal of Child Psychology and Psychiatry* 35, pp.283–92.

Linn, M.C. and Petersen, A.C. (1985), "Emergence and characterisation of sex differences in spatial ability: a meta-analysis," *Child Development* 56, pp.1479–98.

Lloyd, B. and Smith, C. (1986), "The effects of age and gender on social behaviour in very young children," *British Journal of Social Psychology* 25, pp.33–41.

Lord, C. and Schopler, E. (1985), "Brief report: differences in sex ratios in autism as a function of measured intelligence," *Journal of Autism and Developmental Disorders* 15, pp.185–93.

Lovejoy, J. and Wallen, K. (1988), "Sexually dimorphic behavior in group-housed rhesus monkeys (Macaca mulatta) at 1 year of age," *Psychobiology* 16, pp.348–56.

Lubinski, D. and Benbow, C.P. (1992), "Gender differences in abilities and preferences among the gifted: implications for the math-science pipeline," *Current Directions in Psychological Science* 1, pp.61–6.

Lucas, T.H., Lombardino, L.J., Roper, S.N. and Leonard, C.M. (1996), "Effects of handedness and gender on hippocampal size in normal children: an MRI study," *Society for Neuroscience Abstracts* 22, pp.1860ff.

Lummis, M. and Stevenson, H.W. (1990), "Gender differences in beliefs and achievement: a cross-cultural study," *Developmental Psychology* 26, pp.254–63.

Lutchmaya, S. and Baron-Cohen, S. (2002), "Human sex differences in social and non-social looking preferences at 12 months of age," *Infant Behaviour and Development* 25 (3), pp.319–25.

Lutchmaya, S., and Baron-Cohen, S. and Raggatt, P. (2002a), "Foetal testosterone and vocabulary size in 18- and 24-month-old infants," *Infant Behaviour and Development* 24 (4), pp.418–24.

_____(2002b), "Foetal testosterone and eye contact at 12 months," *Infant Behaviour and Development* 25 (3), pp.327–35.

Lytton, H. and Romney, D.M. (1991), "Parents' differential socialization of boys and girls: a meta-analysis," *Psychological Bulletin* 109, pp.267–96.

Maccoby, E.E. (1966), *The Development of Sex Differences*, Stanford University Press.

_____(1990), "Gender and relationships: a developmental account," *American Psychologist* 45, pp.513–520.

_____(1998), *The Two Sexes: Growing Apart, Coming Together*, Cambridge, Mass., Harvard University Press.

Maccoby, E.E. and Jacklin, N. (1974), *The Psychology of Sex Differences*, Stanford University Press.

Maccoby, E.E., Snow, M.E. and Jacklin, C.N. (1984), "Children's dispositions and mother-child interaction at 12 and 18 months: a short-term longitudinal study," *Developmental Psychology* 20, pp.459–72.

Mackintosh, N.J. (1998), *IQ and Human Intelligence*, Oxford University Press.

MacLean, P. (1985), "Brain evolution relating to family, play, and the separation call," *Archives of General Psychiatry* 42, pp.405–17.

MacLusky, N. and Naftolin, F. (1981), "Sexual differentiation of the central nervous system," *Science* 211, pp.1294–1303.

Maguire, E.A., Frackowiak, R.S.J. and Frith, C.D. (1997), "Recalling routes around London: activation of the right hippocampus in taxi drivers," *Journal of Neuroscience* 17, pp.7103–10.

Maltz, D. and Borker, R. (1983), "A cultural approach to male-female miscommunication" in J. Gumperz (ed.), *Language and Social Identity*, New York, Cambridge University Press.

Mann, V.A., Sasanuma, S., Sakuma, N. and Masaki, S. (1990), "Sex differences in cognitive abilities: a cross-cultural perspective," *Neuropsychologia* 28, pp.1063–77.

Manning, J., Baron-Cohen, S., Wheelwright, S. and Sanders, G. (2001), "Autism and the ratio between 2nd and 4th digit length," *Developmental Medicine and Child Neurology* 43, pp.160–4.

Mannle, S. and Tomasello, M. (1987), "Fathers, siblings, and the bridge hypothesis" in K.A. Nelson and A van Kleek (eds.), *Children's Language*, Hillsdale, N.J., Erlbaum.

.rtino, G. and Winner, E. (1995), "Talents and disorders: relationships among handedness, sex, and college major," *Brain and Cognition*, 29, pp.66–84.

Masica, D., Money, J., Erhardt, A. and Lewis, V. (1968), "IQ, fetal sex hormones and cognitive patterns: studies of the testicular feminizing syndrome of androgen insensitivity" *Johns Hopkins Medical Journal* 124, pp.34–43.

Masters, M.S. and Sanders, B. (1993), "Is the gender difference in mental rotation disappearing?" *Behavior Genetics* 23, pp.337–41.

Matthews, K., Batson, C., Horn, J. and Rosenman, R. (1981), "Principles in his nature which interest him in the fortunes of others: the heritability of empathic concern for others," *Journal of Personality* 49, pp.237–47.

Matthews, M.H. (1987), "Sex differences in spatial competence: the ability of young children to map 'primed' unfamiliar environments," *Educational Psychology* 7, pp.77–90.

_____(1992), *Making Sense of Place: Children's Understanding of Large-scale Environments*, Savage, Maryland, Barnes & Noble Books.

Maxson, S.C. (1997), "Sex differences in genetic mechanisms for mammalian brain and behavior," *Biomedical Reviews* 7, pp.85–90.

Mayes, J.T. and Jahoda, G. (1988), "Patterns of visual-spatial performance and 'spatial ability': dissociation of ethnic and sex difference," *British Journal of Psychology* 79, pp.105–19.

McBurney, D.H., Gaulin, S.J.C., Deviineni, T. and Adams, C. (1997), "Superior spatial memory of women: stronger evidence for the gathering hypothesis," *Evolution and Human Behavior* 18, pp.165–74.

McGee, M. (1979), "Human spatial abilities: psychometric studies and environmental, genetic, hormonal, and neurological influences," *Psychological Bulletin* 86, pp.889–918.

McGlone, J. (1980), "Sex differences in human brain asymmetry: a critical survey," *Behavioural and Brain Sciences* 3, pp.215–63.

McGlone, J. and Fox, A.J. (1982), "Evidence from sodium amytal studies of greater asymmetry of verbal representation in men compared to women" in H. Akimoto, H. Kazamatsuri, M. Seino and A. Ward (eds.), *Advances in Epileptology: XIIIth Epilepsy International Symposium*, New York, McGraw-Hill.

McGuinness, D. and Morley, C. (1991), "Sex differences in the development of visuo-spatial ability in pre-school children," *Journal of Mental Imagery* 15, pp.143–50.

McGuinness, D., Olson, A. and Chapman, J. (1990), "Sex differences in incidental recall for words and pictures," *Learning and Individual Differences* 2, pp.263–85.

McGuinness, D. and Symonds, J. (1977), "Sex differences in choice behavior: the object-person dimension," *Perception* 6, pp.691–94.

McManus, I. and Bryden, M. (1991), "Geschwind's theory of cerebral lateralization: developing a formal, causal model," *Psychological Bulletin* 110, pp.237–53.

Mealey, L. (1995), "The sociobiology of sociopathy: an integrated evolutionary model," *Behavioral and Brain Sciences* 18, pp.523–99.

Meaney, M. and McEwen, B. (1986), "Testosterone implants into the amygdala during the neonatal period masculinizes the social play of juvenile female rats," *Brain Research* 398, pp.324–8.

Meaney, M.J., Stewart, J. and Beatty, W.W. (1985), "Sex differences in social play: the socialization of sex roles" in J.S. Rosenblatt, C. Beer, C.M. Busnell and P. Stater (eds.), *Advances in the Study of Behavior*, New York, Academic Press.

Michael, R.P. and Zumpe, D. (1998), "Development changes in behavior and in steroid uptake by the male and female macaque brain," *Development Neuropsychology* 14, pp.233–60.

Miller, L.K. and Santoni, V. (1986), "Sex differences in spatial abilities: strategic and experiential correlates," *Acta Psychologia* 62, pp.225–35.

Miller, P.M., Danaher, D.L. and Forbes, D. (1986), "Sex-related strategies for coping with interpersonal conflict in children aged five and seven," *Developmental Psychology* 22, pp.543–48.

Mills, C.J., Ablard, K.E. and Stumpf, H. (1993), "Gender differences in academically talented young students' mathematical reasoning: patterns across age and subskills," *Journal of Educational Psychology* 85, pp.340–46.

Mitchell, A. (1999), "UK women lead the way on interdisciplinary research," *Nature* 397, pp.282ff.

Mithen, S. (1996), *The Prehistory of the Mind*, Harmondsworth, Penguin Books.

Murdock, G.P. (1981), *Atlas of World Cultures*, University of Pittsburgh Press.

Myers, P., Baron-Cohen, S. and Wheelwright, S. (2003), *The Exact Mind*, London, Jessica Kingsley Publishers.

NAE 1989 Almanac of Higher Education, The (1989), Washington DC.

Nicholson, K.G., and Kimura, D. (1996), "Sex differences for speech and manual skill," *Perceptual and Motor Skills* 82, pp.3–13.

O' Riordan, M., Plaisted, K., Driver, J. and Baron-Cohen, S. (2001), "Superior visual search in autism," *Journal of Experimental Psychology: Human Perception and Performance* 5, pp.47–78.

Ozonoff, S., South, M. and Miller, J. (2001), "DSM-IV defined Asperger Syndrome: cognitive, behavioural, and early history differentiation from high-functioning autism," *Autism* 4, pp.29–46.

Pakkenberg, B. and Gundersen, H.J.G. (1997), "Neocortical neuron number in humans: effect of sex and age," *Journal of Comparative Neurology* 384, pp.312–20.

Pearson, J.L. and Ferguson, L.R. (1989), "Gender differences in patterns of spatial ability, environmental cognition, and math and English achievement in late adolescence," *Adolescence* 24, pp.421–31.

Perrett, D., Smith, P., Potter, D., Mistlin, A., Head, A., Milner, A. and Jeeves, M. (1985), "Visual cells in the temporal cortex sensitive to face view and gaze direction," *Proceedings of the Royal Society of London*, B223, pp.292–317.

Perry, D.G. and Bussey, K. (1979), "The social learning theory of sex differences: limitation is alive and well," *Journal of Personality and Social Psychology* 37, pp.1699–1712.

Perry, D.G., White, A.J. and Perry, L.C. (1984), "Does early sex typing result from children's attempts to match their behavior to sex role stereotypes?" *Child Development* 55, pp.2114–21.

Peterson, J. (1978), "Left handedness: differences between student artists and scientists," *Perceptual and Motor Skills* 48, pp.961–2.

Peterson, J. and Lansky, L. (1974), "Left handedness among architects: some facts and speculation," *Perceptual and Motor Skills* 38, pp.547–50.

Phillips, W., Baron-Cohen, S. and Rutter, M. (1992), "The role of eye contact in the detection of goals: evidence from normal toddlers, and children with autism or mental handicap," *Development and Psychopathology* 4, pp.375–83.

Piaget, J. and Inhelder, B. (1956), *The Child's Conception of Space*, London, Routledge and Kegan Paul.

Pitcher, E.G. and Schultz, L.H. (1983), *Boys and Girls at Play: The Development of Sex Roles*, South Hadley, Mass., Bergin and Garvey.

Pizzamiglio, L. and Mammucari, A. (1985), "Evidence for sex differences in brain organization in recovery in aphasia," *Brain & Language* 25, pp.213–23.

Plaisted, K., O'Riordan, M., and Baron-Cohen, S. (1998a), "Enhanced discrimination of novel, highly similar stimuli by adults with autism during a perceptual learning task," *Journal of Child Psychology and Psychiatry* 39, pp.765–75.

_____(1998b), "Enhanced visual search for a conjunctive target in autism: a research note," *Journal of Child Psychology and Psychiatry* 39, pp.777–83.

Povinelli, D. (2000), *Folk Physics for Apes*, Oxford University Press.

Power, T.G. (1985), "Mother- and father-infant play: a developmental analysis," *Child Development* 56, pp.1514–24.

Pratto, F. (1996), "Sexual politics: the gender gap in the bedroom, the cupboard, and the cabinet" in D.M. Buss and N.M. Malamuth (eds.), *Sex, Power, Conflict: Evolutionary and Feminist Perspectives*, New York, Oxford University Press.

Premack, D. (1995), *Causal Cognition*, Oxford University Press.

Pugh, K.R., Fletcher, J.M., Skudlarski, P., Fulbright, R.K., Constable, R.T., Bronen, R.A., Lacadie, C. and Gore, J.C. (1997), "Predicting reading performance from neuroimaging profiles: the cerebral basis of phonological effects in printed word identification," *Journal of Experimental Psychology: Human Perception and Performance* 23, pp.299–318.

Pugh, K.R., Shaywitz, B.A., Shaywitz, S.E., Fulbright, R.K., Byrd, D. and Skudlarski, P. (1996), "Auditory selective attention: an MRI investigation," *Neuroimage* 4, pp.159–73.

Rammsayer, T. and Lustnauer, S. (1989), "Sex differences in time perception," *Perceptual and Motor Skills* 68, pp.195–8.

Rasia-Filho, A., Londero, R. and Achaval, M. (1999), "Effects of gonadal hormones on the morphology of neurons from the medial amygdaloid nucleus of rats," *Brain Research Bulletin* 48, pp.173–83.

Reinisch, J.M. (1977), "Pre-natal exposure of human foetuses to synthetic progestin and oestrogen affects personality," *Nature* 266, pp.561–2.

_____(1981), "Pre-natal exposure to synthetic progestins increases potential for aggression in humans," *Science* 211, pp.1171–3.

Reinisch, J.M. and Saunders, S.A. (1984), "Pre-natal gonadal steroid influences on gender-related behaviour" in G.J. De Vries (ed.), *Progress in Brain Research*, Amsterdam, Elsevier, p.61.

Resnick, S., Berenbaum, S., Gottesman, I. and Bouchard, T. (1986), "Early hormonal influences on cognitive functioning in congenital adrenal hyperplasia," *Developmental Psychology* 22, pp.191–8.

Robert, M. and Chaperon, H. (1989), "Cognitive and exemplary modelling of horizontal representation on the Piagetian water-level task," *International Journal of Behavioural Development* 12, pp.453–72.

Robert, M. and Ohlmann, T. (1994), "Water-level representation by men and women as a function of rod-and-frame test proficiency and visual and postural information," *Perception* 23, pp.1321–33.

Robert, M. and Tanguay, M. (1990), "Perception and representation of the Euclidean coordinates in mature and elderly men and women," *Experimental Aging Research* 16, pp.123–31.

Robertson, I. (1999), *Mind Sculpture*, London, Bantam Press.

Roof, R.L. and Havens, M.D. (1992), "Testosterone improves maze performance and induces development of a male hippocampus in females," *Brain Research* 572, pp.310–13.

Rosenthal, R., Hall, J.A., DiMatteo, M.R., Rogers, P.L. and Archer, D. (1979), *Sensitivity to Nonverbal Communication: The PONS Test*, Baltimore, Johns Hopkins University Press.

Rosser, R.A., Ensing, S.S., Glider, P.J. and Lane, S. (1984), "An information-processing analysis of children's accuracy in predicting the appearance of rotated stimuli," *Child Development* 55, pp.2204–11.

Rotter, N.G. and Rotter, G.S. (1988), "Sex differences in the encoding and decoding of negative facial emotions," *Journal of Nonverbal Behavior* 12, pp.139–48.

Rowe, A., Bullock, P., Polkey, C. and Morris, R. (2001), " 'Theory of mind'" impairments and their relationship to executive functioning following frontal lobe excisions," *Brain* 124, pp.600–616.

Rubin, K.H., Fein, G.G. and Vandenberg, B. (1983), "Play" in P. Mussen and E.M. Hetherington (eds.), *Handbook of Child Psychology: Socialization, Personality, and Social Development*, 4th edn., New York, John Wiley & Sons Inc.

Rushton, J.P., Fulker, D.W., Neale, M.C., Nias, D.K.B. and Eysenck, H.J. (1986), "Altruism and aggression: the heritability of individual differences," *Journal of Personality and Social Psychology* 50, pp.1192–8.

Russell, G. and Russell, A. (1987), "Mother-child and father-child relationships in middle childhood," *Child Development* 58, pp.1573–85.

Russell, J. (ed.) (1997), *Autism as an Executive Disorder*, Oxford University Press.

Rutter, M. (1978), "Diagnosis and definition" in M. Rutter and E. Schopler (eds.), *Autism: A Reappraisal of Concepts and Treatment*, New York, Plenum Press, pp.1–26.

Sainsbury, C. (2000), *Martian in the Playground*, Bristol, Lucky Duck Publishing.

Sandberg, D.E. and Meyer-Bahlburg, H.F.L. (1994), "Variability in middle childhood play behavior: effects of gender, age, and family background," *Archives of Sexual Behavior* 23, pp.645–63.

Sanders, B., Soares, M.P. and D'Aguila, J.M. (1982), "The sex difference on one test of spatial visualisation: a nontrivial difference," *Child Development* 53, pp.1106–10.

Sanders, G., Aubert, F. and Kadam, A. (1995), "Asymmetries in finger ridge count correlate with performance on sexually dimorphic tasks in children and adults," *International Academy of Sex Research, XXI Annual Meeting*, pp.20–24.

Saunders, S.A. and Reinisch, J.M. (1985), "Behavioural effect on humans of progesterone related compounds during development in the adult," *Current Topics of Neuroendocrinology* 15, pp.175–98.

Savin-Williams, R.C. (1987), *Adolescence: An Ethological Perspective*, New York, Springer-Verlag.

Scheuffgen, K., Happe, F., Anderson, M., and Frith, U. (2000), "High 'intelligence,' low 'IQ'? Speed of processing and measured IQ in children with autism," *Development and Psychopathology* 12, pp.83–90.

Schiff, W. and Oldak, R. (1990), "Accuracy of judging time to arrival: effects of modality, trajectory and gender," *Journal of Experimental Psychology, Human Perception and Performance* 16, pp.303–16.

Scourfield, J., Martin, N., Lewis, G. and McGuffin, P. (1999), "Heritability of social cognitive skills in children and adolescents," *British Journal of Psychiatry* 175, pp.559–64.

Seavey, A., Katz, P. and Zalk, S. (1975), "Baby x: the effect of gender label on adult responses to infant," *Sex Roles* 1, pp.103–9.

Shah, A. and Frith, U. (1983), "An islet of ability in autism: a research note," *Journal of Child Psychology and Psychiatry* 24, pp.613–20.

――――(1993), "Why do autistic individuals show superior performance on the block design test?" *Journal of Child Psychology and Psychiatry* 34, pp.1351–64.

Shaywitz, B., Shaywitz, S., Pugh, K., Constables, R., Skudlarski, P., Fulbright, R., Bronen, R., Fletcher, J., Shankweiler, D., Katz, L. and Gore, J. (1995), "Sex differences in the functional organization of the brain for language," *Nature* 373, pp.607–9.

Sheldon, A. (1992), "Preschool girls' discourse competence: managing conflict and negotiating power" in M. Bucholtz, K. Hall and B. Moonwomon (eds.), *Locating Power*, Proceedings of the 1992 Berkeley Women and Language Conference, Berkeley Linguistic Society, vol. 2, pp.528–39.

Shephard, R.N. and Metzler, J. (1971), "Mental rotation of three dimensional objects," *Science* 171, pp.701–3.

Sherman, J.A. (1967), "Problems of sex differences in space perception and aspects of intellectual functioning," *Psychological Review* 74, pp.290–99.

Sherry, D.F., Jacobs, L.F. and Gaulin, S.J.C. (1992), "Spatial memory and adaptive specialization of the hippocampus," *Trends in Neurosciences* 15, pp.298–303.

Sherry, D.F., Vaccarino, A.L., Buckenham, K. and Herz, R.S. (1989), "The hippocampal complex of food-storing birds," *Brain, Behavior and Evolution* 34, pp.308–17.

Shucard, D.W., Shucard, J.L. and Thomas, D.G. (1987), "Sex differences in electrophysiological activity in infancy: possible implications for language development" in S. Philips, S. Steele and C. Tanz (eds.), *Language, Gender, and Sex in Comparative Perspective*, Cambridge University Press.

Shute, V.J., Pellegrino, J., Hubert, L. and Reynolds, R. (1983), "The relationship between androgen levels and human spatial abilities," *Bulletin of the Psychonomic Society* 21, pp.465–8.

Siddiqui, A. and Shah, B. (1997), "Neonatal androgen manipulation differentially affects the development of monoamine systems in rat cerebral cortex, amygdala, and hypothalamus," *Brain Research and Development* 98, pp.247–52.

Sidorowicz, L. and Lunney, G. (1980), "Baby x revisited," *Sex Roles* 6, pp.67–73.

Silverman, I. and Eals, M. (1992), "Sex differences in spatial abilities: evolutionary theory and data" in J.H. Barkow, L. Cosmides and J. Tooby (eds.), *The Adapted Mind: Evolutionary Psychology and the Generation of a Culture*, New York, Oxford University Press.

Skuse, D. (2000), "Imprinting, the X chromosome, and the male brain: explaining sex differences in the liability to autism," *Paediatric Research* 47, pp.9–16.

Skuse, D.H., James, R.S., Bisop, D.V.M., Coppin, B., Dalton, P., Aamodt-Leeper, G., Bacarese-Hamilton, M., Cresswell, C., McGurk, R. and Jacobs, P.A. (1997), "Evidence from Turner's syndrome of an imprinted X-linked locus affecting cognitive function," *Nature* 387, pp.705–8.

Smith, G.A. and McPhee, K.A. (1987), "Performance on a coincidence timing task correlates with intelligence," *Intelligence* 11, pp.161–7.

Smith, P.M. (1985), *Language, the Sexes and Society*, Oxford, Basil Blackwell.

Snow, M.E., Jacklin, C.N. and Maccoby, E.E. (1983), "Sex-of-child differences in father-child interaction at one year of age," *Child Development* 54, pp.227–32.

Stanley, J.C. (1990), "We need to know why women falter in math," *The Chronicle of Higher Education*.

Stefanova, N. (1998), "Gamma-aminobutyric acid-immunoreactive neurons in the amygdala of the rat: sex differences and effect of early postnatal castration," *Neuroscience Letters* 255, pp.175–7.

Stern, J.M. (1989), "Maternal behavior: sensory, hormonal, and neural determinants" in F.R. Brush and S. Levine (eds.), *Psychoendocrinology*, San Diego, Academic Press.

Stern, M. and Karraker, K.H. (1989), "Sex stereotyping of infants: a review of gender labeling studies," *Sex Roles* 20, pp.501–22.

Stone, V., Baron-Cohen, S. and Knight, K. (1999), "Frontal lobe contributions to theory of mind," *Journal of Cognitive Neuroscience* 10, pp.640–56.

Strayer, F.F. (1980), "Child ethology and the study of preschool social relations" in H.C. Foot, A.J. Chapman and J.R. Smith (eds.), *Friendship and Social Relations in Children*, New York, John Wiley & Sons Inc.

Stumpf, H. and Eliot, J. (1995), "Gender-related differences in spatial ability and the k factor of general spatial ability in a population of academically talented students," *Personality and Individual Differences* 19, pp.33–45.

Stumpf, H. and Jackson, D.N. (1994), "Gender-related differences in cognitive abilities: evidence from a medical school admissions program," *Personality and Individual Differences* 17, pp.335–44.

Surian, L., Baron-Cohen, S. and Van der Lely, H. (1996), "Are children with autism deaf to Gricean Maxims?" *Cognitive Neuropsychiatry*, 1, 55–72.

Sutton-Smith, B., Rosenberg, B.G. and Morgan, E.F. (1963), "Development of sex differences in play choices during preadolescence," *Child Development* 34, pp.119–26.

Swaab, D.F. and Hofman, M.A. (1995), "Sexual differentiation of the human hypothalamus in relation to gender and sexual orientation," *Trends in Neurosciences* 18, pp.264–70.

Swettenham, J., Baron-Cohen, S., Charman, T., Cox, A., Baird, G., Drew, A., Rees, L. and Wheelwright, S. (1998), "The frequency and distribution of spontaneous attention shifts between social and non-social stimuli in autistic, typically developing and non-autistic developmentally delayed infants," *Journal of Child Psychology and Psychiatry*, 39, pp.747–53.

Symons, D. (1979), *The Evolution of Human Sexuality*, New York, Oxford University Press.

Szatmari, P. (1999), "Heterogeneity and the genetics of autism," *Journal of Psychiatry and Neuroscience* 24, pp.159–65.

Tager-Flusberg, H. and Sullivan, K. (2000), "A componential view of theory of mind: evidence from Williams Syndrome," *Cognition* 76, pp.59–89.

Tannen, D. (1990), *You Just Don't Understand: Women and Men in Conversation*, New York, William Morrow.

_____(1994), *Talking from Nine to Five*, New York, William Morrow.

Tanner, J.M. (1970), "Physical growth" in P. Mussen (ed.), *Carmichael's Manual of Child Psychology*, 3rd edn, New York, John Wiley & Sons Inc.

Tanner, J.M. (1990), *Foetus into Man: Physical Growth from Conception to Maturity*, Cambridge, Mass., Harvard University Press.

Tantam, D. (2001), "Psychological disorder in adolescents and adults with Asperger Syndrome," *Autism* 4, pp.47–62.

Thomas, H., Jamison, W. and Hummel, D.D. (1973), "Observation is insufficient for discovering that the surface of still water is invariantly horizontal," *Science* 181, pp.173–4.

Thomas, J.R. and French, K.E. (1985), "Gender differences across age in motor performance: A meta-analysis," *Psychological Bulletin* 98, pp.260–82.

Tordjman, S., Ferrari, P., Sulmont, V., Duyme, M. and Roubertoux, P. (1997), "Androgenic activity in autism," *American Journal of Psychiatry* 154, pp.1626–7.

Tronick, E.Z. and Cohn, J.F. (1989), "Infant-mother face to face interaction: age and gender differences in coordination and the occurrence of miscoordination," *Child Development* 60, pp.85–92.

Tsai, L. and Beisler, J. (1983), "The development of sex differences in infantile autism," *British Journal of Psychiatry* 142, pp.373–78.

Tsai, L., Stewart, M. and August, G. (1981), "Implications of sex differences in the familial transmission of infantile autism," *Journal of Autism and Developmental Disorders* 11, pp.165–73.

Tucker, J.S., Friedman, H.S., Schwartz, J.E., Criqui, M.H., Tomlinson-Keasey, C., Wingard, D.L. and Martin, L.R. (1997), "Parental divorce: effects on individual behavior and longevity," *Journal of Personality and Social Psychology* 73, pp. 381–91.

Valian, V. (1999), *Why So Slow? The Advancement of Women*, Cambridge, Mass., MIT Press.

Van Goozen, S.H.M., Cohen-Kettenis, P.T., Gooren, L.J.G., Frijda, N.H. and Van de Poll, N.E. (1995), "Gender differences in behavior: activating effects of cross-sex hormones," *Psychoneuroendocrinology* 20, pp.343–63.

Vandenberg, S.G. and Kuse, A.R. (1978), "Mental rotations, a group test of three-dimensional spatial visualization," *Perceptual and Motor Skills* 47, pp.599–604.

Velle, W. (1987), "Sex differences in sensory functions," *Perspectives in Biology and Medicine* 30, pp.490–522.

Vetter, B. (1979), "Working women scientists and engineers," *Science* 207, pp.28–34.

Vinader-Caerols, C., Collado, P., Segovia, S. and Guillamon, A. (2000), "Estradiol masculinizes the posteromedial cortical nucleus of the amygdala in the rat," *Brain Research Bulletin* 53, pp.269–73.

Voyer, D., Voyer, S. and Bryden, M. (1995), "Magnitude of sex differences in spatial abilities: a meta-analysis and consideration of critical variables," *Psychological Bulletin* 117, pp.250–70.

Wagner, H.L., Buck, R. and Winterbotham, M. (1993), "Communication of specific emotions: gender differences in sending accuracy and communication measures," *Journal of Nonverbal Behavior* 17, pp.29–53.

Watson, N. (2001), "Sex differences in throwing: monkeys have a fling," *Trends in Cognitive Neurosciences* 5, pp.98–9.

Watson, N.V. and Kimura, D. (1991), "Nontrivial sex differences in throwing and intercepting: relation to psychometrically-defined spatial functions," *Personality and Individual Differences* 12, pp.375–85.

Weekes, N.Y. and Zaidel, D.W. (1995), "Effects of sex and sex role attributions on the ear advantage in dichotic listening," *Neuropsychology* 9, pp.62–7.

Wellman, H. (1990), *Children's Theories of Mind*, Oxford University Press.

Wentzel, K.R. (1988), "Gender differences in math and English achievement: a longitudinal study," *Sex Roles* 18, pp.691–9.

Whiting, B.B. and Edwards, C.P. (1988), *Children of Different Worlds: The Forma-tion of Social Behavior*, Cambridge, Mass., Harvard University Press.

Whitten, P.L. (1987), "Infants and adult males" in B.B. Smuts, D.L. Cheney, R.M. Seyfarth, R.W. Wrangham, T.T. Struhsaker (eds.), *Primate Societies*, University of Chicago Press.

Widener, A. (1979), *Gustav Le Bon: The Man and his Works*. Liberty Fund, Inc.

Willey, L. (1999), *Pretending to be Normal*, London, Jessica Kingsley Publishers.

Williams, C., Barnett, A. and Meck, W. (1990), "Organisational effects of early go-nadal secretions on sexual differentiation in spatial memory," *Behavioural Neu-roscience* 104, pp.84–97.

Willingham, W.W. and Cole, N.S. (1997), *Gender Fair Assessment*, Hillsdale, NJ, Erlbaum.

Willis, S.L. and Schaie, K.W. (1988), "Gender differences in spatial ability in old age: longitudinal and intervention findings," *Sex Roles* 18, pp.189–203.

Wilson, G. and Jackson, C. (1994), "The personality of physicists," *Personality and Individual Differences* 16, pp.187–9.

Wing, L. (1976), *Early Childhood Autism*, Oxford, Pergamon Press.

———(1981a), "Asperger Syndrome: a clinical account," *Psychological Medicine* 11, pp.115–30.

———(1981b), "Sex ratios in early childhood autism and related conditions," *Psy-chiatry Research* 5, pp.129–37.

———(1988), "The Autistic Continuum" in L. Wing (ed.), *Aspects of Autism: Bio-logical Research*, London, Gaskell/Royal College of Psychiatrists.

Witelson, S. (1985), "The brain connection: the corpus callosum is larger in left-handers," *Science* 229, pp.665–8.

———(1989), "Hand and sex differences in the isthmus and genu of the human corpus callosum," *Brain* 112, pp.799–835.

———(1976), "Sex and the single hemisphere: specialization of the right hemi-sphere for spatial processing," *Science* 193, pp.425–7.

Witkin, H.A., Dyk, R.B., Faterson, H.F., Goodenough, D.G. and Karp, S.A., *Per-sonality through Perception*, New York, Harper & Row.

Wittig, M.A. and Allen, M.J. (1984), "Measurement of adult performance on Pi-aget's water horizontality task," *Intelligence* 8, pp.305–13.

Wolterink, G., Daenen, L., Dubbeldam, S., Gerrits, M., Rijn, R., Kruse, C., Van Der Heijden, J. and Van Ree, J. (2001), "Early amygdala damage in the rat as a model for neurodevelopmental psychopathological disorders," *European Neu-ropsychopharmacology* 11, pp.51–9.

Wright, P. (1998), "Towards an expanded orientation to the study of sex differences in friendship" in D. Canary and K. Dindia (eds.), *Sex Differences and Similarities in Communication*, Brighton, Lawrence Erlbaum Associates.

Zahn-Waxler, C., Radke-Yarrow, M., Wagner, E. and Chapman, M. (1992), "Development of concern for others," *Developmental Psychology* 28, pp.126–36.

INDEX

Simon Baron-Cohen is professor of psychology and psychiatry at Cambridge University and co-director its Autism Research Centre. He has carried out research into both autism and sex differences over a twenty-year career. He is the author of *Autism: The Facts* and *Mindblindness*.